The
Fun Seeker's
Chicago

THE ULTIMATE GUIDE TO ONE
OF THE WORLD'S HOTTEST CITIES

THE FUN ALSO RISES TRAVEL SERIES

. We accept no payment of any
this book. We welcome your views

Credits

Executive Editor	Alan S. Davis
Series Editor	Peter Cieply
Contributing Editor	Wendy Wollenberg
Copyeditor	Gail Nelson-Bonebrake
Book Design	DeVa Communications
Maps	Chris Gillis
Production	Samia Afra
	Jo Farrell

Special Sales

For information about bulk purchases of Greenline books (ten copies or more), email us at info@greenlinepub.com. Special bulk rates are available for charities, corporations, institutions, and online and mail-order catalogs, and our books can be customized to suit your company's needs.

GREENLINE PUBLICATIONS
Extraordinary Guides for Extraordinary Travelers
P.O. Box 590780
San Francisco, CA 94159-0780

The
Fun Seeker's Chicago

**THE ULTIMATE GUIDE TO ONE
OF THE WORLD'S HOTTEST CITIES**

Ryan Ver Berkmoes

GREENLINE PUBLICATIONS

To Our Readers:

In 1998 I wrote and published *The Fun Also Rises Travel Guide North America*, followed in 1999 by *The Fun Also Rises International Travel Guide*. Together, these books covered the world's most fun places to be at the right time—from the Opera Ball in Vienna to the Calgary Stampede.

The success of these guides persuaded me of the need for a different approach to travel book publishing—*extraordinary guides for extraordinary travelers*. Greenline Publications was launched as a full-scale travel book publisher in December 2002, with **The 25 Best World War II Sites: Pacific Theater**, the first book in the **Greenline Historic Travel Series**.

The Fun Also Rises Travel Series was introduced in 2003 with an updated version of the first book—now called **The Fun Seeker's North America**. Like Ernest Hemingway's *The Sun Also Rises*, which helped popularize what has become perhaps the most thrilling party on earth (Pamplona's Fiesta de San Fermín, also known as the Running of the Bulls), **The Fun Also Rises** travel books take readers to the world's most fun places.

For the series, we have identified 21 cities worthy of five-star ratings for fun. Greenline will be releasing original, single-destination guides for each of these cities, including Las Vegas, Los Angeles, New York, San Francisco, Athens, and London.

Greenline's guiding principle is simple: Never settle for the ordinary. We hope that a willingness to explore new approaches to guidebooks, combined with meticulous research, provides readers with unique and significant travel experiences.

Please let me know if our guides fail to meet your expectations in any way. To reach us, or for updated information on all Greenline books, please visit our website at www.greenlinepub.com.

Wishing you extraordinary travels,

Alan S. Davis
Publisher

This book is dedicated to the memory of
Miriam Hope Bass,
whose guidance, sense of humor, and spirit
helped many of us find the joy in publishing.

– Alan S. Davis

ACKNOWLEDGMENTS

Derrek Hull is a proud inheritor of the amazing legacy of Patricia Sullivan. Thanks to the many people who work to make Chicago such a wonderful place to visit, including Susan Ellefson and Stacey Koerner. Then there's those special people who always make me wish I didn't have to leave. Kelly McGrath helped through a lifetime of meals and drinks, Sandy Eitel picked up the slack, John Holden ran me around, and Kate Campion led me astray.

Ryan Ver Berkmoes

I would like to add my thanks to Archie Beaton and John Hart and to Ronald Gryzwinski and the board and officers of the Shorebank Corporation for giving me the opportunity to develop my affection for Chicago.

Alan S. Davis
Executive Editor

ABOUT THE AUTHOR

Ryan Ver Berkmoes first fell in love with Chicago when he got lost in Marshall Field's vast department store when he was four. What a place of wonder! Years later, when he was working as a journalist in the city, his horizons spread much farther but he still thought, What a place of wonder! Today his writing takes him around the world, but he still comes home to Chicago every chance he gets.

How to Use This Book

The Fun Seeker's Chicago takes a selective approach to the city that saves you days of figuring out what to see, where to go, and which El station to use. You'll be taken beyond the humdrum that awaits the undiscerning and right into the heart of this heaving, rollicking city. First we key you in to **City Essentials**, travel tips for getting to and around Chicago, and provide you with a **Cheat Sheet** filled with savvy tips, trivia, and the very least you need to know about this town.

Next you'll find **The Perfect Chicago**, a compilation of The Fun Seeker's "best" picks for hot and happening restaurants, clubs, museums, tours, shopping experiences, and other activities and attractions.

Then, while most other guidebooks are organized geographically, *The Fun Seeker's Chicago* offers a unique approach to exploring a city. **The Chicago Experience** gives you five different ways to explore the Windy City, each focused on a different theme. Each experience begins with a detailed three-day itinerary that gives you insider tips on where to be when for maximum fun. Following that, you'll find in-depth reviews of all the best hotels (upper-tier only), restaurants, bars, clubs, theatres, and attractions related to that particular experience (these listings appear in bold in the itineraries).

We've customized five different Chicago experiences—*Classic Chicago, Hot & Cool Chicago, Luxe Chicago, Hipster Chicago,* and *Neighborhood Chicago*, so you can go wherever the mood takes you with ease.

• Cool blues, hot jazz, swank lounges, high living—Chicago's image internationally is still rooted in its storied past. The Windy City has been wowing 'em for generations, and the things that made the city famous are still a vital part of what makes it so great today. The Loop, the El, the Art Institute, stellar restaurants, smoky blues bars, corner pubs, hot clubs—here's your chance to plunge into a **Classic Chicago** experience that will have you crooning that it's your kind of town.

• The fact that Chicago is culturally white-hot comes as a surprise to folks who think it's a dumb broad-shouldered regular-guy kinda town. Part of Chicago's incredible appeal is that new clubs, restaurants, galleries and more open daily, and it's been that way for a long time. Chicago produces so much great food, theatre, comedy, art, and design that it can hold its own with any major city. No matter when you visit, you'll soon get caught up in the buzz about the latest opening by a locally vaunted nighttime impresario or chichi chef. **Hot & Cool Chicago** lets you mingle with the hippest locals who *always* know where to go.

• Chicago is not generally about flash, but there's money aplenty here, and no shortage of ways to spend it enjoying the very best in life, as you'll see in **Luxe Chicago**, which shows you how you can savor virtually any luxury in this sophisticated city. Indulge your passion for the finest, whether dining out, clubbing, shopping, golfing—or even sailing or flying. The pleasures of this hot and happening top-shelf town are at your feet, so dive in and experience all it has to offer.

• What defines "hip?" Bars and clubs that are hip but not pretentious? Restaurants that blow you away with their style and savvy without making a big deal of it? A vibrant arts scene that's recognized internationally but is taken for granted as part of the fabric of the city? **Hipster Chicago** lets you

A Quick Guide to Planning Your Trip

The Chicago Calendar (p.206)
When to go (listings of annual events)—a great planning tool for the ultimate vacation.

Hit the Ground Running (p.17)
All the essential information you need for a successful and enjoyable vacation.

The Chicago Experience (p. 69)
Five themed chapters with three-day itineraries, followed by detailed descriptions of all related venues. Choose your approach to the city, or mix and match these extraordinary days.

The Perfect Chicago (p. 35)
Three absolute best-of-the-bests in 33 categories (with descriptions and hot tips)—handy for putting your own itinerary together (naturally, most of these venues also appear in the itineraries).

The Chicago Black Book (p. 213)
A quick way to find a venue—lists all Chicago venues highlighted in the book, with addresses, phone numbers, and page numbers. It also lists the Experience in which each appears and whether it's one of our "bests."

Leaving Chicago (p. 195)
The ten best day-trip and overnight destinations to round out your Chicago visit.

MAPS

Metro Chicagoland (p. 16)
Helps you understand the layout of Chicago and its surrounding area.

Central Chicago (p. 34)
Zooms in to provide key streets in the areas in which you'll find most venues.

Greater Chicago Area (p. 194)
Puts Chicago in perspective and pinpoints each of the "Leaving Chicago" destinations.

in on all this and more. What's so cool about this amazing city on the lake is that there's so much going on but so little attitude. From restaurants, bars, and clubs to boutiques, galleries, and theatres, you'll get the insider info you need to find out why people who live here love Chicago.

• Many Chicagoans will tell you that the real Chicago is found in its neighborhoods, the unique patchwork of evolving ethnic enclaves (and spreading gentrification) that comprises the city and gives it its personality. From the young creative 'hoods like Wicker Park and Bucktown to the hip sophistication of Lincoln Park and lively nightlife of Lakeview and Wrigleyville, **Neighborhood Chicago** gives you a range of experiences that get right to the beating heart of the city.

After all that, if you find yourself needing a bit of open space, then it's time to get out of town for a day. Check out **Leaving Chicago**, a collection of day and overnight trips to great escapes like the wilds of Wisconsin, the villages of Illinois, or the serene beaches of Michigan.

Finally, check your travel dates with **The Chicago Calendar**, a short list of the hottest happenings in the city throughout the year. And for quick reference, you can find in **The Chicago Black Book** all the important addresses and phone numbers you'll need (along with their page numbers in the theme chapters and "best" lists).

Key to Pricing Symbols

Hotel symbols
indicate each hotel's best non-suite double room price per night.

$ =	up to $99
$$ =	$101 to $200
$$$ =	$201 to $300
$$$$ =	$301 to $400
$$$$+ =	more than $400

Restaurant symbols
indicate average cost of one entrée. **Nightclub** and **attraction** symbols indicate cover or entry fee.

$ =	Up to $10
$$ =	$11 to $20
$$$ =	$21 to $30
$$$$ =	$31 to $40
$$$$+ =	more than $40

Table of Contents

Introduction

Chicago: What It Was, What It Is

Welcome to Chicago, the greatest city in the U.S., if we do say so ourselves. Nicknamed and often regarded as the "second city," Chicago these days can legitimately argue that it's as cool as either of its coastal bigger cousins, and it has bloomed as a prime destination for visitors worldwide. If a place with industrial roots that go to the core of U.S. history and one that has always celebrated its "city of big shoulders" image can be called an oasis, then Chicago should be. Here, hard by Lake Michigan, is a truly world-class city, with nonstop nightlife, vibrant and sophisticated culture, great beauty (well, on slush-free days, anyway) and, most important, a self-assurance that keeps propelling it to ever better days. It's also a place of great charm, partly because its self-assurance comes without swagger or the sort of showboating that's a sign of a place trying to puff itself up.

Chicago has a rich and colorful history. French explorer Louis Joliet first arrived in 1673 and found a swampy place with a few Native Americans living off buffalo and other critters and plants. One hundred years later, Jean Baptiste Point du Sable became the first resident when he set up a fur-trading post. The expanding United States arrived in force in the early 1800s. Soon commerce-minded business folk—the first of millions who continue to arrive today—realized that Chicago was uniquely situated to exploit the bounty of America's heartland. Lumber and grain flowed through Chicago's ports and railroad terminals. In fact, the city soon became the hub for the nation's railroad network, and for decades travelers wondered why they couldn't cross the country without changing trains in Chicago (a lament continued by today's travelers at O'Hare International Airport). All those tracks leading to Chicago fueled the city's industrial base, and the infamous Chicago Stockyards on the South Side were built to be the central meat-processing plants for the nation.

In 1871 a fire started near one of the many lumber yards on the near South Side (whether Mrs. O'Leary's cow played a role continues to be debated), and soon grew to a conflagration that destroyed much of the city. However, more than anything this tragedy only fueled the city's growth, as much of the city—especially the downtown—was rebuilt with new and much larger structures in only two years. Growth was so rampant that Chicago led the way in the development of high-rise buildings. At various times, the Loop has been home to the world's tallest building, from the 1889 Monadnock

Building to the 1974 Sears Tower (and Chicago still continues to quibble with Kuala Lumpur about the definition of "tallest"—something about antennae).

Sweet Home Chicago is not only home to the blues, it also boasts one of the best music scenes overall, whether your tastes run to rock, jazz, or classical. And where would Hollywood be without the Second City?

The city's international reputation was secured through notable World's Fairs in 1893 and 1933, then that good news was supplanted by the bad-news gangster wars of the 1920s, when Al Capone battled rivals for control of the city's vice industry. At the same time, expanding factories drew hundreds of thousands of poor African-Americans from the old plantations of the South to new and better-paying jobs in Chicago. The city had largely been populated by white immigrants from Europe—especially Germans, Irish, Italians, and Poles—and the new arrivals became part of a city that would divide and consume itself with poor race relations for decades to come. After World War II, huge numbers of white families left the crowded city for homes in the suburbs, and along with a decline in manufacturing (the last of the stockyards closed in 1971), this caused the city to become poorer and less populated.

But even as events such as the 1968 riots at the Chicago Democratic Convention showed a nasty side to the city, the seeds of a new age were present. Professionals began discovering the joys and vibrancy of urban life, and by the 1980s the city's population had grown, old buildings were rehabbed, and where there had once been factories there were now scores of new businesses, galleries, trendy restaurants, boutiques, and more. Neighborhoods were filled with new life in a process that continues throughout the city today.

Where other cities that had industrial roots all but blew away when the jobs moved out of town, Chicago was able to discover its inherent strengths and use them as the basis for a rebirth that continues unabated. The lakefront and its great parks have always been beautiful and timeless in their pleasures, and now they look better than ever, with lush plantings and continual improvements. Neighborhoods with individual character and charm

> **The beating pulse of fashion can be felt throughout Chicago's neighborhoods, where trendy new boutiques, galleries, shops, and salons—not to mention hot restaurants and cool clubs—open every day.**

have always helped the city's sum add up to be even greater than its parts, and this too continues. From Hyde Park in the south to the West Loop, the Gold Coast, Lakeview, Andersonville, and dozens more, these little urban villages merge to form a whole sophisticated city, unified by a handy and well-run transit system. Formerly humdrum 'hoods like Wicker Park, Ukrainian Village, and Bucktown are now on the cutting edge of style and are home to scores of creative people who make the streets vibrant. Old Town and Lincoln Park are so genteel, leafy, and chicly sophisticated, it's hard to imagine that their thousands of sturdy and lovely brown- and graystones were once badly run down, but both have been reborn into a couple of the city's most lively and fashionable neighborhoods.

The ever growing and changing population of this patchwork drives an unslakable thirst for nightlife. Chicago is regularly named the best restaurant city in the nation. Chefs like Charlie Trotter, Rick Bayless (Frontera Grill), Rick Tramonto (Tru), and Jean Joho (Everest) have achieved international acclaim and are well known to TV food-show aficionados, but there are dozens of other talented chefs, many quite young, who are constantly experimenting with new cuisines and finding innovative ways to push the envelope of dining.

After dinner, nighttime has always been a fun time here in Sweet Home Chicago. Besides the incomparable blues scene, where each night scores of bars feature performances by top local and touring talents, Chicago's music scene can hold its own in any genre, whether jazz, rock, or classical. The theatre scene here gets notice, from Hollywood and Broadway to London's West End—Steppenwolf and the Goodman top the list, but there are so many more, and, most remarkably, Chicagoans actually go out and support local theatre in droves. And let's not forget that huge numbers of the biggest names in comedy got their start at Second City or at one of the improv or sketch comedy clubs.

Nightlife just begins with these early-bird options. As a city where the weather doesn't encourage being outdoors for a good part of the year, Chicago has always had lots of indoor places to party. Many bars and clubs take full advantage of closing times that can go as late as 4 a.m. (5 a.m. Saturdays!) to keep scores of cool cats, hipsters, scenesters, and others living large until dawn. Venues range from the friendly corner pub to hip, swank scenester hangouts where it's hard to decide what's more beautiful—the staff, the patrons, or the decor.

In the daytime, Chicago easily separates itself from wannabe-great cities. There are an almost infinite number of sites to see just strolling around, from the historical, awe-inspiring, world-class architecture of the Loop to the parks and lakefront, and on to all those neighborhoods. Along the way are scores of museums and attractions like the Art Institute with its vast collections, which is in itself a major draw for visitors worldwide. South of Grant Park, the Museum Campus is home to the Field Museum of Natural History, the Shedd Aquarium, and the Adler Planetarium, each of which can keep you hopping for half a day or more. Toss in the hugely popular Museum of Science and Industry in Hyde Park, the Chicago Historical Society in Lincoln Park, plus about a dozen others, and you have a lineup that caters to every interest.

Shopping regularly tops visitor polls as a favorite reason to come here, and it's easy to see why, starting on North Michigan Avenue with its hundreds of stylish and famous stores. But to find the contemporary pulse of fashion, look to the neighborhoods, like ultraposh Oak Street in the Gold Coast, trendy Armitage Avenue in Lincoln Park, and cutting-edge Milwaukee and Damen Avenues in Wicker Park.

The city has been riding a wave of success for more than a decade now. Much of Chicago has never looked better, especially along the lakefront, where the $500 million Millennium Park (finally) opened in 2004. But throughout the city, you'll also see continual growth and rebirth, with new clubs, restaurants, boutiques, shops, salons, galleries, studios, theatres, dance spaces, and more opening each day. So dive in to one of the most enjoyable cities on the planet, and no matter how long your current trip is— start planning the next one, because you'll be back.

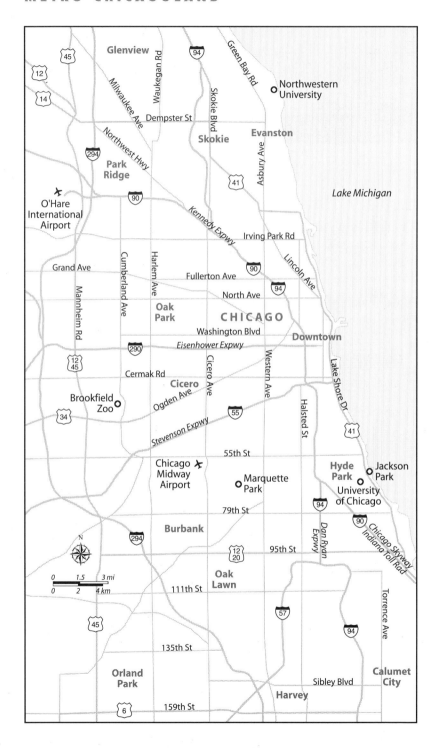

Hit the Ground Running

If you've never been here before—or even if you live here—Chicago can be overwhelming. Which neighborhood is where? What park is that? Should I take the El? Will I freeze in April? Bake in July? If you want to make like a local, you need to know the basics. Here are most of the facts and figures, including our Cheat Sheet, a quick-reference countdown of vital information that'll help you feel like an instant Chicagoan.

City Essentials

Getting to Chicago

By Air: Chicago has two airports: O'Hare International Airport (ORD, 800-832-6352, www.ohare.com) which perennially vies for the title as "The World's Busiest," and Midway International (MDW, 5700 S. Cicero Ave., 773-838-0600, www.ohare.com/midway/home.asp).

O'Hare, with its vast size, can confound and confuse. But given its traffic—close to 60 million passengers a year—it's well managed. Domestic airlines are based out of Terminals 1, 2, and 3. All international flights arrive at Terminal 5, but many foreign airlines depart from the terminals of their U.S. partners, as with Lufthansa from United's Terminal 1. The domestic terminals (there

Flying Times to Chicago	
Atlanta	2 hours
Dallas/Fort Worth	2.5 hours
Denver	2.5 hours
Las Vegas	4 hours
London	7.5 hours
Los Angeles	4.5 hours
Miami	3 hours
New York	2 hours
San Francisco	4.5 hours
Seattle	4.5 hours
Tokyo	13.5 hours
Washington, D.C.	2 hours

is no number 4) are linked by various passages above and below ground as well as by the quick and efficient Airport Transit System (ATS) people mover. Terminal 5 is also a stop on the ATS, which also serves some of the remote parking lots. Departures are from the upper level, while arrivals, baggage claim, shuttle buses, and taxis leave from the lower level. The highly useful Chicago Transit Authority (CTA) station for trains downtown is underground near Terminals 1, 2, and 3, and you can reach it by ATS from Terminal 5. There is a wide range of food and beverage outlets in the terminals, many of them outposts of classic Chicago restaurants. Good bookstores can be found in Terminals 1, 2, and 3. If you have lots of time, there's an excellent exhibit on the airport's namesake, WWII U.S. Navy fighter ace "Butch" O'Hare, in Terminal 2.

In contrast to O'Hare, navigating Midway is relatively easy. Whereas the larger facility on the city's northwest side is a hub for huge carriers United and American as well as the terminus for almost all international flights, Midway, on the southwest side, is the primary destination for budget carriers such as Southwest and AirTran. All travel begins and ends in the light and airy Terminal Building, which was completed in 2001. Various concourses, which serve upward of 20 million passengers a year, branch off from the Terminal Building. As in O'Hare, departures are on the upper level and arrivals are on the lower level. The CTA station is nearby. There are plenty of cafes, bars, and newsstands (and in fact food options here may be better than at O'Hare).

Airlines Serving Chicago

Close to 50 airlines serve Chicago with some serving both airports. Note that all international flights to O'Hare arrive at Terminal 5, but many depart from Terminals 1, 2, and 3.

Air Canada (888-247-2262, www.aircanada.com) O'Hare Terminal 2

Air France (800-237-2747, www.airfrance.com) O'Hare Terminal 5

Air Tran (800-825-8538, www.airtran.com) Midway

Alaska Airlines (800-426-0333, www.alaskaair.com) O'Hare Terminal 3

America West (800-235-9292, www.americawest.com) O'Hare Terminal 2

American Airlines (800-443-7300, www.aa.com) O'Hare Terminal 3; Midway

ATA (800-225-2995, www.ata.com) Midway

British Airways (800-247-9297, www.british-airways.com) O'Hare Terminal 5

BMI British Midland (800-788-0555, www.flybmi.com) O'Hare Terminal 5

Continental Airlines (800-525-0280, www.continental.com) O'Hare Terminal 2; Midway

Delta Air Lines (800-221-1212, www.delta.com) O'Hare Terminal 3; Midway

Frontier Airlines (800-432-1359; www.frontierairlines.com) Midway

Japan Airlines (800-525-3663, www.japanair.com) O'Hare Terminal 5

KLM Royal Dutch (www.klm.com, 800-374-7747) O'Hare Terminal 5

Lufthansa (800-645-3880, www.lufthansa.com) O'Hare Terminal 1

Mexicana (800-531-7921, www.mexicana.com) O'Hare Terminal 5

Northwest Airlines (800-225-2525, www.nwa.com) O'Hare Terminal 2; Midway

Southwest Airlines (800-435-9792, www.southwest.com) Midway

United Airlines (800-241-6522, www.united.com) O'Hare Terminal 1

US Airways (800-428-4322, www.usairways.com) O'Hare Terminal 2; Midway

To and From the Airports

O'Hare is 13 miles northwest of downtown Chicago on I-90 and I-190. Midway is 7 miles southwest of downtown off I-55 on Cicero Avenue. Travel time to both can be as short as 30 minutes, but easily can be an hour or more during rush hour and other random traffic-jammed times throughout the week (though Midway is almost always quicker to get to).

Cabs: Taxis are plentiful, although they can easily be stranded in traffic. Expect to spend roughly $35 to $40 from O'Hare and $25 from Midway to downtown.

Shuttles: Continental Airport Express (312-454-7800, 800-654-7871, www.airportexpress.com) has a near monopoly on shuttle services to and from the airports. Fares average $18 to or from O'Hare or $16 to and from Midway. Travel times can be long since besides traffic, you may have to wait for the shuttle to fill the van and then wander around dropping people off. The service operates 6 a.m. to 11:30 p.m.

CTA: Chicago Transit Authority trains (commonly called the El) operate around the clock from O'Hare and 4 a.m. to midnight from Midway. The fare is $1.75 and the cars are clean and air-conditioned. O'Hare is served by the Blue Line from the Loop, and trains take about 40 minutes. The Orange Line goes to Midway from the Loop, with trains taking about 30 minutes. Once in the Loop, you can exit the trains and get a cab to your final destination.

By Car: Interstate highways converge on Chicago, but the big decision is what you'll do with the car once you arrive, given that it's easier to see the city without a car.

Driving to Chicago by Car

From	Distance (mi.)	Time (hr.)
Atlanta	710	11
Boston	980	15
Dallas	915	15
Denver	1,000	15
Detroit	260	4
Los Angeles	2,000	32
Miami	1,350	22
New Orleans	920	14
New York	780	12
Saint Louis	300	5
San Francisco	2,100	33
Seattle	2,000	31
Washington, D.C.	700	11

Getting Around Chicago

By Car: You can get around Chicago by car, but it's unlikely that this will add pleasure to your journey. Traffic is rarely good, both on expressways and surface roads, and parking can be hard to find, expensive, or both. However, one detail that will prove helpful is Chicago's remarkably sensible and easy-to-understand street numbering system (see the sidebar "Street Numbers in Chicago"). In the Loop, Near North, and other areas in the center, parking in garages will run $20 a day or more. Top-end hotels and restaurants offer valet parking, which runs upward of $10 for a couple of hours. There is some street parking, but you'll need a fistful of quarters. Out in the neighborhoods you may not find parking at all as garages are few and in many areas street parking is limited to cars displaying proper permits. And don't think you can get away with breaking the law; like many cities, Chicago has discovered that parking tickets are a good source of revenue, and cops will track you down regardless of whether you had a rental car or out-of-state plates. Truly, public transit and cabs are the way to get around. Should you find yourself driving at a busy time (most days until 8 p.m.), tune in to WBBM AM 740 for traffic reports every few minutes. Speed limits are 35 mph in the city and 55 mph on the expressways unless otherwise posted.

Rental Cars

If you're just coming to see the city, it doesn't make sense to rent a car. If you plan on leaving Chicago, you might wait to pick up your car until you're ready for your journey. The companies listed below have locations at both O'Hare and Midway airports as well as city locations in the center of town (note that rates can vary widely between a rental company's city and airport locations).

Alamo (800-327-9633, www.alamo.com)

Avis (800-831-2847, www.avis.com)

Budget (800-517-0700, www.budget.com)

Dollar (800-800-4000, www.dollarcar.com)

Enterprise (800-566-9249, www.enterprise.com)

Hertz (800-654-3131, www.hertz.com)

National (800-227-7368, www.nationalcar.com)

Thrifty (800-527-7075, www.thrifty.com)

By Public Transit: The Chicago Transit Authority (CTA, 800-968-7282, www.transitchicago.com) operates the trains and buses in Chicago. The train lines, which are generically called "the El," are not only a great way to get around but also an attraction in their own right. Consisting of six color-coded lines, the El serves most parts of the city and close-in suburbs that will be of interest to visitors. The Red Line is the busiest and is the vital north-south spine of the system, serving the Loop, Near North, Gold Coast, Lincoln Park, and points near the waterfront including Wrigley Field. The Purple Line links Evanston and Wilmette with the North Side. The Brown Line goes through Lincoln Park and the gentrified neighborhoods of Lakeview and the northwest. The Blue Line serves Bucktown and then follows the Kennedy Expressway (I-80) to O'Hare International Airport. It also runs through neighborhoods on the west and southwest sides, including Pilsen. The Green Line goes through the heart of the South Side and gets close to Hyde Park as well as going west to Garfield Park and Oak Park. The Orange Line travels south of the Loop and then southwest past the vestiges of the old stockyards and on to Midway International Airport.

Although El is short for *elevated*, two of the key lines serving the center (the Red and Blue Lines) run as underground subways when they pass through the Loop. But the other lines make use of all or portions of the famous circle of elevated tracks downtown that give the Loop its name. The trains are air-conditioned, usually clean, and often safer than the neighborhoods that they pass through. The lines run at least 5 a.m.–10 p.m., with most running later and the Red Line as well as the portion of the Blue Line from the Loop to O'Hare running 24 hours. The fare for one trip is $1.75, but you can purchase tickets in whatever increments you'd like from machines in the stations, and the fare and/or transfer (an additional 25 cents) is automatically deducted as you go through the fare gate. If you're going to ride a few times, it makes sense to purchase a ticket for $10 or more so you're not always lining up to buy one. It's also worth considering a Visitor Pass, which provides unlimited travel on CTA trains and buses. The cost for a pass is: one-day, $5; two-day, $9; three-day, $12; and five-day, $18. They are available at visitor centers, airport CTA stops, museums, or on the internet. Where sights and neighborhoods in this book are convenient to the El, it is noted.

Compared to the El, buses are much less fun. Although their route plan is comprehensive, service can be slow due to traffic, and as you stand at a stop waiting, you never know if the next bus will be in 3 or 30 minutes. Still, some of the lines are useful, most notably the 151-Sheridan (which runs right along the lakefront) and the 22-Clark (which goes through the heart of the North Side). Fares are the same as for the El, and you can transfer between the two (25 cents). Buses lack fare-card machines, so if you don't have a fare card already, you have to pay cash (exact change!) to the driver.

Metra (312-836-7000—and all other local area codes work with that number as well—www.metrarail.com) is the name for the collection of commuter train lines that fan out in all directions from Chicago. Service is fast and efficient, and many outlying points of interest in the Leaving Chicago chapter can be reached by Metra trains. Be sure to check in advance from which of the four terminals near the Loop your train leaves.

Street Numbers in Chicago

Chicago is laid out in a grid of north-south and east-west streets (with a few diagonals like Clark Street and Lincoln Avenue thrown in for efficiency of getting around). Street numbers conform to a grid reference system. Numbering starts at the intersection of State and Madison Sts. in the Loop. From there (effectively number zero), street numbers radiate out in the four directions of the compass in consistent increments on all streets that parallel one another, so 400 N. State St. and 400 N. Halsted St. are both the same distance north of Madison Street; 400 W. Madison St. and 400 W. Chicago Ave. are both the same distance west of State Street. Each 800 in street numbers is about a mile, and major streets occur at about every 400 in numbers. This is especially useful to know if you are walking. If you're going from 900 N. Michigan to the Lincoln Park Zoo (which is almost due north at 2100 N.), you know you have a 1-1/2 mile stroll (which happens to go through some of Chicago's nicest neighborhoods!).

Besides street numbers, Chicagoans generally navigate by talking about which part of the city they're going to in relation to the Loop: the North Side, South Side, northwest, and so on, as well as by neighborhood: Streeterville, Lincoln Park, Bucktown, Lakeview, and about 50 others.

Taxis

Chicago taxis are plentiful and are a common way of getting around. Fares start at $1.90 and are $1.60 for each additional mile. In addition—to make up for slow traffic—it is $2 for every six minutes you are stopped or are moving slowly. Drivers range from chatty to indifferent or surly, with no particular personality type having a lock on the city's geography. It's important that you know the address of your destination as well as a cross street or grid reference number (see the box "Street Numbers in Chicago"), as your cabbie may or may not be familiar with where you want to go. No matter how good or bad the service, the driver will expect a tip of 15% to 20%.

Cabs can be hailed on the street in all busy parts of the city. Hotels, restaurants, and clubs often have cab stands or can hail one for you. Even small bars are happy to call you a cab. Should you seek out your own, try Yellow Cab (312-829-4222) or Flash (773-561-4444).

Emergency

Call 911 for the police, fire department, ambulance, and paramedics. The two main 24-hour emergency rooms are at Northwestern Memorial Hospital (251 E. Huron St., 312-633-6000) on the Near North Side and Cook County Hospital (1835 W. Harrison, 312-633-6000) southwest of the Loop. The latter is the city's designated trauma center for life-threatening injuries and is the inspiration for the TV show *ER*.

If you need a pharmacy, your hotel will be able to steer you to one. Otherwise, Walgreen's (800-289-2273) has three 24-hour pharmacies convenient to most hotels: 641 N. Clark St., 312-587-1416; 757 N. Michigan Ave., 312-664-4000; and 1200 N. Dearborn St., 312-943-0973. Hotlines: Alcoholics Anonymous Greater Chicagoland 800-371-1475; Chicago Rape Crisis Hotline 888-293-2080.

General Information for Visitors

The city's Office of Tourism operates a website (www.877chicago.com) and information service (877-CHICAGO) in conjunction with the state, which has wealth of links to information as well as offers for various travel packages and room deals.

The city also operates two full-featured information centers that make good early stops and have their own attractions: the Chicago Cultural Center in the Loop (77 E. Randolph St. at Michigan Ave., open Mon.-Fri. 10 a.m.–6 p.m., Sat.–Sun. 11 a.m.–5 p.m.) and across from the Water Tower at the Chicago Water Works (163 E. Pearson St. at Michigan Ave., daily 7:30 a.m.–7 p.m.). There are also two small booths inside the Sears Store (State St. and Madison Ave.) and at Navy Pier (700 E. Grand Ave.).

The city also operates the unique, fun, and free Chicago Greeter program (312-744-8000, www.chicagogreeter.com), which pairs visitors with local volunteers who take them for rides on the CTA and on walks around their favorite neighborhoods.

Safety

Like any large city, Chicago has areas where your personal safety is far from assured. These are primarily high-crime neighborhoods on the South and West Sides. Since it's unlikely you'll be venturing into these areas, you shouldn't worry much. However, no matter where you are, it's important to stay street smart: Avoid desolate areas; keep your personal belongings nearby (especially in crowded areas, and, guys, you might want to put your wallet in your front pocket); don't venture into poorly lit streets, alleys, or parks; and heed the inner voice that tells you whether a situation feels comfortable or not. Clubs, restaurants, and bars in edgier parts of town will hail you a cab, and if you're uncertain of the safety of an area, ask a local for advice.

Weather

Like people in cities worldwide who claim the bromide as their own, Chicagoans like to say, "If you don't like the weather, wait five minutes." True, you're safe assuming it'll be cold in January and hot in August, but random days of oddball weather regularly occur. What's important to know is that it's cloudy more than 60% of the time; that the nickname "the Windy City" (although derived from another meaning; see "Party Conversation" later in the chapter) is often true; and that it can precipitate in one form or another on any given day.

Average Monthly Temperatures

Month	High	Low
January	32°	17°
February	38°	24°
March	47°	32°
April	59°	42°
May	70°	51°
June	80°	61°
July	85°	66°
August	84°	65°
September	76°	57°
October	64°	46°
November	46°	35°
December	37°	24°

Generally, it's cold from November through April, with the occasional day of relative warmth when Chicagoans all dash out in shorts even though it's only 50. In January and February especially, it can get down in the teens (best case) or into subzero land with killer wind chills (worst case), and snow is likely. Spring and fall can be gorgeous, but the days of sunny, moderate temps can be short, confined to fleeting periods of May, June, September, and October. Summer temps in the 80s are likely in July, August, and even into September, but temperatures can soar into the high 90s or more with humidity levels to match (oh, that's the other thing Chicagoans say: "It's not the heat, it's the humidity!"). One benefit of the dodgy weather, however, is that Chicago has so many good restaurants, bars, theatres, museums, and shops because for much of the year people can't bear to be outside.

Attire

Let the unpredictable weather be your guide, and come prepared. Layers are key, so you can peel a few off if there's a deep winter thaw or pile a few on if an Arctic breeze blasts down from Canada in the summer. Bring something for rain or wet snow, since walking the streets is one of Chicago's great joys, and you don't want a little bad weather to spoil your fun. Dress is generally casual here, although jeans are frowned upon at high-end places. When in doubt, just wear black and you'll fit in anywhere (except maybe at the ballpark in summer). Or, what the heck, you needed another excuse to shop, didn't you?

Gay Travelers

Despite the vibrant gay scene found along North Halsted Street, Chicagoans of a more loutish type can be conservative when it comes to homosexuality. As with life in most cosmopolitan cities these days, you should not have to think about it much, but if for example you're around the ballparks at game time, you may or may not want to hold hands with your partner. For information about gay and lesbian venues, events, and attractions, visit www.glchamber.org a gay and lesbian tourist guide to Chicago. In addition, the following U.S. organizations provide information about travel and accommodation in Chicago:

- **Damron Company**, www.damron.com
- **International Gay and Lesbian Travel Association**, www.iglta.org

Media

Chicago has two daily newspapers: the multisection *Chicago Tribune,* which is legendary, wealthy, and fairly conservative; and the tabloid *Chicago Sun-Times,* which is historically regarded as liberal but is actually pretty conservative, as well as cash-strapped and scrappy. Both are essential reads to see what's happening locally. Each Thursday, the free weekly alternative and left-leaning *Reader* lands with a thump in the entrances of bars, cafes, and shops all over town. Its copious coverage includes just about everything happening in town, from entertainment to the arts. A local tradition is planning out your weekend with the *Reader* over coffee or a beer. Numerous other free weeklies compete for upscale advertising dollars, and if you like pictures of folks in frocks at parties, you'll find plenty to sate your desire. *Chicago* magazine is a glossy monthly renowned for its local features and coverage of the vibrant restaurant scene.

Radio Stations (a selection)

FM Stations

88.1 WSSD Classic blues

91.5 WBEZ NPR, local news and features, jazz

93.1 WXRT Progressive rock, excellent DJs

93.9 WLIT Elevator music

95.5 WNUA Jazzy elevator music

96.3 WBBM Top 40, dance

98.7 WFMT Nationally recognized classical station

101.1 WKQX Alternative rock, crude humor

102.7 WVAZ Urban contemporary

107.5 WGCI Bitter rival of WVAZ, urban contemporary

AM Stations

670 WSCR Local sports woes debated at all hours

720 WGN *Tribune*-owned local talk with fun-filled farm reports

780 WBBM All news plus good traffic and weather

890 WLS Talk, from shrill to sensible

1000 WMVP Sports talk from ESPN

1390 WGCI Gospel music

1450 WVON Urban talk

1690 WRLL Oldies with legendary DJs Larry Lujack and Tommy Edwards

Party Conversation—a Few Surprising Facts

• The second largest building in the U.S. (after the Pentagon) is the Merchandise Mart (on the river at Wells Street). The second largest Polish population in any city in the world (after Warsaw) is here in Chicago. Chicago gets its nickname "the Second City" from its historic status as second in population to New York City. (That honor now goes to L.A., but who's counting?).

• Another nickname, "the Windy City," is thought by many to stem from the constant blows. While it is often breezy, the moniker was bestowed on the city by a newspaper editor tired of the boasts of Chicago politicians.

• The Loop is named for the loop of elevated train tracks that circle the downtown. Although some stations have been updated, much of the system dates back to the 1800s.

• Although Chicago is a sports-mad town (or maybe because of it), local teams aren't known for their winning ways: The Cubs last won the World Series in 1908—although they were a big tease in 2003; the White Sox last won the series in 1917; the Bears have been mostly tame since their banner Super Bowl win during the 1985 season; the Bulls have returned to their ineptitude since Michael Jordan left for good in 1999; and hockey's Blackhawks last won a Stanley Cup in 1961.

• Longtime mayor Richard M. Daley was born on Arbor Day, which may explain his almost manic affinity for trees: the city plants thousands a year.

• Most bars are open until 2 a.m., some until 4 a.m., and on Saturday nights (well, Sunday mornings) a few are good until 5 a.m.

• Chicago's mostly unblemished lakefront with its parks and beaches is that way thanks to the tireless efforts a hundred years ago of retail magnate Montgomery Ward, who fought to keep developers at bay.

• A popular winter activity involves drilling a hole in the lakefront ice and fishing for tiny smelt.

• If your hot dog doesn't come on a poppy-seed bun and with enough condiments to fill a refrigerator, you've been robbed.

The Cheat Sheet
The Very Least You Ought to Know About Chicago

Though Chicagoans are a friendly lot, as with travel anywhere it helps to know a bit about the locals and their city if you want to play nice with them. Show that you know something about the cool sophistication of this city and you'll score bonus points. Here's a countdown of the ten most essential facts and factoids you need to pretend you already knew.

Ten Neighborhoods

The Loop is the heart of Chicago, home to government, banks, and business. It is a study of the best of American architecture, from the first high-rise building built more than 100 years ago to the most modern skyscrapers.

River North is the go-go center of shopping and entertainment just north of the Chicago River. Dozens of restaurants and hotels line the streets west of Michigan Avenue and south of Chicago Avenue. It has a bit of a theme-park feel (ESPN Zone, etc.) but is also home to greats like Frontera Grill and designer showrooms.

The Gold Coast is traditionally Chicago's high-rent district, and combines dignified old residential buildings with modern highrises. The neighborhood is bounded by Chicago Avenue on the south, Lincoln Park on the north, the lake to the east, and Wells Street to the west.

Old Town is a charming warren of streets lined with once humble wooden buildings, many of which were spared by the 1871 Chicago Fire. It became Chicago's Haight Ashbury in the 1960s, fashionable in the '80s, and today is a good place for a stroll and for shopping. It's mostly north of North Avenue and west of Clark Street.

Lincoln Park is the upscale neighborhood west of the park with the same name. Its streets are lined with lovingly restored gray- and brownstones. Scores of trendy places to eat, drink, and exhaust your credit card can be found along Clark and Halsted Streets and Armitage Avenue.

Lakeview is north of Diversey Parkway and Lincoln Park and east of Clark Street. A bustling neighborhood, it's a hive of shops, boutiques, restaurants, cafes, and a kaleidoscope of other diversions. Broadway Street and Belmont Avenue have something for almost any taste, and North Halsted Street is the center of Chicago's gay community.

Wrigleyville is a once working-class neighborhood that now rivals Lincoln Park as home to the upscale young. Namesake Wrigley Field is the anchor, and in the nearby streets is a panoply of bars and clubs. Wrigleyville is bounded by Irving Park Boulevard on the north, Halsted Street on the east, Ashland Avenue on the west, and a few blocks south of Addison Avenue on the south.

Wicker Park is the once-gritty home of literary luminaries like Nelson Algren who crafted their hard-edged Chicago prose here. In the blocks around the six-way intersection of North, Damen, and Milwaukee Avenues you can find some of the liveliest bars and best rock clubs, plus a thriving arts scene.

Bucktown is just north of Wicker Park along Damen Avenue and shares the same urban charm, although the gentrification is farther along, with the restaurants chichi-er and the boutiques more exclusive.

Hyde Park is home to the University of Chicago. It almost feels like another town, with its bookstores, Gothic academic buildings, and cafes. The Museum of Science and Industry is another premier attraction.

Nine Streets

Clark Street transverses most of the North Side, from the Loop to River North, the Gold Coast, Lincoln Park, Lakeview, Wrigleyville, Andersonville, and beyond.

Damen Avenue is best known as the lively street linking Wicker Park and Bucktown with neighborhoods north and south.

Fullerton Parkway runs from the lake far out west and is one of the best ways to get in from the expressway or Lake Shore Drive to the North Side nightlife areas.

Halsted Street runs almost the entire length of Chicago and is unmatched for the breadth of neighborhoods, good and bad, it traverses.

Lake Shore Drive is the fabled grand boulevard that runs for 15 miles along Chicago's preserved lakefront with its unbroken string of parks and beaches.

Michigan Avenue parallels State Street but reaches its apotheosis north of the Chicago River, where it is truly one of the nation's finest shopping streets.

Milwaukee Avenue cuts a diagonal path across the city, northwest from the Loop to the middle-class bungalows near O'Hare.

North Avenue is the focus of many revitalized neighborhoods as it runs west from the lake to the suburbs.

State Street is the spine of the Loop and runs from Lincoln Park to the city's southern regions.

Eight Chicago Movies

The Blues Brothers Local boy Jim Belushi literally tears up the town with Dan Ackroyd in this classic farce.

Ferris Bueller's Day Off Matthew Broderick spends an illicit day in the city.

The Fugitive Harrison Ford flees the law while he tries to figure out who really killed his wife.

High Fidelity Local kids John and Joan Cusack in the Chicagoization of Nick Hornby's London novel about a guy obsessed with music.

Hoop Dreams Oscar-winning documentary of two boys from the projects and their dreams of basketball greatness.

Looking for Mr. Goodbar Diane Keaton really picks the *wrong* guy in this story of life in the '70s meet-market bars along Division Street.

Risky Business The movie that made Tom Cruise and his tighty whities famous.

The Untouchables This gangster-era festival of classic Chicago locations features the legendary baby-carriage-on-the-steps scene shot in Union Station.

Seven Performing Arts Venues

Chicago Theatre Classic 1921 movie palace that's been beautifully restored and hosts large traveling shows.
175 N. State St., 312-902-1500

Civic Opera House The Art Deco home to the revered Lyric Opera of Chicago.
20 N. Wacker Dr., 312-332-2244, www.lyricopera.org

Gene Siskel Film Center Vibrant film venue named for the late *Chicago Tribune* film critic.
164 N. State St., 312-846-2600, www.siskelfilmcenter.org

Goodman Theatre Two side-by-side restored movie theatres are now home to the legendary dramatic company, the city's oldest.
170 N. Dearborn St., 312-443-3800, www.goodman-theatre.org

Music Box Theatre A small-scale Wrigleyville movie palace dating from 1929, which unspools a wide range of old, art, and indie films.
3733 N. Southport Ave., 773-871-6604, www.musicboxtheatre.com

Steppenwolf Theatre An upscale home for the theatrical company that helped create modern Chicago's great dramatic reputation.
1650 N. Halsted St., 312-335-1650, www.steppenwolf.org

Symphony Center Home to the renowned Chicago Symphony Orchestra and other smaller music groups.
220 S. Michigan Ave., 312-435-8122, www.cso.com

Six Museums

Adler Planetarium
The heavens in all their glory, plus the StarRider Theatre.
1300 S. Lake Shore Dr., 312-922-7827

The Art Institute of Chicago
One of the world's great art museums.
111 S. Michigan Ave., 312-443-3600

Field Museum
Egyptian tombs, African and Inuit villages, and more, plus Sue the dinosaur.
1400 S. Lake Shore Dr., 312-922-9410

John G. Shedd Aquarium
Some 650 different species of marine life, plus shark and whale exhibits.
1200 S. Lake Shore Dr., 312-939-2438

Museum of Contemporary Art
A stellar collection of modern and contemporary art in a sleek aluminum-clad building off North Michigan Avenue.
220 E. Chicago Ave., 312-280-2660

Museum of Science and Industry
All about technology; interactive exhibits, U-boats, airplanes, and a coal mine.
5700 S. Lake Shore Dr., 773-684-1414

Five Big Deals

The William Wrigley, Jr., Company is the world's largest **chewing-gum manufacturer**, producing more than 20 million packs per day.

The Art Institute of Chicago houses the largest collection of **Impressionist paintings** in the world outside the Louvre.

The John G. Shedd Aquarium is the world's largest **indoor aquarium**, and its Wild Reef exhibit is one of the largest shark habitats in North America.

The Mexican Fine Arts Center Museum is the largest **Latino cultural institution** in the United States.

The Field Museum is home to Sue, the largest, most complete, and best preserved **Tyrannosaurus rex** ever discovered.

Four Chicago Eats

Deep-Dish Pizza A local favorite for over 60 years; piles of cheese and ingredients like sausage are layered with sauce and crust for the kind of pizza where you say, "I'll try to have one piece."

Hot Dogs The Chicago version takes a steamed or grilled all-beef hot dog, nestles it into a soft poppy-seed bun, and then piles on everything from fresh tomatoes to relish to pickles to mustard and much more, as long as it's not ketchup.

Baby-Back Ribs Meltingly soft pork ribs in a sweet and tangy sauce that will have you licking your fingers clean.

Cracker Jack "Candy-coated popcorn, peanuts, and a prize, that's what you get in Cracker Jack." The ubiquitous treat was invented for the 1893 Columbian Exposition and went on to become a staple of both childhood and baseball games. It's also one of many popular candies that are made in the city, including Tootsie Rolls.

Three Tall Buildings

Sears Tower By some measures, the tallest in the world at 110 stories and 1,707 feet. 233 S. Wacker Dr.

Aon Building The Second City's second-tallest structure (1,136 feet) gets no respect, especially after its marble exterior started to crumble and had to be replaced by granite. 200 E. Randolph St.

John Hancock Center The third-tallest building (1,127 feet) combines offices with some of the highest condos in the world. 875 N. Michigan Ave.

Two Parks

Grant Park
Chicago's front yard is home to the soaring Buckingham Fountain, formal gardens, and a long stretch of lakefront.

Lincoln Park
America's largest urban park stretches almost seven miles along the lake and has a wealth of attractions, from a wonderful zoo to sailboats to beaches.

One Time Zone

Central time is one hour earlier than New York and two hours later than L.A.

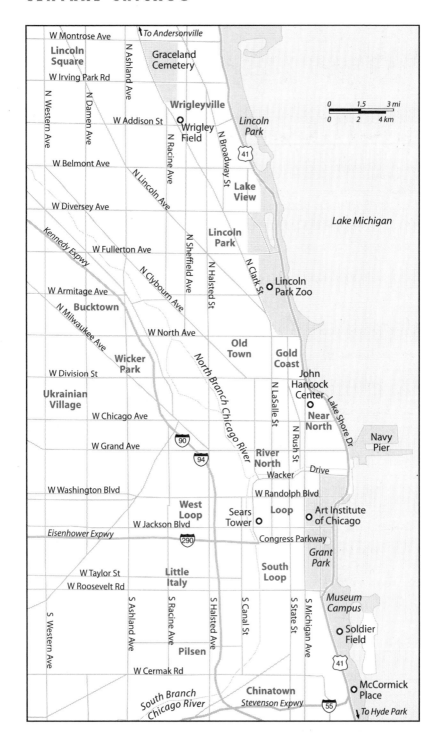

The Perfect Chicago

When you're on a trip, you don't want a city with all its little flaws and inconsistencies, you want a perfect city. You want the hottest, hippest, coolest, best places to be. We've taken the guesswork out of finding what's where in Chicago by putting the best the city has to offer right at your fingertips. Here are the best places to eat, drink, dance, lounge, see, be seen, get jazzed up, or get weighed down with shopping bags. From steaks to blues and outdoor adventures, it's all here.

Always-Hot Restaurants

Places of the moment come and go, but these three have real staying power and keep packing 'em in year after year, thanks to top food and a great scene. Mention that you've dined at any of them to a local and you'll have immediate street cred.

Frontera Grill
445 N. Clark St., River North, 312-661-1434

The Draw: Innovative regional Mexican cooking that for nearly 20 years has brought raves and fame to chef/owner Rick Bayless.

The Scene: Boldly designed, with a riot of color coming from the Mexican art collection on the walls. Packed all the time with an attractive, lively crowd tossing back unusual tequilas, everyone happy that they got here before all those other people. What are they waiting for? The revelatory food: dishes like masa crusted shrimp, duck breast with peanut mole, hurraches with black beans and partridge—who knew Mexican food could be like this?
Open for lunch Tues.–Fri. 11:30 a.m.– 2:30 p.m., Sat. 10:30 a.m.– 2:30 p.m.; dinner Tues.–Thurs. 5–10 p.m., Fri.–Sat. 5–11 p.m. $$–$$$$

Hot Tip: For a less frenetic (and even more transcendent foodie) experience, reserve well in advance for the fine-dining room, Topolobampo.

Red Light
820 W. Randolph St., West Loop, 312-733-8880

The Draw: Chef Jackie Shen has built a budding TV career based on her fusion Asian cooking. The action never stops in the explosive open kitchen.

The Scene: There's wild style inside here, from the grinning huge Thai stone Buddha head in the middle of the main room to the Gaudi-esque copper forms in the unisex bathrooms, and the food is as dazzling as the room.
Open for lunch Mon.–Fri. 11:30 a.m.–2 p.m.; dinner Sun.–Wed. 5:30–10 p.m., Thurs. 5:30–11 p.m., Fri.–Sat. 5:30 p.m.–midnight. $$$

Hot Tip: Somehow save room for Shen's trademark "chocolate bag" dessert.

Wishbone
1001 W. Washington Blvd., West Loop, 312-850-2663

The Draw: Mouth-watering "Southern reconstruction cooking," and its adoring fans.

The Scene: Oprah and her staff (her studio's across the street) and zillions of others, clamoring for the shrimp and grits, crispy French toast, chicken-fried steak, blackened fresh fish, and other comfort food that's gotten raves from everyone from *Gourmet* to *Rolling Stone.*
Open for breakfast Mon.–Fri. 7–11 a.m.; brunch Sat.–Sun. 8 a.m.–2:30 p.m.; lunch Mon.–Fri. 11 a.m.–3 p.m., dinner Tues.–Sat. 5–10 p.m. $

Hot Tip: There's another location in Lincoln Square, 3300 N. Lincoln Ave., 773-549-2663.

Architecture Sightings

This really should be a category of about 50, there's so much to see—Chicago's architecture is one of the reasons many people visit the city. Here are just three of the dozens of buildings in town that shaped the future of architecture.

Carson Pirie Scott & Company
1 S. State St., Loop/Downtown, 312-641-7000

The Draw: Louis Sullivan is one of Chicago's most influential architects, and his dictum "form follows function" is quoted to this day. This grand department store is a festival of cast-iron ornamentation on its first two floors that culminates in its spectacular rotunda at the corner of State and Madison Streets.

The Scene: Otherwise ignored by time-pressed Loop shoppers, Sullivan's work here (1899) is a spot of pilgrimage for architecture buffs. The building is significant for its modular design and construction and for Sullivan's genius for ornamentation.

Hot Tip: Step back across the street to fully appreciate the contrast of the ornamentation against the simple geometry of the large windows, which made this building a timeless trendsetter.

Glessner House
1800 S. Prairie Ave., South Loop, 312-326-1480

The Draw: An H.H. Richardson masterpiece, carefully restored.

The Scene: The Prairie Avenue district on the near South Side was home to Chicago's millionaires (the Armours, Fields, and Pullmans among them) in the 1800s, before they moved up to the Gold Coast. The neo-Romanesqe Glessner House influenced many architects, including Louis Sullivan and Frank Lloyd Wright.
Tours Wed.–Sun. at 1, 2, and 3 p.m. $

Hot Tip: Walk over to neighboring Indiana Avenue to see one of Chicago's oldest buildings, the Greek Revival Clarke House.

Robie House
5757 S. Woodlawn Ave., Hyde Park, 708-848-1976

The Draw: The culmination of Frank Lloyd Wright's Prairie style of architecture. Wright himself described this building as "the cornerstone of modern architecture."

The Scene: The living space reinvented: Wright's objective was to eliminate the sense of rooms as boxes, and that's accomplished here beautifully with the 174 Wright-designed art-glass windows that serve to "dissolve" the outer walls. The mostly restored house is run as a museum by the Frank Lloyd Wright Preservation Trust.
Tours Mon.–Fri. 11 a.m., 1 p.m., 3 p.m., Sat.–Sun. every 30 minutes 11 a.m.–3:30 p.m. $

Hot Tip: Steel beams were used for the first time here in residential architecture, allowing the roof to reach twenty feet beyond the walls at each end of the house.

Blues Bars

Best

Chicago has been singin' the blues for decades, and choosing the best places to hear them is tough since they are legion and legendary—the Checkerboard Lounge, B.L.U.E.S., Lee's Unleaded Blues...the list is long. A great Chicago blues bar should be like the music itself: unadorned, honest, and gritty. Here's a few to get you going.

Buddy Guy's Legends
754 S. Wabash Ave., South Loop, 312-427-0333

The Draw: A classic blues club in the South Loop, owned and operated by a genuine blues legend whose buddies play here regularly.

The Scene: A room a few steps up the ladder from other blues clubs in terms of decor. The Louisiana-style food isn't half bad.
Open Mon.–Thurs. 5 p.m.–2 a.m., Fri. 4 p.m.–2 a.m., Sat. 5 p.m.–3 a.m., Sun. 6 p.m.–2 a.m. $$

Hot Tip: You can reserve for dinner in order to get a better table.

Kingston Mines
2548 N. Halsted St., Lincoln Park, 773-477-4646

The Draw: This always-jammed blues club has continuous music on two stages until the 4–5 a.m. closing time. Expect to hear top talent.

The Scene: Lincoln Park yuppies mix it up with suburbanites, tourists, and die-hard fans in a rough-edged place that doesn't pander to amateurs, despite the crowd. As long as you only expect your beer to be cold and not to be some swank microbrew, you'll do fine here.
Open Sun.–Wed. 9 p.m.–4 a.m., Thurs.–Fri. 8 p.m –4 a.m., Sat. 8 p.m.–5 a.m. $

Hot Tip: Get here early and find a place where you can hear both stages. If you're going late, be sure to arrive before the 2–3 a.m. closing times of other bars to avoid the descending hordes.

Rosa's Lounge
3420 W. Armitage Ave., Bucktown, 773-342-0452

The Draw: The best blues played locally in the most authentic place to hear them. There's nothing fancy, nor should there be in this bare-bones family-run operation.

The Scene: Mismatched chairs face a small stage under a low ceiling. The men's john opens right near the drummer. But the wildly diverse crowds don't notice because they're too busy listening to the terrific national and local acts.
Open Tues.–Fri. 8 p.m.–2 a.m., Sat. 8 p.m.–3 a.m. $

Hot Tip: Watch for nights when Rosa cooks Maxwell Street sausages. This almost-forgotten old Chicago culinary staple puts a grilled Polish sausage in a bed of onions on a soft bun.

Breakfast/Brunch Places

There are at least two dozen choices on the cutting-room floor that could have made this list—Chicagoans love their breakfasts, and on weekends every place that serves even a merely good breakfast is positively packed.

Ina's
1235 W. Randolph St., West Loop, 312-226-8227

The Draw: Stylish breakfast comfort food draws folks to Ina's. The breakfast breads are baked onsite and the coffee comes in carafes—no waiting for refills here.

The Scene: The dining room is classy and lively, with Ina's collection of kooky salt and pepper shakers literally and figuratively adding spice to every table. Surprising specials appear daily.
Open Mon.–Thurs. 7 a.m.–9 p.m., Fri. 7 a.m.–10 p.m., Sat. 8 a.m.–10 p.m., Sun. 8 a.m.–2 p.m. $$

Hot Tip: The pancakes and the vegetable hash are legendary. Chat up the gracious and lovely Ina and wait for an outdoor table if the weather's nice.

Lou Mitchell's
565 W. Jackson Blvd., West Loop, 312-939-3111

The Draw: Skillet-filling omelets, double-yolk eggs, fluffy-as-a-pillow pancakes, and addictive marmalade. No matter what you order, the chow is at least a notch better than you'd expect.

The Scene: Long tables abuzz with business all morning. Veteran servers have an uncanny ability to thread the crowds while dodging errant feet.
Open Mon.–Sat. 5:30 a.m.–3 p.m., Sun. 7 a.m.–3 p.m. $

Hot Tip: Best on weekdays when people are in a hurry to get in and out to their business of the day. Weekends are mob scenes, as people hang around enjoying every last bite.

Orange
3231 N. Clark St., Lakeview, 773-549-4400,

The Draw: This trendy take on a breakfast joint serves up style with your morning joe. The kitchen knows how to fry an egg, fluff an omelet, hash-brown a potato, and more.

The Scene: Dr. Seuss fans will like the Green Eggs and Ham. Many other dishes are creative in both concept and execution, including the Breakfast Brochettes—skewers of little French toast cubes and strawberries. As the good coffee takes effect, you may notice that someone who caught your eye in the club a few hours before amid the mobs of somnolent noshers.
Open daily 8 a.m.–3 p.m. $

Hot Tip: Lay waste to some of the crates of oranges lining the walls by ordering the fresh juice.

Celebrity Launching Pads

Chicago has produced a long list of celebrities, and agents and producers from both coasts arrive daily, scouting for new talent. The incredibly fertile theatre scene is a prime breeding ground for the stars of tomorrow, and dozens of theatres big and small burst with energy. The city's winning comic track record means that no new casting of *Saturday Night Live* is complete without a swing through town to Hoover-up talent.

Lookingglass Theatre
821 N. Michigan Ave., Near North, 312-337-0665

The Draw: A white-hot theatre company in a new high-profile home in the Water Tower Pumping Station.

The Scene: Two of the founders are David Schwimmer of *Friends* and Tony Award winner Mary Zimmerman (both of whom remain in the ensemble). The company favors adaptations and original works by lesser-known playwrights, and the staging is often both highly physical and metaphorical—past productions saw cast members swinging in on meat hooks or performing Ovid in a large pool of water. $$$

Hot Tip: This is a company you can take a chance on—no matter what's on, if you can get a ticket, check it out, it's bound to be interesting.

The Second City
1616 N. Wells St., Old Town, 312-337-3992

The Draw: Knowing that at least one of the half-dozen or so people onstage is likely to become a household name.

The Scene: Past members of Second City include Mike Nichols and Elaine May, Dan Akroyd, John Belushi, Bill Murray, and Gilda Radner, Mike Myers, George Wendt, Bonnie Hunt, and many, many others. Every night the current crew performs sketches, does improvisational comedy, and otherwise hones its timing and wit until it's razor sharp. $$

Hot Tip: Stick around after the final show on weeknights (after 11 p.m.) for free improv as the cast cuts loose and pushes the limits of its talents.

Steppenwolf Theatre Company
1650 N. Halsted St., Old Town, 312-335-1650

The Draw: Dramatic, risky ensemble work, performed by a company that's consistently at the top of its game; great American theatre.

The Scene: A lavish three-stage complex in Old Town attests to the success of this theatrical group, founded by nine actors in 1976. Notable company members in this starry ensemble include Joan Allen, Gary Cole, John Malkovich, Laurie Metcalf, John Mahoney, and Gary Sinese. $$$$+

Hot Tip: Look for Steppenwolf's premieres of original works—more often than not they will soon be Broadway-bound.

Chicago Pizza

Chicago-style pizza is thick and juicy—no wimpy thin-crust pizzas for the city of big shoulders. But it's not thick-crust (a common mistake made by imitators). It's either deep-dish or double-crust, and although toppings may vary and many are popular, to stay really true to the classic, make sure there's sausage on that pie.

Giordano's
730 N. Rush St., River North, 312-951-0747

The Draw: This is the second type of Chicago pizza, which wasn't invented until about the '70s: stuffed, with a crust on the bottom, cheese and stuff in the middle, and another crust on top, topped with sauce.

The Scene: The Rush Street location is always busy with diverse groups of people loyal to type-two pizza. The date tables are the ones not having the fresh garlic, an otherwise must-have option.
Open Sun.–Wed. 11 a.m.–10 p.m., Thurs.–Sat. 11 a.m.–midnight. $$

Hot Tip: In a hurry? Call your pizza order in and they can get that big ol' bugger baking while you make that last purchase on the Mag Mile. Or call for delivery to your hotel.

Pizzeria Uno
29 E. Ohio St., River North, 312-321-1000

The Draw: The reason for coming here has not changed since 1943: deep-dish pizza with savory sausage and a piquant and chunky tomato sauce. The crust is heavy but not thick and not doughy; in fact, it's rather flaky. This is what they mean when they say "Chicago pizza," and don't believe them if it doesn't taste like this.

The Scene: A line of people waiting in the diminutive waiting area, some with a bit of drool visible as pizzas arrive for those lucky ones that got in first.
Open Mon.–Fri. 11:30 a.m.–1 a.m., Sat. 11:30 a.m.–2 a.m., Sun. 11:30 a.m.–11:30 p.m. $$

Hot Tip: Nab seats in the cozy entranceway and send somebody in to get a round of beer or the gulpable cheap red from the bar while you wait. (Let him pick up the tab, too.)

Ranalli's
2301 N. Clark St., Lincoln Park, 773-244-2300

The Draw: Though this is not classic Chicago pizza per se, it's an institution in its own right. A long menu features every kind of pizza you could want: thin, thick, stuffed, and panzerottis.

The Scene: Ranalli's huge patio is justifiably popular all summer long, and you can join the hordes of happy Lincoln Parkers enjoying themselves in the sunshine or under the stars. The beer menu boasts more than 100 choices from around the world.
Open Mon.–Fri. 7 a.m.–2 a.m., Sat.–Sun. 8 a.m.–2 a.m. $$

Hot Tip: After your meal, stroll the streets of Chicago's most pleasant neighborhoods.

Best

Classic Restaurants

It's comforting to know there are places in Chicago where you can have virtually the same experience—and maybe even the same meal—that your parents or grandparents had.

The Berghoff
17 W. Adams St., Loop/Downtown, 312-427-3170

The Draw: The oldest restaurant in the Loop never loses its appeal, thanks to the Berghoff family, who knows what to preserve and what to change.

The Scene: Busy old wooden dining rooms on two floors, with efficient waiters carrying trays of German classics, homemade rye breads, Berghoff-brewed beers, plus more modern fare. Smart diners have the sublime creamed spinach.
Open Mon.–Thurs. 11 a.m.–9 p.m., Fri. 11 a.m.–9:30 p.m., Sat. 11:30 a.m.–10 p.m. $$

Hot Tip: If you don't have time for the full treatment, stop in next door at the stand-up bar for a sandwich. You'll rub elbows with bike messengers and federal judges alike.

Italian Village
71 W. Monroe St., Loop/Downtown, 312-332-7005

The Draw: First opened in 1927, this is really a village, as there are three restaurants under one roof. Vivere draws foodies, La Cantina draws romantics downstairs, and the real classic, the Village, draws everybody for solid Italian fare in a kitsch setting.

The Scene: Couples, families, folks going to the theatre, and more lap up lasagne in the Village while dining at red checked tablecloths under twinkling star lights in the ceiling. Vivere is a copper-and-mahogany fantasy with fantastic food to match.
Village open Mon.–Thurs. 11 a.m.–1 a.m., Fri.–Sat. 11 a.m.–2 a.m., Sun. noon–midnight. $–$$; Vivere open for lunch Mon.–Fri. 11:30–2:30; dinner Mon.–Thurs. 5–10 p.m., Fri.–Sat. 5–11 p.m. $$$

Hot Tip: If you can forgo the classic charms of the Village, have a more memorable meal with cutting-edge cuisine in Vivere. Book a table for after the theatre crowd has left, and spend time with the *Wine Spectator* "Grand Award"–winning wine list.

Pump Room
1301 N. State Pkwy., Gold Coast, 312-266-0360

The Draw: The famous fine dining room in the Ambassador East Hotel keeps its kitchen fresh by employing young chefs on the way up. The atmosphere drips with 1930s opulence.

The Scene: Don't even try to take in all the celebrity photos as you enter, you'll never get to your food (or drink). Many come for the meals, others to dance cheek-to-cheek; the smart ones come for it all.
Open for breakfast Mon.–Fri. 6:30–11 a.m., Sat.–Sun. 7–11 a.m.; lunch Mon.–Sat. 11 a.m.–2 p.m.; dinner daily 6–10 p.m. $$$$

Hot Tip: It's also a great place just for a drink, and they have live music in the evenings.

Best

Clubs for Live Music

It's not enough for a live venue to have a good sound system. A truly great place for live music should have a personality that enhances the music and makes going to hear the band an experience in itself, whether it's the bartenders, the drinks, the crowd, or any other tangible that sets the scene. Although the music is obviously what you're there for, these cool places are worth a visit no matter who's playing.

Double Door
1572 N. Milwaukee Ave., Wicker Park, 773-489-3160

The Draw: Smallish music club in Wicker Park with an international reputation as *the* place to catch top bands looking to perform in an intimate venue. Music can range from hard rock to acid jazz or even country.

The Scene: A low-ceilinged club where not many folks can fit, in so you'll be close to the front. Decor is limited to a nude mural above the bar. One way to judge the quality of the band is to see how many people are playing pool in the basement. *Open Sun.–Fri. 8 p.m.–2 a.m., Sat. 8 p.m.–3 a.m.* $$

Hot Tip: If you hear the Rolling Stones are anywhere near Chicago, run to the Double Door. They are known to play here when they're in town, and it's always unannounced.

Empty Bottle
1035 N. Western Ave., Ukrainian Village, 773-276-3600

The Draw: A Ukrainian Village rock venue without frills that books solid acts almost every night.

The Scene: People who know their way around indie music and are really pissed off that there's not a better selection on iTunes; people quaffing bad domestic beer while debating the talents of the band performing. Dressing up here is wearing jeans without holes in them. *Open Mon.–Wed. 5 p.m.–2 a.m., Thurs.–Fri. 3 p.m.–2 a.m., Sat. noon–3 a.m., Sun. noon–2 a.m.* $

Hot Tip: Stop by for a beer late in the afternoon and let the clued-in bartender tell you which groups are worth seeing and which aren't.

Metro
3730 N. Clark St., Wrigleyville, 773-549-0203

The Draw: The bookers here have an uncanny ability to attract bands on their way up. The savvy have already heard of them, and everybody else will tomorrow, but Metro has them tonight.

The Scene: An old movie theatre with the seats removed; great sight lines, and you can get close to the stage. Who the crowd is depends on who's playing. *Call for hours.* $$$$

Hot Tip: After the show, head to the basement Smart Bar for some of the best cutting-edge dance music in Chicago.

Dance Clubs

Dance clubs in Chicago are as varied as styles of dance, and just like the looks of the people jamming the dance floors, there's always something new. Choices range from the posh places of River North to less-vaunted outposts in the neighborhoods. DJs are celebrities in themselves and are followed from club to club. After visiting just a couple of places, you'll probably have a favorite of your own.

Berlin
954 W. Belmont Ave., Lakeview, 773-348-4975

The Draw: A wild mix of people, clothes (or lack thereof), and dance styles at a Lakeview club that's a melting pot for the masses.

The Scene: A plethora of monitors showing videos chosen by the DJs, most of which would immediately cause a fatal constriction of John Ashcroft's gullet. Gay, straight, young, old, getting down in a smallish, party-atmosphere club where the music is as varied as the clubbers.
Open Mon. 8 p.m.–4 a.m., Tues.–Fri. 5 p.m.–4 a.m., Sat. 5 p.m.–5 a.m., Sun. 8 p.m.–4 a.m. $

Hot Tip: Watch for theme nights dedicated to one music style or artist.

Crobar
1543 N. Kingsbury St., Old Town, 312-266-1900

The Draw: Possibly the flashiest club in town. The music, the scene, the crowd, the vibe—flash, flash, flash, flash. There are different DJs on different nights; Saturday with Teri Bristol is the hottest.

The Scene: The name is an artifact of the club's original postindustrial motif. A recent makeover has brought in the cool colors and warm feelings of South Beach. You'll fit right in if it never even occurs to you to gawk at the crowd of beautiful and sometimes famous people.
Open Thurs.–Fri., Sun. 9 p.m.–4 a.m., Sat. 9 p.m.–5 a.m. $$

Hot Tip: To beat the competition, remember that the tough-minded doormen favor the brave and daring of dress.

Smart Bar
3730 N. Clark St., Wrigleyville, 773-549-4140

The Draw: The best DJs playing the best in dance music to an appreciative crowd. Expect all styles, from house to hip-hop.

The Scene: Stays crowded right through to closing, and the crowds don't mind the lack of gimmicks or froufrous. People are here first to hear the DJ, second to dance, and a distant third, to pick somebody up.
Open Sun.–Fri. 9 p.m.–4 a.m., Sat. 9 p.m.–5 a.m. $$

Hot Tip: Wear what you want, there's no designer-eyed doorman vetting your looks. Typical nights see everything from T-shirts to tuxes.

Don't-Miss Attractions

Hopefully you don't need to be told, but just in case: Don't miss these. You could easily spend an entire week devoted to these three only-in-Chicago spots, though your feet (and your credit card) might get worn out.

Art Institute of Chicago
111 S. Michigan Ave., Loop/Downtown, 312-443-3600

The Draw: The Monet haystacks, Grant Wood's *American Gothic*, Hopper's *Nighthawks*, Seurat's *Sunday on La Grande Jatte*, Lautrec's *At the Moulin Rouge*, Picasso's *Old Guitarist*...one of the world's great art collections, all under one sprawling multilevel roof.

The Scene: Swarms of people looking, a little slack-jawed, at world-class collections spanning the history of human existence. By the time they reach the French Impressionists, they're almost giddy.
Open Mon.–Fri. 10:30 a.m.–4:30 p.m. (until 8 p.m. Tues.), Sat.–Sun. 10 a.m.–5 p.m. $

Hot Tip: Don't just get one of the free maps to plan your visit, find out what's going on: frequent guided tours and entertaining talks by curators are free.

Lakefront/Lincoln Park
Runs from Oak Street Beach north past Belmont Harbor

The Draw: One of the world's largest urban parks combines beaches, miles of strolling or running and bike paths, museums, a world-class zoo, cute lakes, fine dining, and much, much more.

The Scene: Depending on the weather, you'll find everybody here, from the beautiful bods at the beaches to families pondering the apes at the zoo. Summer weekends see picnickers from all over the city, some parties hosting dozens of folks happily munching away or barbecuing on cut-in-half oil drums.

Hot Tip: Hit the park and zoo in winter. With warm clothes, you'll enjoy the serene solitude and the crunch-crunch of the snow underfoot.

North Michigan Avenue
"Magnificent Mile" runs north from the Chicago River to the lake, Near North

The Draw: The shopping street many consider the best in the United States. Landmark stores, national chains, and vertical malls jostle for frontage on the street. You'll likely find most anything you're looking for, and it's a lovely walk.

The Scene: Everybody and everyone loves to shop along the Mag Mile. It's pretty much crowded year-round but reaches its peak during Christmas, when the trees twinkle with a gazillion white lights.

Hot Tip: Take a look at the walls of the Tribune Tower. The paper's editor at the time of building, Robert McCormick, got his foreign stringers to collect chunks of famous buildings, which he embedded into the structure, including the Arc de Triomphe, Notre Dame, the Taj Mahal, Westminster Abbey, and many others.

Ethnic Dining

Chicago's ethnic dining scene is vast, vibrant, and always changing. New immigrants arrive daily, and many of them can really cook. Besides these three, your best bet is to pick a neighborhood popular with one ethnic group and go sidewalk-shopping, looking for the restaurant that's serving the biggest crowd of locals.

Pegasus
130 S. Halsted St., West Loop, 312-226-3377

The Draw: Great Greek seafood in a setting that might be Mykonos—if they'd just install a beach outside.

The Scene: A typical boisterous Greek Town restaurant, with the added bonus of better-than-average food. And yes, they have saganaki. A small band provides atmosphere in a restaurant where the good food keeps people happy.
Open Mon.–Thurs. 11 a.m.–11 p.m., Fri. 11 a.m.–midnight, Sat. noon–1 a.m., Sun. noon–midnight. $$

Hot Tip: On summer nights, bypass the patio tables with their obvious allure and head up to the rooftop deck, where the skyline looms large.

Penny's Noodle Shop
3400 N. Sheffield Ave., Lakeview, 773-281-8222

The Draw: Steaming bowls of Asian noodles and soups in a minimalist setting and at minimalist prices.

The Scene: The combination of simple, fresh, and tasty Thai noodles, soups, and other treats served with a dash of style have proved an unbeatable draw for Chicago's young, creative community.
Open Sun., Tues.–Thurs. 11 a.m.–10 p.m., Fri.–Sat. 11 a.m.–10:30 p.m. $

Hot Tip: To see a full cross-section of Chicago hipsters, hit all three Penny's locations. (See the listing in Neighborhood Chicago.)

Russian Tea Time
77 E. Adams St., Loop/Downtown, 312-360-0000

The Draw: Where else would you go for caviar and blinis with a horseradish-infused–vodka chaser?

The Scene: Lunching Loop workers, folks on their way to or from the Art Institute, and theatre and symphony patrons grabbing dinner. Besides blinis, this red velvet vision of the good life in Mother Russia also has great samsas (meat pies), chicken and dumplings, and of course, chicken Kiev.
Open Sun.–Mon. 11 a.m.–9 p.m., Tues.–Thurs. 11 a.m.–11 p.m., Fri.–Sat. 11 a.m.–midnight. $$

Hot Tip: Try a tasting flight of infused vodkas, which might include coffee, coriander, or pineapple, to name just a few.

Best

Fine Dining

Chicago takes its culinary reputation quite seriously, which explains why it has a bit of a chip on its broad shoulder about not being more widely known. Competition for best restaurant is tough; the scores in the annual best restaurant edition of *Chicago* magazine are debated like college football rankings.

Charlie Trotter's
816 W. Armitage Ave., Lincoln Park, 773-248-6228

The Draw: One of America's best restaurants, owned by a chef with a legion of admirers and protégés. It's a fabled dining experience, and it bestows bragging rights on its alums.

The Scene: A perfectly conceived restaurant in the heart of Lincoln Park with superlative service that begins with the valet and continues right through the meal. Set menus allow for wide-ranging tasting of Trotter's exquisite and diverse creations. *Open Tues.–Sat. 5:30 p.m.–11 p.m.* $$$$

Hot Tip: Plan far in advance and book the kitchen table. Trotter will wow you with technique, and the food will just keep coming.

Everest
440 S. LaSalle St., 40th Floor, Loop/Downtown, 312-663-8920

The Draw: The very personal and very good cuisine prepared by Jean Joho; it's French with an Alsatian accent, which is an excuse for especially hearty preparations.

The Scene: A Masters of the Universe perch atop a 40-story office building with flawless service and a wine list that goes on for pages. The gregarious Joho loves chatting up the diners. *Open Tues.–Thurs. 5:30–9 p.m., Fri.–Sat. 5:30–10 p.m.* $$$$

Hot Tip: Scan the menu for Joho's signature salmon soufflé; if you don't see it, hint that you've heard it's good...

Tru
676 N. Saint Clair St., Near North, 312-202-0001

The Draw: A fine dining restaurant at the top of its game that infuses its food not just with flavor but also with fun.

The Scene: A suitably dramatic Streeterville location exudes drama, from the dark and moody entrance to the luminescent dining room. Diners exchange refined banter with the servers, who get a kick out of surprising people with yet another unannounced course of extraordinary food. The trademark caviar service on a small glass staircase is an example of Tru's flair. *Open Mon.–Thurs. 5:30–10 p.m., Fri.–Sat. 5:30–10:30 p.m.* $$$$

Hot Tip: By all means order the Grand Degustation, but keep the following day free so you can recuperate from an evening of wonderful excess.

Best

Gallery Spaces

Art galleries in Chicago come in all shapes and sizes and cater to all tastes. They can be found in four areas (with rough focus of works): North Michigan Avenue (famous dead artists), River North Gallery District (famous living artists), West Loop (artists you've never heard of, yet) and Wicker Park and Bucktown (artists you may never hear of, but who knows?).

Donald Young Gallery
933 W. Washington Blvd., West Loop, 312-455-0100

The Draw: Hot nationally known gallery for contemporary art. Young has a flair for finding works by artists who create buzz.

The Scene: It's a huge space in the burgeoning West Loop gallery district, and the size is needed, since 2-D pictures are only a part of the artworks offered. Expect to see videos, sculptures, and works in nontraditional media.
Open Tues.–Fri. 10 a.m.–5:30 p.m., Sat. 11 a.m.–5:30 p.m.

Hot Tip: Take time to chat up the staff. They're happy to give you a grounding in the latest art trends.

Flat Iron Building
1579 N. Milwaukee Ave., Wicker Park

The Draw: A huge collection of cutting-edge galleries in an angled brick building dating from the 1920s.

The Scene: The galleries offer an overview of current Chicago art—many are run by the artists themselves. Among the spaces to check out: photographer Diane Solis's Art Studio 210 and the Around the Coyote (ATC) Gallery, which shows some of the best works from the annual art festival.

Hot Tip: Drop by on the evening of the first Friday of the month, when all the galleries and spaces in the building are open. At other times, hours for some galleries can be erratic.

Richard Gray Gallery
875 N. Michigan Ave., Ste. 2503, Near North, 312-642-8877

The Draw: Top works by European and American artists of the 20th century, from Calder to Picasso.

The Scene: A large and refined gallery in the John Hancock Center on the Mag Mile. Works are well spaced and it is easy to focus on each one. Discreet salespeople soft-pedal the sell.
Open Tues.–Sat. 10 a.m.–5:30 p.m.

Hot Tip: Subscribe to the gallery's newsletter to get advance word on the arrival of major works.

Gay Bars

Halsted Street north of Belmont is Chicago's main neighborhood for gay culture and is affectionately known as Boystown—gay bars and clubs line its length to Addison Avenue. But that's not the only place for gay bars; several can be found on Clark Street in Andersonville and elsewhere around town.

Big Chicks
5024 N. Sheridan Rd., Andersonville, 773-728-5511

The Draw: A narrow, hip bar, renowned for its friendly vibe, that draws an unparalleled assortment of patrons from the lesbigay and straight communities.

The Scene: Murals of nude "big chicks" line the walls—try to guess which one is owner Michelle Fire (who says she got the moniker from locals while traveling in India). Works by artist regulars are also mounted. The bar can get very crowded, but a DJ keeps things movin' and groovin'.
Open Mon.–Fri. 4 p.m.–2 a.m., Sat. 3 p.m.–3 a.m., Sun. 11 a.m.–2 p.m. No cover.

Hot Tip: Sunday afternoons in warm weather are the time for free hot dogs, which draws retirees from the surrounding highrises, creating a curiously delightful scene.

SideTrack
3349 N. Halsted, Lakeview, 773-477-9189

The Draw: This video bar—Chicago's largest and most popular gay bar—is a veritable playground, with multiple rooms and bars (and large and small screens), a deck, and popular theme nights, all overseen by very talented VJs and friendly bartenders.

The Scene: Everyone. This anchor of Boystown (along with Roscoe's across the street, with which it might as well be connected by tunnels for all the cross-traffic) is a mandatory destination in Boystown for all except perhaps the serious leather crowd. Monday nights are show-tune nights (it's hilarious to see a bar packed with men singing along with *Oklahoma* and *God Bless America*); Thursdays are comedy nights, also very popular—the VJs scour sources to find offbeat stuff, and put it together with style.
Open Sun.–Fri. 3 p.m.–2 a.m., Sat. 3 p.m.–3 a.m. No cover.

Hot Tip: Supposedly SideTrack sells more Absolut vodka than any other American bar, and Absolut's president made a trip here to see the place for himself.

Spin
800 W. Belmont Ave., Lakeview, 773-327-7711

The Draw: The Friday-night shower contests, the Wednesday-night dollar-drink nights....

The Scene: Droves of guys ramble to and from this large lively dance club at the south end of the North Halsted strip, famous for its theme nights. DJs/VJs, a great sound system, and numerous video monitors keep the crowd happily spinning.
Open Sun.–Fri. 4 p.m.–2 a.m., Sat. 4 p.m.–3 a.m. $

Hot Tip: Thursday nights, Spin spins alternative music on the dance floor.

Guided Tours

It shouldn't be a surprise that in this town, where an appreciation of architecture is ingrained in the cultural fabric, there are numerous great tours to be found, and the Chicago Architecture Foundation offers enough great tours to fill ten "bests." But guided tours can also help you get to know other aspects of the city—focus on art, or experience Chicago's varied neighborhoods.

Art on the Move
Various locations, 847-432-6265

The Draw: Whatever interests you—a tour is customized to your tastes.

The Scene: Just you and a friend, or a large group, you decide. These folks organize scheduled and custom tours of art galleries, artists' studios, museums, and even private collectors' homes to show you whatever type of art you follow. $$

Hot Tip: If gardens are your thing, they can even do a botanic gardens tour.

Chicago Architecture Foundation
224 S. Michigan Ave., Loop/Downtown, 312-922-3432

The Draw: Enthusiastic guides take you on jaunts through the Loop and various neighborhoods and give you a chance to learn about important buildings you might have otherwise simply regarded as "cool" or "pretty."

The Scene: More than 40 tours are offered by the CAF, and they're simply some of the best activities you can sign up for. From Bucktown and Uptown to Hyde Park (and of course the Loop), the tours explain the fascinating and at times dramatic history of Chicago as told by its buildings. There are walking and bus tours, from a Loop photography tour to Mies and Modernism or Frank Lloyd Wright tours, and there's even an architecture river cruise—highly recommended. *Tours daily year-round.* $$$$

Hot Tip: Ask questions! The number one complaint from guides is that crowds stand around mute and don't take advantage of their knowledge.

Chicago Neighborhood Tours
78 E. Washington St., Loop/Downtown, 312-742-1190

The Draw: Unique and personal city-run tours that employ local residents as guides to explore the fabric of a different neighborhood each week.

The Scene: A luxury bus loaded with a diverse crowd of locals and visitors who are having fun learning the history of a neighborhood while stopping often to sample its cultural and commercial delights. *Tours Sat. 10 a.m.* $$$$

Hot Tip: Don't worry about which tour is offered when you're here, just go—they're all worth it.

Hip Museums

In a town filled with great and famous museums, ones like these are the places that help define Chicago's current culture. Each is known for its vibrant, ever-changing collection. A visit to them won't just give you a static look at some art, it will plug you in to the latest happenings in the zeitgeist.

Chicago Cultural Center
78 E. Washington St., Loop/Downtown, 312-744-6630

The Draw: A plethora of galleries and attractions, all housed in the grand 1897 former Chicago Public Library and all free.

The Scene: Always bustling, from the ground-floor cafe to the visitor information center and the galleries located on three floors. Rotating shows cover architecture, fine arts, folk arts, crafts, and cultural studies by nationally known artists as well as prominent Chicagoans. Lunchtime performances showcase a range of musical talent, including the nationally-broadcast Dame Myra Hess concerts.
Open Mon.–Fri. 10 a.m.–6 p.m., Sat. 10 a.m.–5 p.m., Sun. 11 a.m.–5 p.m.

Hot Tip: Explore the Beaux Arts interior with its rich ornamentation, especially the mosaic tiles around the two main staircases and in Preston Bradley Hall.

Mexican Fine Arts Center Museum
1852 W. 19th St., Pilsen, 312-738-1503

The Draw: A vibrant museum in Pilsen with a mix of Mexican art old and new, featuring many works by Chicago artists.

The Scene: An old field house on Harrison Park in Pilsen is the museum's original home; renovations and expansions have turned it into a showplace. The permanent collection has more than 3,500 items, some dating back to the pre-Columbian period.
Open Tues.–Sun. 10 a.m.–5 p.m. $

Hot Tip: On the important Mexican holiday of November 1, the Day of the Dead, the museum and Harrison Park come alive with festivities and art shows.

Museum of Contemporary Art
220 E. Chicago Ave., Near North, 312-280-2660

The Draw: The permanent collection includes Magritte, Duchamp, Miro, and of course Warhol, and the museum also presents rotating exhibits of modern and contemporary art.

The Scene: A cool and stylish viewer-friendly museum, looming large off the Mag Mile, with five floors of galleries branching off one main sunlit atrium. Spaces on the top floor feature performance art and other esoteric installations. There's a large sculpture garden, and Wolfgang Puck's cafe patio is a hidden gem.
Open Wed.–Sun. 10 a.m.–5 p.m., Tues. 10 a.m.–8 p.m. $

Hot Tip: Take one of the many free tours offered: introduction (daily at 1 p.m.), curator's (Tues., Sat., Sun.), and artist's (Tues.).

Hipster Hangouts

Hunting down hipsters can be as tough as tracking the rare and elusive jackalope. But while their tastes may be fickle and this week's watering hole is next week's...well, hole, the hip and those who follow them have a few places that always seem to remain on their migratory paths.

Le Passage
937 N. Rush St., Gold Coast, 312-255-0022

The Draw: A swank club/lounge/restaurant with a colonial tropics motif that delivers the goods, thanks to the tireless efforts of nightlife impresario Billy Dec. Very much an A-list place in the heart of the Gold Coast.

The Scene: Who's more beautiful, the crowd or the staff? It's hard to tell, especially after 10 p.m. when Le Passage fills up, heats up, and takes off with a trendy vibe that gets its beat from the pulsing action on the dance floor.
Open Wed.–Fri. 7 p.m.–4 a.m., Sat. 7 p.m.–5 a.m. $$

Hot Tip: Work your way back into the Yow bar with its dark and mysterious booths.

Sonotheque
1444 W. Chicago Ave., Wicker Park, 312-226-7600

The Draw: A hot and sexy yet surprisingly attitude-free club that is off the tourist beat and is known for its great DJ beats.

The Scene: Hipsters here to groove, drink, and hang with their tribes in a minimalist modern setting where the decor is designed to serve the sound: all materials used in the room both contribute to the space-age design and enhance the acoustics. Top DJs spin every night.
Open Tues.–Fri. 8 p.m.–2 a.m., Sat. 8 p.m.–3 a.m. $

Hot Tip: Wear whatever you like.

Wicker Park
Neighborhood centered on the intersection of North, Milwaukee, and Damen Avenues, Wicker Park

The Draw: Not just one club but an entire neighborhood. Hit the sidewalks and find some of the best bars and clubs in the city, as well as top venues for live music.

The Scene: Truly being hip means not trying to be, and that's the case in Wicker Park. Double Door (1572 N. Milwaukee Ave.) is the best music venue, Caffe Deluca (1721 N. Damen Ave.) is the best place for a shot of coffee, Davenport's Piano Bar and Cabaret (1383 N. Milwaukee Ave.) is the best place to sing a song, Ohba (2049 W. Division St.) is the best place for dinner...the beat goes on.

Hot Tip: Drop by Reckless Records (1532 N. Milwaukee Ave.), the unofficial neighborhood cultural center, and find out what's hot in the 'hood.

Jazz Clubs

Second only to the blues, jazz is the other sound of Chicago. A number of clubs book occasional jazz acts, but these three joints are prime venues for jazz every day of the year. These are the kinds of places you see in your mind when you hear a great jazz recording.

Green Dolphin Street
2200 N. Ashland Ave., Lincoln Park, 773-395-0066

The Draw: A sophisticated supper club whose swank decor harks back to the golden days of jazz, complete with candlelit tables.

The Scene: Chicago's largest jazz club is peopled with dressed-up, cocktail-swilling, cigar-smoking glitterati listening to regular acts like the Christian McBride Band or other major touring acts, from Big Band to Latin. There's also an outdoor atrium garden. *Club open Tues.–Thurs. 9 p.m.–2 a.m., Fri.–Sat. 8 p.m.–3 a.m., Sun. 8 p.m.–midnight (Sundays spring and summer only).* $$

Hot Tip: If you're hungry, the onsite restaurant offers a full menu of contemporary American cuisine, from foie gras to Columbia river sturgeon or Indiana pork chops.

Green Mill
4802 N. Broadway St., Uptown, 773-878-5552

The Draw: A 100-year-old bar that's as cool inside as the large stylized neon sign outside. The oldest jazz club in the U.S.

The Scene: Night owls of all stripes clamor for martinis at this storied club, which in the Prohibition era was a mobster hangout. Since then, it's stayed cool and remains on the hipster A-list (besides being a great place for jazz, swing, and blues, this is where poetry slams were invented). Do yourself a favor and get there early to snag one of the round booths. *Open Sun.–Thurs. 11 a.m.–4 a.m., Sat. noon–5 a.m.* $

Hot Tip: This is the best late-closing bar in the city north of Fullerton.

Jazz Showcase
59 W. Grand Ave., River North, 312-670-2473

The Draw: More than 50 years of experience presenting the best jazz to Chicago—owner Joe Segal does not book second-string acts.

The Scene: The showcase is no showplace, but that's just what you want from a great jazz club. The focus here is on the music. Segal helped launch Dave Brubeck back in the day, and he's still finding new talent today. *Shows Tues.–Thurs. 8 and 10 p.m., Fri.–Sat. 9 and 11 p.m., Sun. 4, 8, and 10 p.m.* $$$

Hot Tip: Parents are encouraged to bring kids to Sunday matinees. You've been warned.

Late-Night Eats

In a city where many bars and clubs go well past 2 a.m., late-night eateries need to be able to go the distance. The best joints have plenty of hangover-busting treats and patient servers able to interpret the most addled of orders.

Bar Louie
226 W. Chicago Ave., River North, 312-337-3313

The Draw: A long menu of favorite foods served right up until the last minute before closing. There are very few places in Chicago where you can get freshly fried calamari and a good Caesar salad at 3:30 a.m.

The Scene: This hip little spot on the border of River North and the Gold Coast has proven to be an unbeatable combination of cheerful, casual, and tasty. At any given hour, half the crowd is just having drinks while the other half is enjoying the food. The staff is laid-back and the jukebox has lots of good jazz and rock classics.
Open Sun.–Fri. 11 a.m.–4 a.m., Sat. 11 a.m.–5 a.m. $–$

Hot Tip: This first outpost of the citywide chain of Bar Louies still embodies all the cool traits that spawned its siblings. Come to this one first.

Iggy's
700 N. Milwaukee Ave., Wicker Park, 312-829-4449

The Draw: Lots of low-slung lounging, so you can coast through to the wee hours with someone special.

The Scene: Heavy velvet curtains confound prying eyes. Attentive servers mean you won't go thirsty or hungry (the kitchen serves major items like burgers and pasta right up to closing), or you can get it yourself at either of two bars. A walled-in patio serves the same refreshing function as a porch at a party.
Open Sun.–Fri. 7 p.m.–4 a.m., Sat. 7 p.m.–5 a.m. $

Hot Tip: Booths near the front are the most secluded.

Tempo
6 E. Chestnut St., Gold Coast, 312-943-4373

The Draw: A wall of glowing newspaper reviews greets you as you enter, which tells you that either the place is really good or that newspaper people often stay out late drinking. Actually, both are true.

The Scene: Coffee shop–simple and always crowded. A long menu, with anything egg being a standout (the apple-cheddar omelet is a classic), and the thick toast is a perfect delivery vehicle for the addictive jams. And when's the last time you had a Monte Cristo sandwich?
Open daily 24 hours. $

Hot Tip: If the sun's up and it's not snowing, sit out on the patio.

Best

Late-Night Hangouts

In a town where 25% of the bars and clubs have licenses until 4 a.m. (5 a.m. early Sunday), competition is fierce for the best places to stay up until the birds are chirping and Mr. Sun is getting ready to do his thing. What these three have in common is a vibe that's so transporting that when you glance at your watch you think, "What?!"

Exit
1315 W. North Ave., Wicker Park, 773-395-2700

The Draw: The best punk club between the coasts doesn't let up until they're chaining the doors shut.

The Scene: Death metal, Brit rock, and classic '80s punk are all played by the expert DJs, who each have their own following. There's enough black leather on display to outfit a fetish convention. Come to think of it, Exit *is* a fetish convention. *Open Sun.–Fri. 5 p.m.–4 a.m., Sat. 5 p.m.–5 a.m. $$*

Hot Tip: If you remember the punk bar scene in *After Hours*, you're probably too old.

Katacomb
1909 N. Lincoln Ave., Lincoln Park, 312-337-4040

The Draw: A laid-back and comfy cavern of a lounge full of beautiful people grooving to everything from classic rock to hip-hop and urban jazz.

The Scene: Scenesters, celebs, Lincoln Park loungers, and lots of industry types (the food and beverage industry, that is) congregate at this urban oasis designed by New York's Bogdanow Partners (Union Square Cafe, Cub Room). More hanging out and schmoozing than dancing, even on the DJed weekends. *Open Wed.–Fri. 8 p.m.–4 a.m., Sat. 8 p.m.–5 a.m. $*

Hot Tip: Heats up after midnight, gets really busy after 2 a.m. when other bars close.

Zentra
923 W. Weed St., Old Town, 312-787-0400

The Draw: A large and diverse club that takes in all stylish comers right up until closing, with plenty of places to hang, whether you're dancing or not.

The Scene: Something of the Kasbah, with lots of pillows and comfy sofas and seating. Go for the semiprivate booths with chain-mail shields to keep out the uninvited. Dancing on two floors means you have your choice of styles, which can be anything from disco to house. *Open Sun.–Fri. 10 p.m.–4 a.m., Sat. 10 p.m.–5 a.m. $*

Hot Tip: Go on Saturday nights to hear sensational DJ Psycho Bitch, who plays from an open booth.

Outdoor Activities

While you can get out in the winter and have a blast cross-country skiing through Lincoln Park or ice-fishing on Lake Michigan, let's face it—Chicago is much more fun in the summertime. From the first unseasonably warm weekend in March through the halcyon days of Indian summer, you'll find Chicagoans soaking up every minute of the great outdoors. Here are three unbeatable ways to do this.

Chicago River Canoe & Kayak
3400 N. Rockwell St., west of Lakeview, 773-252-3307

The Draw: A chance to explore an urban waterway from a vantage point 99% of Chicagoans have never enjoyed.

The Scene: Forget those stories about the river catching fire (that was Cleveland) — the North Branch of the Chicago River doesn't share the same industrial past as the waterways to the south. It flows with clean lake water, let in at Wilmette. Expect to see herons and many other birds along the river's leafy banks. *Open April–Oct.* $$$

Hot Tip: Make like a real explorer and rent a canoe; a coonskin cap is optional.

Grant Park/Millennium Park Concerts

The Draw: Sit near Lake Michigan under the stars and listen to some fabulous music while enjoying a picnic.

The Scene: For decades, Grant Park has been the home to a range of summer concerts performed for free in the open air. Besides special events like the Blues and Jazz Festivals, groups such as the Grant Park Symphony Orchestra play a full schedule. Now with the completion of Millennium Park and the stunning Frank Gehry–designed Pritzker Pavilion, many of these performances are moving to the new digs. Given the state-of-the-art sound system, that's all for the good. Free.

Hot Tip: Stake out space on the lawn in the front half of the Pritzker Pavilion for the best views of the stage.

Ravinia Festival
200–231 Ravinia Park Rd., Highland Park, IL, 847-266-5100

The Draw: Performers ranging from Deborah Voigt to Lyle Lovett—most everyone in showbiz in any form has appeared at this 100-year-old concert hall under the stars.

The Scene: Chicagoland's elite, trying to outdo one another with linens and silver candelabra at their picnic spreads; families with buckets of KFC; everyone else grabbing what they can from the onsite restaurants. *Park opens Mon.–Sat. at 5 p.m., Sun. at 4 p.m., with some exceptions, and showtimes vary; box office hours Mon.–Sat. 10 a.m.–6 p.m., Sun. 1–6 p.m.* $$$$+

Hot Tip: You can rent chairs if you don't want to sit on the lawn, or buy pavilion seats. You can also arrange to have a picnic catered for you by the restaurant staff.

Best

Over-the-Top Nightspots

A really over-the-top place leaves your head spinning even before you've had a drink. What qualifies? Wretched excess, for one—having a good idea and then taking it farther than anyone can imagine. Chicago always has a few of these places, maybe because the weather makes people stay indoors half the year.

Domaine
1045 N. Rush St., Gold Coast, 312-397-1045

The Draw: A chance to enjoy the extravagance of Versailles without leaving Chicago.

The Scene: Mirrors and gold everywhere you look. And as if red velvet wasn't posh enough for the chairs, some have coverings modeled after famous Chanel outfits. Bars on two floors serve a long list of French wines and—of course—many bubblies. Sit back and try to figure out which models are serving and which are there being served. *Open Sun.–Fri. 5 p.m.–4 a.m., Sat. 5 p.m.–5 a.m.* $$

Hot Tip: Book a Tribute Room, a private space where you can summon more wine using phones linked to the bar.

Kit Kat Lounge and Supper Club
3700 N. Halsted St., Wrigleyville, 773-525-1111

The Draw: Marilyn Monroe, Rita Hayworth, Bette Davis, Carmen Miranda, and a passel of other faux celebrities working the crowd in the Chicago outpost of the Puerto Vallarta cabaret/restaurant.

The Scene: Light and tropical seafood is served at supper while lip-synchers stroll through serenading; later it's all drinks (with and without umbrellas). White floors and banquettes are a sleek backdrop for black-and-white films projected on the walls, as well as for the performers, who, after several of the 82 available martinis, may seem to have walked right out of the movies. *Open daily 5:30 p.m.–1 a.m.* $

Hot Tip: Yes, they're all men.

Sugar
108 W. Kinzie St., River North, 312-822-9999

The Draw: Desserts aren't just eye candy at this plush lounge. Besides being a dance club, it also has a daring pastry chef who creates wild treats like a trio of warm chocolate cake, chocolate pot de crème, and chocolate sorbet, or a crème brûlée spiked with passion fruit and topped with roasted pineapple.

The Scene: Like something out of Candyland: tables that look like ribbons of candy, booths that look like white chocolate, and lights that look like beehives. House music reverberates in the background and you can take to the dance floor to burn it all off. *Open Sun.–Fri. 5 p.m.–2 a.m., Sat. 5 p.m.–3 a.m.* $$

Hot Tip: Pair your dessert with choices from the long list of wines and liqueurs.

Best

Plush Hotel Rooms

Ahhh, the joys and comforts of capitalism. Tough competition means that for a Chicago hotel to be king of the hill or top of the heap, its rooms have to be truly extraordinary. It's not an easy battle for hotels, but you the guest benefit from the competition. Any of the following have—let's be honest—rooms much nicer than the one you grew up in.

Four Seasons
120 E. Delaware Pl., Gold Coast, 312-280-8800

The Draw: Gracious rooms that are luxurious and comfortable without being fussy. Every need seems to have been anticipated, from the plush seating areas to the large marble bathrooms with large tubs for restful baths.

The Scene: Photo-shoot–worthy rooms decked out in warm colors that vary by room, separate sitting areas or sitting rooms, and stupendous views since all rooms are above the 30th floor. $$$$

Hot Tip: Go ahead, get the 900-square-foot one-bedroom deluxe suite. You can entertain and no one will even see your bedroom and bathroom (they'll use the guest bath).

Park Hyatt Chicago
800 N. Michigan Ave., Near North, 312-335-1234

The Draw: Stylish and modern rooms that are also slightly hedonistic and deeply comfortable. Also home to one of the city's most in-demand dining emporia.

The Scene: Rooms have Eames chairs for lounging, window seats for viewing, large glass-topped desks for working, deep tubs for soaking, and plush beds for sleeping. Clever touches abound, like the cherrywood window panels that open and allow you to enjoy the view while taking a long bath. $$$$

Hot Tip: Get a room facing the Water Tower. Try to make yourself get out and see the city.

The Peninsula Chicago
108 E. Superior St., Near North, 312-337-2888

The Draw: Rooms that seem comfortable and traditional until you discover that in reality they're high-tech marvels. Little touches like steam-proof screens on the bathroom TVs tell you that they've thought of everything.

The Scene: Luxurious rooms with comfortable furnishings in light colors and bedside control panels with which you can knock yourself out adjusting the lights, temperature, and just about every other aspect of the room; gracious public spaces popular with guests and nonguests alike; a sensational spa—in short, heaven. $$$$

Hot Tip: Get one of the rooms facing the Mag Mile for early morning sunshine, and do a few laps in the pool, which has the same great views.

Restaurants with a View

Chicago is its own view. There's nothing nearby like, say, a range of mountains to provide a vista in the distance. And unlike the pounding waves on view at the ocean, Lake Michigan tends to just sit there. But the city itself has remarkable views, from its soaring buildings to its intricate web of streets and railroads. And sometimes the best Chicago views are small and exquisite, a single stunning scene.

NoMi
800 N. Michigan Ave., Near North, 312-239-4030

The Draw: Postcard-perfect views out its windows, which frame the Water Tower and Michigan Avenue.

The Scene: One of Chicago's best restaurants serves creative fusion cuisine that changes to reflect the seasons. When snow is falling on the Water Tower, expect hearty and comforting fare. When the sidewalks are awash in sundresses, you can feast on the rich berries and extraordinary tomatoes of the Midwest summer.
Open for breakfast Mon.–Fri. 6:30–10:30 a.m., Sat. 7–11 a.m., Sun. 7–10:30 a.m.; brunch Sun. 10:30 a.m.–2:30 p.m.; lunch Mon.–Fri. 11:30 a.m.–2:30 p.m., Sat. noon–2:30 p.m.; dinner daily 5:30–10 p.m. $$$$

Hot Tip: Book a window table early, since there are only seven.

North Pond
2610 N. Cannon Dr., Lincoln Park, 773-477-5845

The Draw: A jewel of a restaurant overlooking the pond for which it's named, in the leafiest part of Lincoln Park.

The Scene: A former park warming shed has been given a splendid Arts and Crafts makeover and is now home to hot young chef Bruce Sherman and his inviting regional cuisine. The views out the windows of the pond and the trees beyond could be those of a remote lakeside retreat.
Open for brunch Sat.–Sun. 11 a.m.–2 p.m.; lunch (summer only) Tues.–Fri. 11:30 a.m.–2 p.m.; dinner Tues.–Sun. 5:30–10 p.m. $$$

Hot Tip: On clear summer nights, you can't beat a table on the patio under the stars.

The Signature Room (at the 95th)
John Hancock Center, 875 N. Michigan Ave., Near North, 312-787-9596

The Draw: Views of three states, with sustenance handy to help you through the experience. The elevator ride up is the world's fastest.

The Scene: Lunch is a buffet with tasty salads, dinner has the usual mix of steaks, seafood, and pasta. But your attention will be elsewhere as you contemplate the third largest urban area in the U.S.
Open daily for lunch 11 a.m.–2:30 p.m.; dinner 5–10 p.m. $$$

Hot Tip: A drink here costs less than admission to the observation deck one floor below.

Romantic Rendezvous

Any place can be romantic, as you'll know if you've ever fallen in love at, say, rehab or Weight Watcher's. There's plenty of punks at Exit that will tell you that they met their, er, you know, "person" at that raucous club. But for a romantic spot that needs no explaining, go all gooey inside at one of these three places.

Buckingham Fountain
Grant Park, Loop/Downtown

The Draw: An enormous fountain modeled on one at Versailles that pumps 14,000 gallons per minute through 133 jets. The formal piazzalike setting in Grant Park helps set a hushed mood.

The Scene: The fountain is in a vast open area that can accommodate scores of couples who are able to keep a discreet distance from everyone else. At night, a multitude of lights hit the surging streams with a constantly changing rainbow of colors. The effect is at once powerful and soothing—you can't help but start smooching whomever you're there with.
Operates 10 a.m.–11 p.m. May–Oct.

Hot Tip: Every hour, Buckingham Fountain climaxes, sending its central stream 150 feet into the air.

Opera
1301 S. Wabash Ave., South Loop, 312-461-0161

The Draw: Six tables at this bustling South Loop restaurant are set in the old film vaults of this former movie distribution warehouse, letting you lock yourself away with the one you love.

The Scene: The restaurant bustles, except within the quiet confines of the vault tables, where the world can be easily forgotten. The daring Asian food invites sharing, which adds to the mood.
Open Sun.–Wed. 5–10 p.m., Thurs. 5–11 p.m., Fri.–Sat. 5 p.m.–midnight. $$$

Hot Tip: Let your server pair your dishes with wines from the long list—ahh, romance.

Pops for Champagne
2934 N. Sheffield Ave., Lakeview, 773-472-1000

The Draw: More than 130 champagnes poured in a quiet setting, with small jazz groups providing the score.

The Scene: Dim lights, candles, a fireplace, an intimate room with a tiny stage, champagne and caviar—what more could you ask of a romantic venue? If champagne is not your thing, they also have an extensive selection of single-malt scotches, cognacs, and liqueurs.
Open Sun.–Fri. 6 p.m.–2 a.m., Sat. 8 p.m.–2 a.m. $

Hot Tip: For a more casual place without the live music, call in next door at Pops' sibling, Star Bar, which offers the same champagne list if you ask.

Scene Bars

Not content to merely peddle drinks, these bars peddle attitude and glamour as well, to insatiable throngs who wouldn't think of going anywhere else—at least until a new bar opens and steals the scene. Get 'em while they're hot.

Base Bar
Hard Rock Hotel, 230 N. Michigan Ave., Loop/Downtown, 312-345-1000

The Draw: The hippest place in the Loop to enjoy a cocktail, which puts it solidly on every scenester's itinerary.

The Scene: Low leather sofas and chairs are well spaced so you can ignore those other people even as you're checking out their clothes. A dark backlit bar mixes a long list of cocktails served by a responsive staff that makes sure you don't go dry. *Open Sun.–Fri. 5 p.m.–2 a.m., Sat. 5 p.m.–3 a.m.* No cover.

Hot Tip: The inverted-mushroom–shaped white leather chairs in the middle look comfortable, but there's a reason no one stays in them long.

Ghost
440 W. Randolph St., West Loop, 312-575-9900

The Draw: An A-list bar over an A-list restaurant (Nine) run by two A-list guys (Michael Morton and Scott DeGraff) whose every A-list friend is here.

The Scene: The chic, sleek design complements the figures of the crowd. It's all freeform futuristic shapes and forms, and it's also very dark. But aside from the intimacy it engenders, it also lets you appreciate the various theme drinks like the glow-in-the-dark Ghostini, which mixes Midori and vodka and comes with Casper on the swizzle stick. For something a little more devilish, go for the Ghost, which adds champagne to Midori. *Open Thurs.–Fri. 9 p.m.–2 a.m., Sat. 9 p.m.–3 a.m.* $$

Hot Tip: Get there before 11 p.m. or you won't have a ghost of a chance of getting in— unless you have dinner at Nine first, where patrons are given priority if it's crowded.

Y/Sound-Bar
224–226 W. Ontario St., River North, 312-274-1880

The Draw: Y is an intimate space that caters to a very exclusive group of people: those who are loaded with looks, money, and attitude.

The Scene: Various shades of yellow are combined with patterns such as faux ostrich and alligator to create a minimalist space that still manages to exude wealth. You can pour from your own $200 bottle of vodka or $1,000 bottle of champagne, or let the solicitous staff earn its keep. Got a hankering for a snack? There's a full range of caviar available. *Open Thurs.–Fri. 9 p.m.–2 a.m., Sat. 9 p.m.–3 a.m.* $$

Hot Tip: The adjoining Sound-Bar is not as exclusive as it would pretend to be, due to a need to fill its vast space. Come to Y to canoodle, go to Sound-Bar to dance.

Sexy Lounges

A sexy lounge gets your pheromones flowing as soon as you enter, and the best sexy lounges—like these three—offer you plenty of places to hide away and let the juices flow. The ingredients: places to cavort in seclusion, sensual libations, enticing decor, and just the right mood.

Harry's Velvet Room
56 W. Illinois St., River North, 312-527-5600

The Draw: Sexy, funky music wafts through this plush room, which features nests of secluded booths and sofas lit dimly by candlelight. Are you ready to make out yet?

The Scene: Harry's is below street level, and that adds to the secretive mood of its intimate interior. Several champagnes by the glass are available, as well as more exotic elixirs. Crowds of the unattached hang around the bars and look enviously at those in the shadows.
Open Mon.–Wed. 6 p.m.–4 a.m., Thurs.–Fri. 5 p.m.–4 a.m., Sat. 8 p.m.–5 a.m., Sun. 9 p.m.–4 a.m. $

Hot Tip: Head back to the even more secluded back room for the fireplace.

Moda
25 W. Hubbard St., River North, 312-670-2200

The Draw: *Moda* means "fashion" in Italian—and that pretty much tells you everything you need to know.

The Scene: Models (and that includes the staff) and wannabes lounging around on low sofas while videos of fashion shows play on a multitude of monitors. Less frenetic club music than usual means you won't mess up your outfit dancing. Huge red leaves climb the walls from the stylized bar, and the effect is reminiscent of the old Paris Metro entrances.
Open Thurs.–Fri. 8 p.m.–2 a.m., Sat. 8 p.m.–3 a.m. $$

Hot Tip: Monthly fashion shows are heaven for patrons.

Narcisse
710 N. Clark St., River North, 312-787-2675

The Draw: A lavish bar that would do Narcissus proud. Stop looking in that mirror and pay attention to your companion.

The Scene: Gold, mirrors, brocade, velvet; if it's opulence you want, you'll luxuriate in it here. Settle back into one of the private booths and work your way through the menu of eleven champagnes by the glass (more than a hundred by the bottle) and caviar from three continents.
Open Mon.–Fri. 5 p.m.–2 a.m., Sat. 5 p.m.–3 a.m., Sun. 7 p.m.–2 a.m. $$

Hot Tip: Get there slightly ahead of the 11 p.m. weekend rush to beat the odds and score a booth. You can have a classic French dinner here, but Narcisse is really about cooing and purring by the reflected light of a champagne glass.

Shopping Streets

Everyone knows Michigan Avenue—the Mag Mile—but it has so many stores and malls that it's almost a shopping town rather than a street. For the best shopping and a more intimate experience, head to the streets you can cover in an afternoon or a day (okay, we heard that shopaholic voice say "a week") and find more unique stuff for your spree.

Armitage Avenue
West from Lincoln Ave. to Sheffield Ave., Lincoln Park

The Draw: Designer boutiques, salons, and stores geared to the two-income vibe of posh Lincoln Park. Armitage chicly balances the trendy scene of Bucktown's Damen Avenue with the traditional luxuries of Oak Street.

The Scene: Two professional women on maternity leave talking gibberish on cell phones, to each other, and to their babies in the strollers. Retail highlights include Lori's (a women's shoe Mecca, No. 824), A Unique Presence (custom furniture and design, No. 837), Barker & Meowsky (pet accoutrements, No. 1003), Faded Rose (exquisite interior items, No. 1017), and Jane Hamill (light and airy frocks, No. 1115),

Hot Tip: Take a breather from your browsing and stop at Argo Tea Café (No. 958).

Damen Avenue
North of Milwaukee Ave. to Webster Ave., Bucktown

The Draw: Hip and trendy shopping among young designers and their boutiques in Bucktown.

The Scene: Fashion-conscious folk under 30 looking for the right outfit to wear to the hottest new club. Don't miss Daffodil Hill (date clothes, No. 1659), Running Away (sporty wear, No. 1753), lille (home and personal accessories, No. 1923), and iCandy (clothes for a night out, No. 1960).

Hot Tip: Recover from the stresses of consumerism at Meritage Wine Bar (No. 2118).

Oak Street
The block between Michigan Ave. and Rush St., Gold Coast

The Draw: More than 50 high-end salons and boutiques in one long tree-lined city block that anchors the Gold Coast. It doesn't get any more exclusive (or pricier) than this.

The Scene: Not only would a fur-draped woman walking a coiffed poodle not look out of place here, you'd expect to see one. Among the current retail stars are Prada (No. 30), Chacok (No. 47), Luca Luca (No. 59), Kate Spade (No. 101), Hermès (No. 110), and Marina Rinaldi (No. 113). Barney's New York, the très chic department store, anchors the west end (No. 25).

Hot Tip: Join the ladies who lunch having a late-afternoon martini at Gibson's Steak House (1028 N. Rush St.).

Spas

A great spa rejuvenates you through a series of therapies and techniques using lotions, potions, and other treatments that often sound so exotic they may as well have been plucked from Mars. But the time spent will be worth it. You'll be a new you, ready for more of Chicago's razzmatazz.

Honey Child Salon and Spa
735 N. LaSalle St., River North, 312-573-1300

The Draw: You can't help but giggle and feel good at a spa that describes every service as a "treat."

The Scene: A warm-hued complex where the staff is sweet as sugar but manages to avoid parody by not calling you "honey." A pollen byproduct figures in numerous treats, including the mango honey sugar scrub, the honey quench skin mask, and the crème and honey hand treatment.
Open Tues.–Wed. 10 a.m.–6 p.m., Thurs.–Fri. 10 a.m.–9 p.m., Sat. 9 a.m.–5 p.m., Sun. 11 a.m.–5 p.m. $$$$+

Hot Tip: Obviously, you'll want the "Taste of Honey" treatment, which combines a honey rock massage with a facial, pedicure, and manicure.

Nordstrom Spa
55 E. Grand Ave., Near North, 312-464-1515

The Draw: The same customer service that has made the store legendary can be found in its spa. Expect to be pampered and have your every wish catered to.

The Scene: Nordstrom eschews the gimmicks popular at many spas. There's a range of skin therapies and exfoliations, and they're simply wonderful. Special baths can include essential oils and mustard essence, and you can envelop yourself in a full body wrap based either on mud or algae. Numerous forms of massage are available.
Open daily by appointment. $$$$+

Hot Tip: Opt for the enticingly named "Spa Euphoria," which gives you 2-1/2 hours of skin treatments and massage.

The Peninsula Spa
The Peninsula Chicago, 108 E. Superior St., Near North, 312-337-2888

The Draw: A luxurious and spacious spa at one of the city's best hotels. Individual and personalized attention.

The Scene: Set on two levels, the spa opens on to the Peninsula's sun-drenched palatial pool. Everything is light and airy, and the therapies make use of many organic fruit products. The goal is to "rejuvenate and refresh," and they certainly achieve it.
Open Mon.–Fri. 6 a.m.–10 p.m., Sat.–Sun. 7 a.m.–8 p.m. $$$$+

Hot Tip: Seclude yourself with the "Sanctuary for the Senses," a 2-1/2-hour series of therapies that includes massage, detoxification, and a body polishing.

Sports Bars

Chicago is a great sports town, and there are hundreds of bars that cater to fans of every stripe. In fact, no matter how obscure your university or college, you can probably find a bar that has been claimed by fans. The best sports bars carry all the games of the moment in an atmosphere that offers enough fun that you may miss the game.

Bernie's
3664 N. Clark St., Wrigleyville, 773-525-1898

The Draw: The one honest sports bar in Wrigleyville is right across from the ballpark and attracts hard-core fans as well as a few players and journalists before and after the game.

The Scene: Wrigleyville is filled with cynical sports bars that fleece the fans and suburban day-trippers by jacking up their beer prices on game days. Bernie's stays true to its humble roots and keeps its prices cheap for the loyal crowd of gritty regulars.
Open Sun.–Fri. 8 a.m.–2 a.m., Sat. 8 a.m.–3 a.m. No cover.

Hot Tip: Whatever you do, don't speak the name Bartman (the grabby fan who helped ensure the playoff fiasco in 2003).

Gamekeeper's
1971 N. Lincoln Ave., Lincoln Park, 773-549-0400

The Draw: Roughly 50 TVs, in sizes ranging from big to huge, showing a dozen or more games at all times.

The Scene: What you'd expect in a clubby sports bar: pennants on the walls, lots of polished wood and brass, cheeseburgers on the menu, lots of guys arguing about statistics, lots of women figuring they've found a good place to find a guy, and constant specials featuring the kinds of beers they make you drink in stadiums.
Open Mon.–Fri. 5 p.m.–4 a.m., Sat. 11 a.m.–5 a.m., Sun. 11 a.m.–4 a.m. No cover.

Hot Tip: On a Chicago Bears football Sunday, don't ever shout, "Go Packers!"

Hi-Tops
3551 N. Sheffield Ave., Wrigleyville, 773-348-0009

The Draw: A huge two-level sports bar near Wrigley Field that's friendly to a fault.

The Scene: When you've counted 60 TVs, quit and have another beer. A crop of satellite dishes brings in every sporting event the video engineer (they do have one) can find. If you're doing a thesis on beer poster design, you'll get all your research done here. In order to broaden the bar's appeal, some TVs show popular entertainment—although *Survivor* probably counts as a sporting event anyway.
Open Sun.–Fri. 11 a.m.–2 a.m., Sat. 11 a.m.–3 a.m. No cover.

Hot Tip: Guys: there are plenty of women around on Tuesday's *Gilmore Girls* night; tear yourself away from the New Zealand rugby.

Steak Houses

Ever since the time when the Stockyards supplied half the meat to the nation, Chicago has loved a good steak—in fact, the city has thrived on them. Even today, most restaurants offer at least a beefy dish or two (although it's kind of comical to see a sirloin creation in a sushi-fusion place). But for real steaks, go to a real steak house.

Chicago Chop House
60 W. Ontario St., River North, 312-787-7100

The Draw: Prime steaks, in sizes from big and bigger to huge, all served in a historic old brownstone in the heart of River North.

The Scene: A no-nonsense collection of sated carnivores surround tables on two floors. Many will be sending their receipts directly to the accounting department because you can't go wrong taking a client here.
Open for lunch Mon–Fri 11:30 a.m.–4 p.m.; dinner Mon.–Thurs. 4–11 p.m., Fri.–Sat. 4–11:30 p.m., Sun. 4–11 p.m. $$$

Hot Tip: Unless you've been boning up on the labels and varietals, let the server guide you through the much-lauded 500-item wine list.

Gene & Georgetti
500 N. Franklin St., River North, 312-527-3718

The Draw: Huge and tender aged steaks, char-grilled to perfection and served by waiters whose tenure is measured in decades.

The Scene: A quaint little wooden building in River North under the El tracks. It's fair to say that almost all of the traditional steak-loving crowd owns one or more Sinatra albums.
Open Mon.–Thurs. 11 a.m.–11 p.m., Fri.–Sat. 11 a.m.–midnight. $$$

Hot Tip: Don't fall for the hype attaching fake cachet to the tables downstairs—they're for status-conscious tourists. Upstairs you'll get a table quicker, which is why half the crowd is local.

Morton's
1050 N. State St., River North, 312-266-4820

The Draw: A local legend that spread to Beverly Hills and elsewhere by serving the finest of steaks and lobster at prices that ensure all future Morton children are trust-fund babies.

The Scene: A vast basement room with exposed brick walls, plush carpet, and large booths. The size of the portions of everything, from the shrimp appetizer and the salads to the hunks of meat, borders on the ridiculous—but you won't be laughing, you'll be grinning with pleasure.
Open Mon.–Sat. 5:30–11 p.m., Sun. 5–10 p.m. $$$$

Hot Tip: To be sure you have room for the signature key lime pie, have it as an appetizer.

Swanky Hotel Bars

There was a time when a hotel bar was *the* place to have a drink. Stylish and sophisticated, these were the places you wanted to meet a client, a date, a lover, or a friend—or just contemplate life and enjoy a moment's solitude. But one too many cookie-cutter chain hotels gave hotel bars a bad name. Happily that's changed. Chicago is in the midst of a renaissance in hotel bars that once again have become *the* places to drink.

The Bar
The Peninsula Chicago, 108 E. Superior St., Near North, 312-573-6766

The Draw: A large bar that feels like your own private club. Don't worry whether they have your drink or label—they do.

The Scene: At once refined yet relaxed, The Bar at the Peninsula has quickly gained a local following, thanks to its careful attention to service and its soothing atmosphere with striking lighting and very comfortable leather seating.
Open Mon.–Thurs. 3 p.m.–1 a.m., Fri. 3 p.m.–2 a.m., Sat. noon–2 a.m., Sun. noon–1 a.m.

Hot Tip: The delicious bar-mix snack that the server gives you is addictive—be careful if you have dinner plans.

Coq d'Or
The Drake, 140 E. Walton Pl., Gold Coast, 312-932-4622

The Draw: A timeless lounge with live piano music most nights and formal servers for whom pouring a good mixed drink never went out of style.

The Scene: "Ahhhh" is the most commonly heard exclamation as patrons enter this distinguished bar. A row of deep red leather booths lines the wall and welcomes you to sit and stay a while.
Open Mon.–Sat. 11 a.m.–2 a.m., Sun. 11 a.m.–1 a.m.

Hot Tip: Several of the classic dishes from the Drake's Cape Cod Room restaurant (like the superb clam chowder) can be ordered at the bar.

Le Bar
Sofitel Chicago Water Tower, 20 E. Chestnut St., Gold Coast, 312-324-4000

The Draw: A beautifully conceived bar with a crowd of cutting-edge Gold Coast types unwinding after work.

The Scene: A visually stunning room with an intriguing overlook on Rush Street and a club music soundtrack. The cool and stylish bar is just one example of the focus on architecture here; it's a motif used throughout the interior, including a lounge area with a library of books on architecture.
Open daily 3 p.m.–1 a.m.

Hot Tip: Order a martini, and the server pours it tableside.

Best

Trendy Tables

Some restaurants are only trendy the night they open—heck, some are only trendy during the preopening press party. Truly trendy restaurants are packed with hipsters night after night, week after week, and month after month. That's what separates the best trendy places from the poseurs, and these are the real deal.

Japonais
600 W. Chicago Ave., River North, 312-822-9600

The Draw: A fusion of two hot concepts by two local restaurateurs brings together trendy sushi with modern and whimsical Japanese cuisine.

The Scene: River North's beautiful people have found a new hangout right on the river. In such a setting you might expect the sensual dining rooms to be a triumph of form over substance, but happily the food's as good as the room looks. Post-meal, there's a cool and groovy lounge downstairs.
Open for lunch Mon.–Fri. noon–2:30 p.m.; dinner Mon.–Thurs. 5–11 p.m., Fri.–Sat. 5–11:30 p.m., Sun. 5–10 p.m. $$$

Hot Tip: The deck overlooking the Chicago River has the hottest-ticket outdoor tables in town.

Nacional 27
325 W. Huron St., River North, 312-664-2727

The Draw: Rich Melman gives his Midas touch to the salsa craze, producing a place that, like all his places, is filled with A-list hipsters having a ball.

The Scene: The name comes from the 27 nations of Latin America and the Caribbean, and influences from all of them can be found on the fun menu, which combines tropical flavors and spicy accents. The staff works the crowd, adding to the already high level of energy fueled by the many fanciful drinks.
Open Mon.–Thurs. 5:30–9:30 p.m., Fri.–Sat. 5:30–11 p.m.; bar Mon.–Thurs. 5 p.m.– midnight, Fri. 5 p.m.–2 a.m., Sat. 5 p.m.–3 a.m. $$$

Hot Tip: At 10 p.m. they start clearing tables for the dancing that doesn't stop until closing.

SushiSamba Rio
504 N. Wells St., River North, 312-595-2300

The Draw: A hyperactive *Sex in the City* vibe where anything feels possible.

The Scene: The restaurant and the patrons are both bold and beautiful. A busy sushi bar rocks to a salsa beat, thanks to the fusion of Latin and Asian cultures. The menu makes sense when you realize that ceviche is made with raw fish and that the Japanese love their steaks.
Open Mon.–Thurs. 11:45 a.m.–1 a.m., Fri.–Sat. 11:45 a.m.–2 a.m., Sun. 11:45 a.m.–midnight. $$$

Hot Tip: Be very careful mixing your sake and your caipirinhas, both of which flow freely.

The Chicago Experience

You've only got three days to squeeze the maximum fun out of Chicago. Where do you begin? That depends on which Chicago you're looking for. We've prepared five Thursday-through-Saturday itineraries geared toward those in the know who start weekends early to catch the hottest crowds (and hang with the locals). Whether you're looking for the best little blues joint or the scene-iest scene lounge, we've got you covered.

Classic Chicago

You can see why Sinatra and other crooners would claim this town as their own. It really is "one town that won't let you down," whether you're looking for cutting-edge style or classic culture, and everywhere you go, people truly seem to be enjoying themselves. The Loop is studded with architectural gems that draw visitors from around the world, the city's well-financed museums fairly burst with famous art and exhibits, and the lakefront and parks are a joy. Though the stockyards are long gone, Chicago continues to be a place where you can get a great steak, and otherwise fortifying yourself is a source of endless pleasure, considering there are scores of classic and ethnic eateries that keep the dining scene white-hot. And that's not counting the iconic local vittles like pizza, ribs, and hot dogs that are grounded in the town's working-class roots but reach their apotheosis here. Entertainment options are even more wide-ranging, whether you're grooving to the local blues, rocking out, dancing cheek-to-cheek, seeing edgy new theatre, or just unwinding over a pint or three until 4 a.m. Chicago's still a town where you can "holler and whoop all through the Loop"—and beyond.

Classic Chicago: The Itinerary

Three Great Days and Nights

Your Hotel: **The Drake**

Day 1

Morning: Get yourself fueled for the big day ahead at **Lou Mitchell's**, where the size and quality of the omelets is legendary, or at the **Original Pancake House**, which has a name that says it all—try the *apple pancakes*.

This morning, take some time to look around this great city and its famous architecture—few other cities can boast seminal works by Daniel Burnham, Frank Lloyd Wright, and Louis Sullivan, not to mention a new Frank Gehry. A Chicago River and lake cruise offers a unique way to *savor the skyline*. The best narration is provided aboard the boat operated by the **Chicago Architecture Foundation** (CAF). On land, you can also experience Chicago's famous architecture up close through a range of CAF Architecture Tours by foot or bus, and it also offers neighborhood and Frank Lloyd Wright tours.

Afternoon: For your first lunch, chomp into famous Chicago eats. Many places outside Chicago claim to have "Chicago pizza," but you'll never get the real thing anywhere else. At **Pizzeria Uno**, they've been making *classic deep-dish pizza* since 1943, and it's the *ne plus ultra*. For a different iconic experience, head down to the authentic **Billy Goat Tavern**, a favorite journalists' hangout and the inspiration for the classic *Saturday Night Live* John Belushi skit "Cheezburger, cheezburger, chips, chips."

First stop this afternoon: the **Chicago Cultural Center**, right on Michigan Avenue in the Loop. Take in the splendors of "the People's Palace," as this beautiful former central library has been called (be sure to check out the elaborate *Tiffany mosaics*). The center is home to several floors of art galleries and a city-run visitor information center where you can book neighborhood or El train tours.

While you're in the Loop, explore some renowned examples of large *public sculpture*: *Flamingo* by Alexander Calder (Dearborn and Adams Streets); *The Four Seasons* mosaic by Marc Chagall (Monroe and Clark

CLASSIC CHICAGO

Streets); *Miro's Chicago* by Joan Miro (Washington Street between Dearborn and Clark Streets); and the most famous of the bunch, *Untitled* by Pablo Picasso, a city icon (Washington and Dearborn Streets).

Now that you've gotten the lay of the land, hit the heights and see it all from above. The **John Hancock Center** is the city's third-tallest building and offers *great views* from its observation deck, or, better yet, from the Signature Lounge at the 96th, which tops the observation deck by two floors and offers cocktails and live jazz with your views.

Evening: For upscale dining with those drop-dead views, try **The Signature Room** (at the 95th), for dinner. Or, back down on terra firma, try to score the fabled Booth One at the **Pump Room**, where stars have gathered since 1938—Bogie and Bacall celebrated their wedding here, and Judy Garland and Frank Sinatra practically camped out in *Booth One* (though not together). For something more Old World, tuck in to some caviar and blinis with one of the many infused vodkas they pour at **Russian Tea Time**.

The Windy City's other famous moniker is also the name of one of its most famous entertainment institutions. **The Second City** is a smart sketch and improv *comedy club* that's been breaking new ground for more than 40 years and has an alumni list that reads like a Hollywood *Who's Who*. Or try some high drama at one of the many theatres in the **Loop Theatre District**.

Close out the day in style. Choose from one of the 135 champagnes in the cellars at **Pops for Champagne** and settle back with someone special, sipping to the sounds of smooth jazz. Or head north to the funky **Green Mill**, which for almost 100 years has been serving up *jazz and booze*. Or just mellow out with a classic martini at **Coq d'Or** in the Drake Hotel.

Day 2

Morning: You can plan for your day ahead with coffee and treats from room service, or head over to the **Oak Tree**, a *classic coffee shop* once found off Michigan Avenue but now high above it. For a perfect continental breakfast, try the pastries and coffee at **Albert's Café & Patisserie**.

This morning, grab your clubs and head for the green—one of the four superior courses at **Cog Hill Golf and Country Club.** Course Four is home to the PGA Western Open and is a beaut of a course. If you're not a fan of the links, take some time today to get to know Chicago's famous Loop. Stroll down *State Street*, the self-proclaimed "great street," with its shops, hotels, and theatres, plus famous landmarks like the Louis Sullivan–designed Carson Pirie Scott store and **Marshall Field's**, Chicago's famed department store.

Afterward, pamper yourself with the classic ministrations at the **Nordstrom Spa**, which offers everything from massages to *algae wraps* to get you ready for your remaining nights on the town.

Afternoon: For lunch, time-warp at **The Berghoff**, a downtown institution that holds its *German Beerhall* roots close as it serves up wurst and schnitzel, homemade rye breads, and its own beers—there's even a carpentry shop on the second floor to keep the vintage oak furniture in shape. Alternately, relive the glories—but not the grease—of a 1950s diner at the ever-popular **Ed Debevic's.** Or go totally casual and head to **Portillo's Hot Dogs**, where you're spared having to choose condiments because in Chicago virtually every condiment is piled on (except ketchup—*never* add ketchup).

This afternoon is reserved for the glories of the **Art Institute of Chicago**, a truly *world-class art museum*. Take your time and choose your rooms—there are more than 100. From Renoir, Degas, and the Monet haystacks to Hopper's *Nighthawks* and Grant Wood's *American Gothic,* they're all here. And don't just concentrate on the acclaimed European art— the Asian collection has amazing treasures from every Chinese dynasty, and special exhibits often bring together works from around the world.

Evening: For dinner, more classics await. **Gene & Georgetti** trades on its status as *Frank Sinatra's favorite steak joint,* while the **Chicago Chop House** simply trades on its excellent meats and its endless wine list.

This evening, settle in under stars twinkling in the ceiling of the **Music Box Theatre**, which shows indie and foreign films in a restored *mini–movie palace* designed to look like an Italian courtyard. If you're not a cineaste, wander over to **Navy Pier** for a stroll along its half-mile of restaurants, bars, shops, museums, and performance spaces—check what's on at their outdoor concert or indoor Shakespeare stages.

CLASSIC CHICAGO

Finish the day with a booty shake. **Excalibur** is an enormous *multilevel dance club* with music from rock to house pulsing through its many spaces—one-stop shopping for any boogie urge you need to itch. For something more traditional, try **Jilly's**, which trades on its Rat Pack associations while letting you dance cheek-to-cheek.

Day 3

Morning: A couple of classic breakfast venues vie for your patronage. At **Tempo**, don't be surprised if you see a few stragglers still in their evening clothes from the previous night. Fortunately the endless cups of coffee and bounteous breakfasts soon set everything straight. Or just grab a quick coffee to get you going, and head down to the classic **Palace Grill**, where the *hash browns* win raves from truckers and visiting prime ministers alike.

The South Loop, which today is a mixture of warehouses and fast-spreading gentrification (Mayor Daley lives here), was once Chicago's *"millionaire's row,"* before all the rich folks moved north to the Gold Coast. This morning, step back into the style of 120 years ago with a walk along Prairie Avenue, stopping in at the **Glessner House**, a neo-Romanesque masterpiece in rose-colored granite with a restored interior.

Nearby, two unique institutions await. You can feel the emotion in the artistic expressions of those Americans who fought in Southeast Asia at the **National Vietnam Veterans Art Museum**. Then, if there were United Nations World Heritage Sites for music, the *Chess Records building*—now home to **Willie Dixon's Blues Heaven Foundation**—would be one. A generation of blues musicians including Dixon recorded here and brought the music to the people (including the Rolling Stones, who came here to record).

Afternoon: For lunch head a bit farther south to Chicago's thriving *Chinatown*. Take your pick at **Emperor's Choice**, where the seafood dishes are as authentic as any this side of Hong Kong. After lunch, enjoy vibrant Wentworth Avenue and its array of unique Chinese shops and grocers.

Spend the afternoon trying to tackle the trio of Chicago cultural icons at the Museum Campus. Take your pick from the **Field Museum**, which celebrates natural history (and houses Sue, the world's largest, most complete *Tyrannosaurus rex*), the **John G. Shedd Aquarium**, which includes the largest marine mammal pavilion in the world, and the **Adler Planetarium**, where you can explore the cosmos.

Then stroll back toward the Loop through Chicago's front yard, **Grant Park**. Its formal gardens give the skyline a dignified setting, and (except in winter) *Buckingham Fountain* provides an exclamation mark with its soaring stream of water that reaches 150 feet.

Evening: Choose from three classics for dinner. **Italian Village** has been a Loop institution since 1927. Among its three restaurants under one roof are The Village, a forever-in-twilight re-creation of an Italian hill town, with twinkling lights in faux courtyard windows and classic spaghetti-and-lasagne fare, and Vivere, serving inventive *upscale Northern Italian cuisine* in a sleek copper-and-mahogany dining room. Falling-off-the-bone baby-back pork ribs are another classic Chicago institution (there's a hotly contested annual "Best Of" contest); choose from **Carson's** in River North or **Twin Anchors**, which has a killer jukebox and is an anchor of Old Town.

Buddy Guy is a Chicago blues legend, and his fittingly named **Buddy Guy's Legends** is the place to hear not just him but also many other top blues artists. For a smoother groove, try the **Jazz Showcase**, Joe Segal's vision of the *perfect jazz club*. If you're more of a classicist, you'll be wanting to hear the internationally acclaimed **Chicago Symphony Orchestra**, which has performed at the acoustically stunning Orchestra Hall for more than 100 years. Check for scheduled "club nights" in Symphony Center for piano jazz and cocktails after concerts—or as an outing itself.

Late at night, there's something for everyone. Strut your stuff and sing along at the **Redhead Piano Bar**, or just sit back and listen to the staff musicians, who happily take requests. Or you can get really down at **Kingston Mines**, where top blues performers provide *nonstop music on two stages* until at least 4 a.m.

CLASSIC CHICAGO

Classic Chicago:
The Hotels

The Drake
140 E. Walton Pl., Gold Coast, 312-787-2200 / 800-774-1500
www.thedrakehotel.com

Sitting at the top of the Magnificent Mile and across from Oak Street Beach, the Drake is Chicago's grand dame of lodging. Opened in 1920, the hotel embodies refined elegance and classic charm (and building practices that make it feel as solid as a bank vault). The 537 rooms include 74 suites, which enjoy views that, coupled with the serene charm, will have you extending your stay. To chase away winter chills, get one of the rooms with a Jacuzzi. The public spaces are a good place to relax—check out the always magnificent flower arrangements in the showpiece lobby—or await a meeting in regal splendor while enjoying wireless internet access. The lounge Coq d'Or is a fabulous place to sip a martini. $$$

Hilton Chicago
720 S. Michigan Ave., South Loop, 312-922-4400 / 800-774-1500
www.chicagohilton.com

Hilton gave this Depression-era classic, once the largest hotel in the world in terms of number of rooms, a lavish renovation in the 1980s that reduced the room count to a still remarkable 1,544. In the process a few quirks were introduced: larger rooms formed from two smaller ones boast not one but two bathrooms. Furnishings are traditional. For added luxury, book a Towers-level room, which gets extra amenities, comfier beds, and access to an exclusive lounge. The hotel has a modern fitness club with one of the best indoor pools in the city. Even if you don't visit it for a function, sneak a peek into the Grand Ballroom, which is swathed in gold leaf and modeled on Versailles. Among the Hilton's historic notes: Chicago cops shoved dozens of young antiwar protesters through the front plate-glass windows during the 1968 Democratic Convention riots, and the hotel plays a pivotal role in the Harrison Ford movie *The Fugitive*. There are good views of Grant Park, and the South Loop neighborhood is booming. $$

Millennium Knickerbocker

163 E. Walton Pl., Gold Coast, 312-751-8100 / 866-866-8086
www.millenniumhotels.com

This carefully updated veteran from 1927 retains all the charm and elegance from the Gold Coast of the Roaring '20s. The lobby spans two floors and includes a bar that harks back to classic private clubs. You might not want to get up from one of the overstuffed chairs. Rooms range from large to small and have traditional furnishings spiced with modern and stylish touches. Some rooms have an Asian flair; others have walk-in marble showers. In keeping with its era, the Knickerbocker's 28-foot-high ceiling in the lobby is gilded and there are enough mirrors to keep you primping for days. $$

Omni Ambassador East

1301 N. State St., Gold Coast, 312-787-7200 / 800-843-6664
www.omnihotels.com

You can live in the swanky Gold Coast without hiring a realtor at the Ambassador East, and its stellar location is only one of its many pluses. This gracious 1926 hotel has 285 rooms and is home to that great Chicago evening institution, the Pump Room. Rooms are large and feature all the expected amenities. It's not surprising that the decor is conservative and the hallways are whisper quiet. Several suites are named for famous guests who made the Ambassador East their Chicago headquarters through the years, including Frank Sinatra. But one especially famous guest was purely fictional: Roger O. Thornhill, the unwilling hero played by Cary Grant in Alfred Hitchcock's *North by Northwest.* $$

Palmer House Hilton

17 E. Monroe St., Loop/Downtown, 312-726-7500 / 800-774-1500
www.chicagohilton.com

This is the fourth hotel in a line started by Chicago real estate mogul Potter Palmer before the Chicago fire in 1871. The most recent version dates from 1927 and features some quite grand public spaces. Sit back on one of the chairs in the second-floor lobby and marvel at the elaborate gold and tile ornamentation that decorate the ceiling. A ground-floor arcade is home to numerous shops. The rooms have been kept up-to-date and feature an airy color scheme in pastels. Most are generous with decent-size windows, but beware of a few tiny rooms that come into play when things are busy. Among the bars and restaurants, Trader Vic's is a longtime local favorite that still knows how to mix a great mai tai. The State Street façade is a famous part of the Loop *mise en scene.* $$

CLASSIC CHICAGO

Classic Chicago:
The Restaurants

Albert's Café & Patisserie
52 W. Elm St., Gold Coast, 312-751-0666

Albert Wolf has been serving up French classics for more than 20 years from this quaint little Gold Coast cafe. You can get breakfast all day, including excellent eggs Benedict, French toast, and scrumptious baked goods like muffins and croissants. Lunch and dinner feature bistro classics like onion soup, salads, and a good steak. *Open Mon.–Fri. 10 a.m.–10 p.m., Sat.–Sun. 9 a.m.–10 p.m.* $

The Berghoff
17 W. Adams St., Loop/Downtown, 312-427-3170

It was started by the Berghoffs in 1898 and the family still guides this Loop stalwart that brews its own beer and boasts Chicago's first post-Prohibition liquor license. Look for all the German standards on the menu (be sure to get a side of creamed spinach), which has been updated with salads, seafood, and sandwiches. For a real throwback experience have a fresh-carved sandwich at the stand-up bar. *Open Mon.–Thurs. 11 a.m.–9 p.m., Fri. 11 a.m.–9:30 p.m., Sat. 11:30 a.m.–10 p.m.* $$

Billy Goat Tavern
430 N. Michigan Ave., Near North, 312-222-1525

Journalists still mingle with tourists at this subterranean landmark that's known for three things: John Belushi immortalized it in the early days of *Saturday Night Live* with the "cheezburger cheezburger" skit; original owner Sam Sianis put a curse on the Chicago Cubs after they wouldn't let him into the park with his pet billy goat (and evidently it worked); and it was a haunt of the now-deceased *Tribune* columnist Mike Royko. Go for the atmosphere and remember: The more pickles on your burger, the better. *Open Mon.–Fri. 7 a.m.–2 a.m., Sat. 10 a.m.–3 a.m., Sun. 11 a.m.–2 a.m.* $

Carson's
612 N. Wells St., River North, 312-280-9200

Billed as "the place for ribs," and it is. There's nothing fancy about the dining room, but that doesn't matter since you'll be chowing down on remarkably tender and flavorful classic Chicago baby-back pork ribs. The accompanying fries are fine, as is the coleslaw, but your growing pile of bones will show that you're really enjoying the main event. *Open Mon.–Thurs. 11 a.m.–11 p.m., Fri. 11 a.m.–12:30 a.m., Sat. noon–12:30 a.m., Sun. noon–11 p.m.* $$

Chicago Chop House
60 W. Ontario St., River North, 312-787-7100

Grilled meats in a variety of glories take center stage here. Star of the menu is the formidable 64-ounce (4-pound) porterhouse steak, but more diminutive diners might get by with the 48-ounce version. Appetizers are of the shrimp cocktail variety and there are no surprises anywhere on the menu, which is just as well since your focus should be on the many steaks and chops—and those who forgo steak for a pork chop do not go wrong. The wine list stretches beyond 500 labels, so you might just save your energy for the meal and ask for ordering assistance. The old brownstone building adds authentic charm. *Open for lunch Mon.–Fri. 11:30 a.m.–4 p.m.; dinner Mon.–Thurs. 4–11 p.m., Fri.–Sat. 4–11:30 p.m., Sun. 4–11 p.m.* $$$

Ed Debevic's
640 N. Wells St., River North, 312-664-1707

At first glance this is just another version of a retro-1950s diner, complete with wisecracking waitresses waiting for their next break in local theatre, but the food delivers real quality. Such seemingly mundane classics as meat loaf and grilled cheese sandwiches are top-notch and help explain why Ed's stays crowded with regulars long after the novelty has worn off. *Open for breakfast Sat.–Sun. 9–11 a.m.; for lunch and dinner Mon.–Thurs. 11 a.m.–9 p.m., Fri.–Sat. 11 a.m.–11 p.m., Sun. 11 a.m.–10 p.m.* $

Emperor's Choice
2238 S. Wentworth Ave., Chinatown, 312-225-8800

Just navigating the long menu at this Chinatown favorite for seafood will keep you entranced for a while. In fact, you might want to take a break and check out some of the fish swimming about in the fish tanks to clear your head before ordering from the long list of fresh fish and shellfish. Do know that once you place your order, the food will come quickly, as most everything is cooked fast in woks with plenty of spices. Dig deep into the menu, or ask your server and you can ponder more exotic Chinese choices. The set meal featuring lobster is justifiably popular. *Open Mon.–Sat. 11:45 a.m.–1 a.m., Sun. 11:45 a.m.–midnight.* $$

CLASSIC CHICAGO

Gene & Georgetti

500 N. Franklin St., River North, 312-527-3718

This longtime Chicago steak house boasts equally longtime waiters. The lengthy list of steaks come char-grilled and are just what you'd want to grill in your own backyard if you could find the same quality of meat. Like many old Chicago joints, this one brags of its Sinatra connections, and in many ways the tradition continues with most diners being out-of-town guests. Don't get hung up on whether you sit in the supposedly more status-conscious downstairs or the more plebeian upstairs. Just enjoy the ancient surroundings of this wood-framed River North survivor and dig into your steak. *Open Mon.–Thurs. 11 a.m.–11 p.m., Fri.–Sat. 11 a.m.–midnight.* $$$

Italian Village

71 W. Monroe St., Loop/Downtown, 312-332-7005

This 1927 complex, run by the Capitanini family since its inception, is a Loop institution, especially popular pre-opera and -theatre, and includes three restaurants. Besides the two detailed below, there's also La Cantina, which serves seafood in a wine cellar setting.

The Village serves Italian food out of central casting—right down to the red-checkered tablecloths—and has been satisfying celebrities, opera stars, and commoners for years. Manicotti is a favorite and there are plenty of other standards like chicken cacciatore and pizza. Save the price of a ticket to Tuscany and revel in the village setting under the perpetual twilight of the star-studded ceiling. *Open Mon.–Thurs. 11 a.m.–1 a.m., Fri.–Sat. 11 a.m.– 2 a.m., Sun. noon–midnight.* $$$

Vivere is the culinary star of the village, with a stunning copper-and-mahogany dining room and fresh and inventive cuisine. Look for seasonal ingredients and interesting combinations that will challenge your notion of Italian fine dining (the pheasant agnelottini are a perennial favorite). The menus change often depending on the chef's inspiration. Don't miss the excellent and wide-ranging Bible-thick wine list. *Open for lunch Mon.–Fri. 11:30 a.m.–2:30 p.m.; dinner Mon.–Thurs. 5–10 p.m., Fri.–Sat. 5–11 p.m.* $$$

Lou Mitchell's

565 W. Jackson Blvd., West Loop, 312-939-3111

Everything is superlative at this West Loop haven for breakfast lovers. The eggs aren't just eggs, they're all double-yolk eggs. And the fluffy huge omelets come in their own pans with excellent potatoes and toast (the preserves are tops as well). Expect lines on the weekends but room on weekdays when busy folks dine and dash from the long communal tables. *Open Mon.–Sat. 5:30 a.m.–3 p.m., Sun. 7 a.m.–3 p.m.* $

Oak Tree
900 N. Michigan Ave., Gold Coast, 312-751-1988

This Gold Coast favorite for breakfast has found its latest home high up in the 900 N. Michigan shopping center. Service bustles, and if you want excessive niceties they'll tell you where you can go. But if you want top-notch coffee-shop fare, this is the place. Many people break with tradition and have one of the massive milkshakes before lunch. *Open Mon.–Thurs. 7:30 a.m.–8:30 p.m., Fri.–Sat. 7:30 a.m.–9:30 p.m., Sun. 7:30 a.m.–8:30 p.m.* $

Original Pancake House
22. E. Bellevue Pl., Gold Coast, 312-642-7917

This a good place to make friends on the Gold Coast, since you'll be rubbing elbows while you're waiting in line and after you've been seated at one of the hemmed-in tables. But your biggest concern should be leaving space in front of you, because the pancakes and waffles are justifiably famous. Come early ahead of late-rising locals and snag one of the popular window seats where you'll have room for the paper—and a side of bacon with your waffle. *Open Mon.–Fri. 7 a.m.–3 p.m., Sat.–Sun. 7 a.m.–5 p.m.* $

Palace Grill
1408 W. Madison Ave., West Loop, 312-226-9529

"The best hash browns on the planet" is how one diner describes the classic breakfast side at this West Side diner. Stainless steel and Formica provide the proper backdrop to the sounds of the sizzling grill, boisterous servers, and satisfied sighs of happy diners. Look for all the breakfast classics here, especially three-egg omelets with those hash browns. Among the more notable patrons who've visited are then–vice president Al Gore and the Russian prime minister, who wanted to see what real Americans ate. *Open Mon.–Fri. 5 a.m.–9 p.m., 5 a.m.–3 p.m.* $

Pizzeria Uno
29 E. Ohio St., River North, 312-321-1000

Home to one of the city's signature dishes since 1943, Pizzeria Uno should not be judged on the (de)merits of its franchised namesakes, which taste nothing like what you get here. The original retains all of its scruffy charm and the wine remains suitably cheap—all the better since you'll have plenty of time to wash it down during the 45 minutes it takes your deep-dish pizza to cook. *Open Mon.–Fri. 11:30 a.m.–1 a.m., Sat. 11:30 a.m.–2 a.m., Sun. 11:30 a.m.–11:30 p.m.* $$

Portillo's Hot Dogs
100 W. Ontario St., River North, 312-587-8930

This River North spot is almost too flash for the working-class roots of the classic Chicago hot dog. But then this big beefy dog deserves a setting that showcases its poppy-seed bun and pile of condiments that include relish, mustard, onions, tomatoes, fresh pickles, and much more. Just don't *ever* ask for ketchup, except on fries—it's just not done in Chicago. Outside tables are a great place to chow down in good weather. *Open Mon.–Thurs. 10:30 a.m.–11 p.m., Fri.–Sat. 10:30 a.m.–midnight., Sun. 11 a.m.–11 p.m.* $

Pump Room
1301 N. State Pkwy., Gold Coast, 312-266-0360

For many years the Pump Room was in danger of becoming either a self-parody or an ossified leftover from a time when you dressed to go out and expected a photographer to snap your picture while ensconced in your booth. But just when the ratio of dead-to-alive for the celebrities whose photos line the walls was shifting decidedly six feet under, new life in the kitchen means that the Pump Room is again known for its excellent classic American food, which varies by season. Service remains formal, but you don't have to be. A new generation of jazzy singers has enlivened the bar and made the Pump Room the place for a civilized drink with someone special. Oh, and Booth One remains, as ever, the table of choice. *Open for breakfast Mon.–Fri. 6:30–11 a.m., Sat.–Sun. 7–11 a.m.; lunch Mon.–Sat. 11 a.m.–2 p.m.; dinner daily 6–10 p.m.* $$$$

Russian Tea Time
77 E. Adams St., Loop/Downtown, 312-360-0000

A real find in the Loop, this vision in red velvet is actually run by immigrants from the old Soviet Union. As one would expect, vodka in its many forms can be found on the menu (try a tasting flight and you'll be flying), and this is a good place to try more unusual variations such as vodkas infused with coffee, coriander, horseradish, or pineapple. But also keep the tea portion of the place's name in mind, and enjoy the classic Russian tea service, with dainty glass cups and steaming samovars. Food is Russian, of course, and for the uninitiated that means plenty of salads using peas, carrots, beets, and cabbage. Other treats include blinis and caviar and various samsas (meat pies), as well as chicken dishes and vareniky (dumplings). Waiters wear white coats. This is an especially good choice if you need sustenance near the Art Institute or Orchestra Hall. Open Sun.–Mon. 11 a.m.–9 p.m., Tue.–Thu. 11 a.m.–11 p.m., Fri.–Sat. 11 a.m.–midnight. $$

The Signature Room (at the 95th)
John Hancock Center, 875 N. Michigan Ave., Near North, 312-787-9596

It's the view, it's the view, it's the view. Restaurants on top of tall buildings are a cliché, but when the restaurant is on the 95th floor of one of the world's tallest buildings, that's not a cliché, that's fun. The views of three states are the real draw at this perennial favorite for visitors and locals celebrating a special event. And the food? Quite good, although don't worry, it's not so showy that you'll take your eyes off the horizon. Steaks, seafood, and pastas dominate the menu, and the service is smooth and unobtrusive. *Open Mon.–Thurs. 11 a.m.–2:30 p.m. and 5–10 p.m., Fri.– Sat. 5 p.m.–11 p.m., Sun. 10:30 a.m.–2:30 p.m. and 5–10 p.m.* $$$

Tempo
6 E. Chestnut St., Gold Coast, 312-943-4373

The top choice among Chicago's many all-night coffee shops, Tempo boasts a hard-earned wall of praise from the local press for its seemingly pedestrian but ultimately superlative menu. Success is in the details, and every dish, from the daily soups to the myriad of sandwiches and the plethora of breakfasts, shows great attention from the kitchen. Dining outside in the sunshine on a warm spring day is one of the joys of the Gold Coast. *Open daily 24 hours.* $

Twin Anchors
1655 N. Sedgwick St., Old Town, 312-266-1616

Twin Anchors is highly popular with the well-heeled residents of Old Town, and with its corner neighborhood location off the major streets, it fits right in to the local ambience. The decor supports the name with a funky '50s nautical theme. The bar is the real deal too, with rows of spirits sparkling seductively in the backlight, and the jukebox is something of a local legend with its solid collection of crooner classics. But the real allure here are the soft and buttery baby-back ribs, which the tangy sauce complements perfectly. Waits on warm summer nights can be long, but that's what a bar—and jukebox—is for. *Open Mon.–Thurs. 5–11:30 p.m., Fri. 5 p.m.–midnight, Sat. noon–midnight, Sun. noon–10:30 p.m.* $$

CLASSIC CHICAGO

Classic Chicago:
The Nightlife

Buddy Guy's Legends
754 S. Wabash Ave., South Loop, 312-427-0333

Mick Jagger and Ron Wood have long said that Chicago blues acts were the inspiration for much of the early work of the Rolling Stones, and in fact, they did a number of early recordings in the South Loop at Chess Studios. Jagger and Wood can still be found jamming here at Buddy Guy's every time they pass through town. Meanwhile, Buddy has achieved his own fame and often can be seen onstage. The caliber of acts is top-notch, varying from the best local talent to touring national acts. Get here early to snag a good table in the large room, and if you're hungry, there's a list of Louisiana staples like jambalaya on the menu. *Open Mon.–Thurs. 5 p.m.–2 a.m., Fri. 4 p.m.–2 a.m., Sat. 5 p.m.–3 a.m., Sun. 6 p.m.–2 a.m.* $$

Chicago Symphony Orchestra
220 S. Michigan Ave., Loop/Downtown, 312-294-3000

Orchestra Hall has been a source of pride for Chicagoans since it was built by Daniel Burnham in 1904. The Chicago Symphony Orchestra has proved to be an equally beloved resident, and its annual season is always sold out. That doesn't keep scores of tickets from regularly being available, and fans hanging out in front of the hall usually find some subscriber willing to sell a couple of tickets for face value. Music Director Daniel Barenboim conducts an orchestra with a stellar international reputation not just for classics but also for discovering new and magnificent works every year. Look for performances by other groups and artists ranging from classical to jazz throughout the year at Symphony Center, where Orchestra Hall is just one of three performance venues, and check out "club nights" for cocktails and piano jazz with great views. $$$$+

Coq d'Or
The Drake, 140 E. Walton St., Gold Coast, 312-932-4622

The banks of red leather booths in this dimly lit classic bar beg you to snuggle up to someone special. Martinis are a specialty, and it's hard to imagine what you would order otherwise in these period surroundings. The bar also offers a menu from the Drake's other restaurants. Nightly live entertainment features plenty of standards from the crooner era. *Open Mon.–Sat. 11 a.m.–2 a.m., Sun. 11 a.m.–1 a.m.*

Excalibur
632 N. Dearborn St., River North, 312-266-1944

A sort of shopping mall for clubbers, Excalibur boasts several clubs on several floors of this huge classic brownstone that was once home to the Chicago Historical Society. One bar invites you to chill out while another boasts every type of arcade game imaginable (for the antisocial kid in everybody). But the real draw is the individual areas with music ranging from rock or house to funk and beyond. On Thursdays you'll find Latin and salsa on one floor. *Open Sun.–Fri. 5 p.m.–4 a.m., Sat. 5 p.m.–5 a.m.* $

Green Mill
4802 N. Broadway St., Uptown, 773-878-5552

How does this nearly 100-year-old club remain hot? By booking true jazz greats and letting them play in a setting that hasn't changed since Capone was a regular (ask the bartender for the scrapbook). Situated in the only very recently gentrifying Uptown neighborhood, the Green Mill is small and intimate with good sight lines and marvelous booths. It gets credit for sparking the swing revival. Poetry slams also began here, and spread nationwide; the one here is still held every Sunday afternoon and still doesn't tolerate any bad verse. *Open Sun.–Thurs. 11 a.m.–4 a.m., Sat. noon–5 a.m.* $

Jazz Showcase
59 W. Grand Ave., River North, 312-670-2473

The name says it all at this large River North hall that has seen every notable jazz musician from the young Dave Brubeck to the Next Big Thing. A no-frills philosophy extends right through to the cash-only policy. But that's all the better since you don't want frills getting in the way of acts carefully booked by local legend Joe Segal. One potentially welcome break with jazz traditions is the club's no-smoking policy. *Shows Tues.–Thurs. 8 and 10 p.m., Fri.–Sat. 9 and 11 p.m., Sun. 4, 8, and 10 p.m.* $$$

Jilly's
1007 N. Rush St., Gold Coast, 312-664-1001

This shrine to Sinatra actually opened after Ol' Blue Eyes had gone on to the big jukebox in the sky, but you'd never know it. The bars pour strong drinks, enjoyed by patrons who are often as carefully poured into their dresses. This is not a place where modern subtleties are respected: Smoke that stogie with abandon. As the night wears on, expect to hear swing standards spiced up with disco classics, and even a few Top 40 tunes from the 1980s. *Open Sun.–Fri. 4 p.m.– 2 a.m., Sat. 4 p.m.–3 a.m.* $

CLASSIC CHICAGO

Kingston Mines
2548 N. Halsted St., Lincoln Park, 773-477-4646

Acts rotate on two stages, so you never need to wait for someone to set up at this Lincoln Park stalwart. It's totally unadorned, but that's the point, right? Saturday nights can get crowded, especially after 3 a.m., when the crowd swells after other places close. But weeknights can be manageable, and after other clubs close at 2 a.m. you don't get just an influx of patrons—many feeling the full effects of their drinks—but an influx of other musicians as well. *Open Sun.–Wed. 9 p.m.–4 a.m., Thurs.–Fri. 8 p.m.–4 a.m., Sat. 8 p.m.–5 a.m.* $

Loop Theatre District
In the late 1990s, the much heralded Loop Theatre District finally took shape after years of false starts. It actually is more than anything a return to the status the Loop once enjoyed before World War II as the heart of Chicago's entertainment world. The bevy of restored theatrical palaces attract a wide range of touring acts and shows. The Goodman Theatre is an important regional theatre that has long been one of Chicago's most respected venues for drama. It is now based in a stunning space carved out of adjoining former cinemas. Except for the Goodman, which is home to the theatrical company of the same name, the rest of the theatres listed below are large spaces that attract large crowds to special and traveling shows.

Cadillac Palace Theatre 151 W. Randolph St., 312-977-1700

Chicago Theatre 175 N. State St., 312-902-1500

Goodman Theatre 170 N. Dearborn St., 312-443-380

Oriental Theatre, Ford Center for the Performing Arts
24 W. Randolph St., 312-977-1700

Shubert Theatre 22 W. Monroe St., 312-977-1700

Music Box Theatre
3733 N. Southport Ave., Wrigleyville, 773-871-6607

This landmark neighborhood theatre is like a trip to a Moorish castle. As the *Chicago Tribune* architectural critic wrote, "the architectural style is an eclectic melange of Italian, Spanish, and Pardon-My-Fantasy put together with passion." Little stars wink from the nighttime sky–painted ceiling, projected clouds scuttle by, and there are lavish and restored statues and decoration all around. Foreign, art, and classic films unspool day and night, and the joy of seeing one here is that even a marginal film looks much better in these surroundings. The butter on the popcorn is real. Call for show times. $

Pops for Champagne
2934 N. Sheffield Ave., Lakeview, 773-472-1000

This place is the real deal, and as clubs come and go in River North and the Gold Coast, Pops just keeps delivering the goods year after year. The setting in a quiet upscale neighborhood of gentrified brownstones is classic. The interior is all burnished woods, and the ceiling is an aquamarine marvel that brightens moods even on the slushiest day. A patio out back provides a welcome place for a sip on warm nights, and if you're lucky you might even see a star. Small jazz groups perform classics nightly—think Louis and Ella. Champagne is obviously the thing, and they have more than 135 on offer. Light snacks of the baked brie and crème brûlée variety are available. *Open Sun.–Fri. 6 p.m.–2 a.m., Sat. 8 p.m.–2 a.m.* $

Redhead Piano Bar
16 W. Ontario St., River North, 312-640-1000

This swellegant piano bar is a haven for swinging nightclubbers and attracts a crowd of upscale regulars, see-and-be-seen singles, snoggling couples, and sing-along groupies perched at the piano. The place gets crowded beginning around 10 p.m. *Open Sun.–Fri. 7 p.m.–4 a.m., Sat. 7 p.m.–5 a.m.; entertainment Mon.–Sat. 8:30 p.m.–2:30 a.m., Sun. 8 p.m.–4 a.m.* No cover.

The Second City
1616 N. Wells St., Old Town, 312-337-3992

The alumni list reads like a who's who of American comedy: Mike Nichols and Elaine May, Dan Akroyd, John Belushi, Bill Murray, and Gilda Radner, George Wendt, Mike Myers, Bonnie Hunt, Tim Meadows, and many, many more. Both Hollywood and New York (Conan, Dave, and *Saturday Night Live*) regularly raid the ranks of this sketch comedy company for writers and performers. The group has presented more than 90 shows since 1959, and they spare few targets in their ensemble mocking. On many nights after the last show, the cast stays on for improvisational comedy, the scriptless hilarity that Chicago has refined to an artform. Shows are performed both on the main stage and at the next-door Second City e.t.c., and there are suburban companies in play as well. *Mainstage shows: Tues.–Thurs. 8:30 p.m., Fri.–Sat. 8 and 11 p.m., Sun. 8 p.m. Second City e.t.c. shows: Thurs. 8:30 p.m., Fri.–Sat. 8 and 11 p.m., Sun. 8 p.m.; check for additional or late weekend shows.* $$

CLASSIC CHICAGO

Classic Chicago: The Attractions

Adler Planetarium

1300 S. Lake Shore Dr., South Loop, 312-922-7827

The heavens are truly awesome, and yet they've been done a disservice for years by dull planetariums that seem inspired by the dustiest of textbooks. The Adler was equally guilty of the drabbing-down of the cosmos until a few years ago when a massive renovation and expansion put the pizzazz back into the universe. The StarRider Theatre puts to shame even the best special effects of Hollywood blockbusters as it takes viewers into the heart of time itself. Rotating shows include a recent one that looked at what the Milky Way will look like in a million years (suffice it to say that Earth property values will be way down). Interactive exhibits include a neat one showing what happens when a meteorite strikes land. *Open Mon.–Fri. 9:30 a.m.–4:30 p.m., Sat.–Sun. 9 a.m.–4:30 p.m.; summer, Sat.–Wed. 9 a.m.–6 p.m., Thurs.–Fri. 9 a.m.–9 p.m.* $

Art Institute of Chicago

111 S. Michigan Ave., Loop/Downtown, 312-443-3600

The star of local cultural institutions, the Art Institute collection covers a range of ancient to modern works from a range of cultures. The Impressionist paintings—including six Monet haystacks—are a legacy of the early Chicago millionaires whose wives (most famously Bertha Palmer) knew good art when they saw it and bought everything in sight in Paris. Other famous pieces can be found throughout the galleries, and first-time visitors are well advised to join one of the many tours that help make sense of the collections. Wandering around the galleries aimlessly can occupy hours, so you may wish to plan your visit using the free maps at the information desks. Often overlooked for the European and American art, the Chinese collection is among the best anywhere and contains treasures from a string of dynasties, and the modern and contemporary collection is also among the world's finest. And those who seek out the rotating photo exhibits in the basement are always rewarded. Watch for the many special shows, which often bring together works from around the world. Take a break from the beauty at the courtyard cafe, and take home a memento from the excellent and vast museum store. *Open Mon.–Fri. 10:30 a.m.–4:30 p.m. (until 8 p.m. Tues.), Sat.–Sun. 10 a.m.–5 p.m.* $

Chicago Architecture Foundation
224 S. Michigan Ave., Loop/Downtown, 312-922-3432

Chicago's reputation as an architectural showplace is richly deserved, and fans travel from all over the world to stand in the shadows of structures both old and new. The Chicago Architecture Foundation celebrates local heritage and offers dozens of tours as well as lectures and rotating exhibits at its headquarters on South Michigan Avenue. Walking tours through the Loop depart several times daily. Other walking tours take in a variety of neighborhoods. Bus tours cover more ground and visit close-in suburbs like Oak Park with its wealth of Frank Lloyd Wright houses. Other tours travel via the El or by boat—the Architecture River Cruise by Chicago's First Lady (at the Michigan Avenue Bridge) is a winner. Guides from the Chicago Architecture Foundation provide narration. *Call for tour times and details. Shop open Mon.–Sat. 9 a.m.–6:30 p.m., Sun. 9 a.m.–6 p.m.* $$$$

Chicago Cultural Center
78 E. Washington St., Loop/Downtown, 312-744-6630

Built in 1897, this block-long building served as the city's main public library until the late 1970s when it could no longer hold all of the books in the collection. Since then it has been carefully renovated and is home to one of the city's two main visitor information centers as well as numerous galleries with rotating art exhibits. Its Tiffany glass and mosaics, especially upstairs in the stunning Preston Bradley Hall where the dome is thought to be the largest Tiffany dome in existence—and worth about $35 million—are a real highlight. It's all free, including weekday lunchtime concerts. *Open Mon.–Wed. 10 a.m.–7 p.m., Thurs. 10 a.m.–9 p.m., Fri. 10 a.m.–6 p.m., Sat. 10 a.m.–5 p.m., Sun. 11 a.m.–5 p.m.* Free.

Cog Hill Golf and Country Club
12294 Archer Ave., Lemont, IL, 630-264-4455

There are four courses at this long-established public club. Course Number 4 Cog Hill (a.k.a. Dubsdread) has been ranked nationally since it opened in 1964. A beautiful course, it is known for its tight landing areas combined with heavily bunkered large undulating greens. It is home to the PGA Western Open, which Tiger Woods won in 2003. Opening hours vary but are generally good for daylight hours. *Opening dates vary by the weather.* $$$$

CLASSIC CHICAGO

Field Museum
1400 S. Lake Shore Dr., South Loop, 312-922-9410

The kid in every adult (and kid) can't resist the dinosaurs in their stupendous glory here at the Field Museum. Center stage is the nearly complete skeleton of Sue, a once-fearsome Tyrannosaurus rex. But many, many more treasures abound in the cavernous halls. As with the Art Institute, you're best taking time to plan your visit before you start wandering around. The Field is renowned for its exhibits celebrating the natural history of Egyptian, African, and Pacific cultures. A natural history museum used to mean dusty cases of dusty artifacts, but here, exhibits are based instead on highly creative and interactive displays that take you inside African and Inuit villages or an Egyptian tomb. The recent opening of a fossil lab takes the preparation of fossils for display out of the back rooms and brings the workings into plain view. *Open daily 9 a.m.–5 p.m.* $

Glessner House
1800 S. Prairie Ave., South Loop, 312-326-1480

Prairie Avenue on the near South Side was the home of Chicago's millionaires in the 1800s before they moved north to the Gold Coast. The Glessner House survives as an astonishing gem of the period; its daring architecture attracted design pilgrims from around the world and had an influence on Louis Sullivan and Frank Lloyd Wright, among many others. Its creator's neo-Romaneque designs even earned their own architecture-style name: Richardson Romanesque, for the architect, H.H. Richardson, famous for his Trinity Church in Boston, among other buildings. Characterized by its massive stone walls and semicircular arches, this 1887 house presents bold pink granite façades to the streets and its interior is considered a marvel of planning for the ways it was designed to capture the often fleeting rays of the sun during the winter (back then, the rich had separate homes they used during the hot summers). Many of the interior furnishings have been restored or re-created. *Tours Wed.–Sun. at 1, 2, and 3 p.m.* $

Grant Park

Bounded by Randolph Drive on the north, Roosevelt Road on the south,
Michigan Avenue on the west, and Lake Michigan on the east,
Loop/Downtown 312-742-7529

Chicago's "front yard" consists of 319 acres of gardens, grass, and trees,
plus the new Millennium Park. The centerpiece and a definite must-see
sight is Buckingham Fountain, which pumps 14,000 gallons per minute in
a changing display of water that regularly climaxes with a central spurt that
shoots 150 feet into the sky, and which has light shows playing nightly—
beginning at dusk, every hour on the hour for 20 minutes, the water display
is accompanied by lights and music; the final display begins at 10 p.m.
Other areas include the nicely scented formal rose garden and the wildflower
garden, which spectacularly re-creates the proliferation of multicolored
plants that once covered the ground for hundreds of miles in the Midwest.
Numerous festivals call Grant Park home, including Taste of Chicago, the
multiday eating and drinking festival around July 4.

John G. Shedd Aquarium

1200 S. Lake Shore Dr., South Loop, 312-939-2438

The world's largest indoor aquarium boasts a range of displays, including
the colorful Caribbean Reef, where you can watch divers hand-feed sharks,
sea turtles, and other hungry sea denizens. The huge indoor Oceanarium
overlooking the lake houses 1,500-pound beluga whales. Smaller aquariums
and pools are home to 650 different species. The constantly changing
Amazon exhibit shows how nature deals with the dramatic variations that
occur every year in a floodplain forest. *Open Mon.–Fri. 9 a.m.–5 p.m.
(until 6 p.m. summer), Sat.–Sun. 9 a.m.–6 p.m.* $

John Hancock Center

875 N. Michigan Ave., Near North, 888-875-8439

Lacking the cachet of being the tallest—the Sears Tower nabs that
honor—the Hancock actually tries a little harder, and the observatory at
the John Hancock Center is convenient to North Michigan Avenue. An area
in the observatory is open to the outdoors, which lets you hear the surprisingly loud sounds of the city from near the top of the tower's 1,127 feet.
You can enjoy the same views from two floors above at the Signature Room,
which offers drinks with the endless views on a clear night. *Open daily
9 a.m.–11 p.m.* $

CLASSIC CHICAGO

Marshall Field's
111 N. State St., Loop/Downtown, 312-781-1000

Covering an entire block and occupying more than eight floors of its land-mark building, Marshall Field's is a local icon that is definitely a must-see sight if for no other reason than to look at its famous Tiffany ceiling. A place of pilgrimage at Christmas, Field's is known for its lavish decorations and entertaining window displays. Goods on offer range from the merely modest to exclusive designer creations, and you can buy everything from obscure kitchen gadgets in the basement to a new sofa on the eighth floor. Be sure to pick up some of the incomparable Frango Mints. *Open Mon.–Fri. 9:45 a.m.–7 p.m. (until 8 p.m. Thurs.), Sat. 10 a.m.–6 p.m., Sun. 11 a.m.–6 p.m.*

National Vietnam Veterans Art Museum
1801 S. Indiana Ave., South Loop, 312-326-0270

The horrors of war and their effects on the people involved are exposed in this highly personal museum filled with the works by more than 150 people who fought in Vietnam. The emotional pain exposed by some of the pieces is searing and shows the struggle many continue to cope with. Most artistic media are represented, and there are displays that put the war in a broader context. Many of the volunteers on hand are veterans. *Open Tues.–Fri. 11 a.m.–6 p.m., Sat. 10 a.m.–5 p.m., Sun. noon–5 p.m.* $

Navy Pier
600 E. Grand Ave., Near North, 312-595-7437

Over a half-mile long, Navy Pier was once the city's hub for lake commerce. In the 1990s it was massively rebuilt and transformed into an entertainment and convention center. There are restaurants, bars, cafes, shops, and several museums and performance venues (see also Hipster Chicago for listings of its many features). The pier is a good place to wander for an hour or two—just getting to the end will take that long, although there is a seasonal beer garden at the east end to reward you. Casual browsers will enjoy the Smith Museum of Stained Glass Buildings, which showcases more than 150 color-ful windows saved from older buildings around the U.S. For color in the sky, look for fireworks shows pegged to various special events throughout the summer. *Open Sun.–Thurs. 10 a.m.–10 p.m., Fri.–Sat. 10 a.m.–midnight.*

Nordstrom Spa
55 E. Grand Ave., Near North, 312-464-1515

This full-range spa is very popular and embodies the attention to customer care for which Nordstrom is noted. Body treatments include a range of skin therapies and exfoliations. Special baths can include essential oils and mustard essence. You can opt for a full body wrap based on either mud or algae. All forms of massage are available and programs are customized for both men and women. Patrons are encouraged to work with the staff to create their own ideal experience based on their personal needs. *Open daily by appointment.* $$$$+

Willie Dixon's Blues Heaven Foundation
2120 S. Michigan Ave., South Loop, 312-808-1286

This pilgrimage spot for music fans is located in the old Chess Records recording studios. Muddy Waters, Chuck Berry, and many more artists recorded here in the 1950s and 1960s, and Chess Records played an instrumental role in breaking the boundaries of what had been called "Negro music" by traditional recording companies. The Rolling Stones recorded many of their early songs here; they were studying at the knees of Chicago blues greats and later named a song 2120 S. Michigan Ave. in honor of the studio. Blues great Willie Dixon also recorded here, and today a foundation named after him works to preserve the legacy of groundbreaking blues artists. Tours include the original studios as well as a wealth of memorabilia and artifacts. *Call for hours.* $

Hot & Cool Chicago

Chicago's down-to-earth image is shattered when you start noticing all the things here that are white-hot and supercool. Stellar restaurants, cafes, clubs, galleries, bars, boutiques, theatres, comedy clubs, and more vie for the affections of the Windy City's scenesters, who are tireless in their pursuit of the latest, greatest, and sharpest cutting edge. In neighborhoods from the Gold Coast to Wicker Park, Bucktown, Lincoln Park, and many others, places are packed with people soaking up the good life in all its forms. Whether you're looking for art, beach-bumming, roller-blading, salsa, shopping, clubbing, or just kicking back in the latest hot spot, it's all here.

Hot & Cool Chicago: The Itinerary

Three Great Days and Nights

Your Hotel: **The Hard Rock Hotel**

Morning: Gird yourself for the swirl of fun that lies ahead by taking the quick walk over to **Atwood Café**, a Loop *power-breakfast spot* where pancakes and other comfort foods are celebrated. If the day has dawned sunny, head west for the shady outdoor tables at **Ina's**, where you can adjust to the morning over French toast with some mighty fine sautéed apples.

Start your day at the top. The **Sears Tower** is the city's tallest building (and some still say it's the world's tallest, arguing about the antenna height), and views from its observation deck give you a spectacular vista of the great grid of the city. Then descend into the pits—the trading floors of the **Chicago Board of Trade** or the **Chicago Mercantile Exchange**, both of which boast great visitor centers and viewing areas. The trading of commodities like wheat and pork bellies made Chicago the financial capital of the Midwest, and this colorful and *rowdy trading* continues, though now it's more often based on foreign currencies or stocks.

Afternoon: Ralph Lauren is known for his classic take on American style, so it's no surprise that his signature restaurant off Michigan Avenue, **RL**, boasts excellent *classic American cuisine*, and there's more of RL here than you might expect: the beef is raised on Ralph's ranch. For a different lunch option, leave the continent and the decade behind at the Gold Coast's **Le Colonial**, which re-creates the Vietnam of when the French were in charge.

It's time to walk off your high-carb start. *North Michigan Avenue* continues to be the hottest shopping street in the country. Start in the Loop and head north along the "Magnificent Mile" over the bridge with its post-card views, past the white terra-cotta 1919 Wrigley Building (400 North Michigan Avenue) and the neo-Gothic 1923 Tribune Tower (435 North Michigan Avenue), and scores of stores stretching all the way up to Oak Street Beach, from Apple and Nike to Bulgari and Chanel, plus the swanky high-rise malls at 900 North Michigan Avenue and Water Tower Place.

For a real workout, hustle over to the sleek, ultramod **Holmes Place**, the trendy *European health club* chain that's made its first U.S. home right here in River East. It offers cardio and weight training, swimming, classes including kickboxing and Pilates, and the full-service Spa Mondial.

Evening: Where to dine? Always a pleasant problem in this very foodie town. **Nine** is always hot. From the *champagne-and-caviar bar* to the make-your-own-s'mores, the food is as much fun as the drinks (glow-in-the-dark martinis) and decor (lotsa stylish metal). A table at any Rich Melman restaurant (one of Chicago's original auteur restaurateurs) is a tough ticket, and that's certainly the case at **Nacional 27**. The food takes its inspiration from a range of cuisines from Peru to Mexico, and there's excellent salsa (the musical kind) to back it up. The *supersleek* **Wave** made a big splash when it opened in the scene-y W Hotel, and it's still going strong. With seafood fare on the menu like spice and molasses–glazed shrimp with candied orange, mulled red wine syrup, and cardamom, you know your dinner will be full of surprises.

Chicago theatre is forceful and direct, and nowhere is this better realized than at **Steppenwolf Theatre Company**, the long-running creation of ensemble members John Malkovich, Gary Sinese, Joan Allen, et al. If you can get tickets to whatever is playing—go. Or check out what's going on at **Lookingglass Theatre**, a younger but no less lauded troupe. Long before David Schwimmer started making *Friends*, he was part of this ensemble, which he helped launch in 1988 (and to which he still belongs). The troupe has a reputation for staging some of Chicago's best original productions. Afterward (or instead), head out just west of Bucktown, where chic **Tini Martini** has *velvet ropes* restraining the crowds on the sidewalk, which gives them a chance to rest up for the raging dance scene inside that ranges from salsa to house. Alternately, try the **Back Room**, a Rush Street institution where crowds compete to snag a romantic table and listen to national jazz acts on tour.

Your late-night options are happily varied. At the top end are the red-hot combo of **Y** and **Sound-Bar**. The former emphasizes lounging, the latter emphasizes dance. At both, expect *extravagant indulgence*. You could also spread yourself out on the velvet banquettes at **BUtterfield 8**, a perfect place for a presleep snuggle, complete with people who'll bring you a nightcap.

Day 2

Morning: Hop in a cab and head up to Lakeview to the hot breakfast sensation, **Orange**, where you'll get *tasty new twists* on old favorites. Or follow the Gold Coast crowds to **Pierrot Gourmet** for its sought-after baked goods.

After breakfast, arrange a morning with **Art on the Move**, a company that specializes in *customized tours* of Chicago's trendiest museums, art galleries, artists' studios, and even private collectors' homes. If you'd rather be outdoors, stop by **Bike and Roll** at North Avenue Beach, rent a bike or *inline skates*, and head north along the lake or through the park. Following the lake you can go almost as far north as Evanston. (There's also a beautiful running path, if that's your thing.)

Afternoon: It's *picnic time* in Lincoln Park, and your purveyor of choice should be **Trotter's To Go**, the storefront deli owned by local legend Charlie Trotter (who also runs Charlie Trotter's Restaurant; see Luxe Chicago). Or join the A-list types dining either on classic Italian at **Carmine's** on Rush Street or on trendy fusion cuisine at **Kevin**.

You probably don't think of Chicago as a beach town, but in fact it has one of the world's great urban beaches—**Oak Street Beach**. This is the place to see and be seen on a hot day—and there's a lot to feast your eyes on, with all the beach bums and babes sunning, splashing, cycling, and blading. You can even soak up a couple of cocktails as you *soak up the sun* at the resident cafe, Oak Street Beachstro.

If you're not in a tanning mood (or if the weather's not cooperating), head down to the happening neighborhood of Pilsen for the morning. This once was home to Chicago's Czech blue-collar workers, but 100 years later it's a *vibrant cultural mix* of Latino families and young artists drawn to lofty spaces and low rents. Check out the recently expanded **Mexican Fine Arts Center Museum**—it's *muy caliente*.

However you've whiled away the afternoon, cap it off with a happy-hour trip to **Whiskey Sky** in the W Lakeshore hotel. The trendy clientele pack themselves in for the comfy leather loungers, good music, and *great vibe*.

HOT & COOL CHICAGO

Evening: Passing the Zen garden as you enter, prepare yourself for creative and exquisite seafood. If you like your Zen with a little more drama, you'll love **Ben Pao**, a trendy *dinner-as-theatre* venue where regional Chinese cuisine is served in a dramatic laquered-pillar dining room. For cuisine closer to home, hot chef Michael Kornick packs in the crowds at **MK**, where Midwestern ingredients shine thanks to French techniques and Asian influences. Yet more culinary artistry is on display at **one sixtyblue**, where you can start with a foie gras sandwich and move on to duck with cherry bread pudding. It's always busy, so book ahead.

After dinner, join the *beautiful people* that haunt **Ghost**, the exclusive mod-chic bar popular with the famous and their followers. Also on the celeb circuit, **Rednofive** is a retro-stylish club that draws crowds to its energetic but surprisingly unpretentious dance floor. For high-concept club action, **Ontourage** offers a vast main dance floor and a far more intimate upper floor that's reached through a startling blue cone. For a mellower vibe, hang out in the sleek setting of **Le Bar** in the Sofitel Hotel.

Day 3

Morning: This morning, head over to **Café des Architectes**, truly an architect's fantasy in the eye-popping Sofitel Hotel, and have some of the perfect *French baked goods*. Or join the masses at **Hillary's Urban Eatery** in Wicker Park for updated American and Mexican classic breakfasts.

Start your day on the greens at **Harborside International Golf Center**, Chicago's most popular *top-level public course*, where Bill Clinton scored a hole-in-one and PGA events are held regularly.

If you're one of those types that think "golf is a good walk spoiled," perhaps you'd rather take a good walk shopping. This morning, prowl the new Mecca of chic Lincoln Park—*Armitage Avenue*. There are designer boutiques aplenty west of Lincoln Avenue; stop in the eponymous **Jane Hamill** for the local designer's made-in-Chicago clothing and accessories, and in **Lori's**, the shoe Mecca that's a compulsory first stop for many women visitors upon arrival in the city.

Afterward, *treat yourself* to a morning at **Honey Child Salon and Spa.** It has attracted a huge following with its range of services, variously described as "artsy," "creative," and "sexy."

Afternoon: After your grueling morning, you're probably ready to kick back with a glass of wine. **Bin 36** has more than 50 available by the glass, along with enticing complex salads and sandwiches, making it a perfect lunch spot. For a lunch with a more impressive pedigree, try **Vong's Thai Kitchen** in River North, a more casual, scaled-down spinoff of chef *Jean-Georges Vongerichten*'s Vong in New York.

After an indulgent lunch, you need a place to stretch your legs. **Millennium Park** is the hottest thing to happen to Chicago in some time, and it should be, given that it cost somewhere in the neighborhood of a half-billion dollars. East of Michigan Avenue and south of Randolph Street, the park occupies a premier position and boasts a range of features including the *Frank Gehry-designed* soaring Pritzker Pavilion for open-air concerts, an outdoor ice rink, enormous outdoor sculptures and fountains, and various lush gardens.

Evening: For dinner, travel to 1940s Paris at **Brasserie Jo**, chef Jean Joho's buzzily *stylish supper salon*. Or try **Mirai**, where sushi is the star and the interior's right out of *Wallpaper*. The fish is ultrafresh (some awaits your plate in a fish tank), and there's techno-beat music filtering down from the lounge upstairs. For sushi with a surprise, try the very scene-y **SushiSamba Rio.** It's a good thing the place has a great bar (choose one of the several caipirinhas), since you and a gaggle of other scenesters will be waiting a while for the Brazilian-Peruvian-Japanese fusion cuisine.

Tonight, dive into Chicago's legendary comedy scene at an improv club. **ComedySportz** and **Improv Olympic** both feature teams of actors performing *hilarious skits* based on the suggestions of the audience. Don't be surprised if you sit next to an agent looking for next year's star.

Late at night, **Crobar** offers high-concept and high-priced clubbing with a South Beach motif. For a more international scene, **Zentra** offers comfy booths in a faux Middle Eastern setting. Like Crobar, Zentra boasts some of *Chicago's best DJs* for house, hip-hop, and other genres. For an alternative scene, join the partying crowds at **Berlin**, a fun, long-running eclectic gay-straight dance club with great, varied music.

Hot & Cool Chicago: The Hotels

Hard Rock Hotel
230 N. Michigan Ave., Loop/Downtown, 312-345-1000 / 877-762-5468
www.hardrock.com

Images of logo T-shirts and "no nukes" signs will be obliterated by this new incarnation of the famous brand. There's nary a rock icon in sight among the cool and muted colors of the lobby and public spaces, although staffers do list their favorite musician on their lapels. Instead, the tone of the hotel is set by its home, the architecturally stunning 1929 Carbide & Carbon Building, which is resplendent now that its deep green and gold terra-cotta Art Deco exterior has been restored. The elevator lobby is true to the original and worth a trip inside even if you're not going to your room. But hopefully you are, because the understated decor extends to the rooms, which feature amazingly comfortable beds, serviced twice a day by the otherwise reclusive housekeepers. Aim high—literally—for one of the suites that cover up to a floor and feature views of Chicago in all directions. $$$

Sofitel Chicago Water Tower
20 E. Chestnut St., Gold Coast, 312-324-4000 / 877-813-7700
www.sofitel.com

The new Sofitel is something of a rarity these days in Chicago—an architectural stunner that isn't a reuse of a building originally intended for something else. Architect Jean-Paul Viguier won a stiff competition for the commission and designed this wild three-sided 33-story white showplace, which increasingly looms over the Gold Coast as it rises. The inside is both bold and chic, with dramatic primary colors vying with modern art galore for attention. The rooms aren't huge but they manage to evoke the same flair for design, albeit in more restful tones. The bathrooms are fully up to the modern trend for large spaces with a wealth of conveniences. $$$

Sutton Place Hotel
21 E. Bellevue Place, Gold Coast, 312-266-2100 / 800-606-8188
www.suttonplace.com

This European-designed hotel on the Gold Coast combines Danish modern decor with Art Deco flair. Opened in 1988, it features large rooms that are open and airy, many boasting exceptional views. The marble bathrooms are almost destinations in themselves, with deep tubs, separate showers, and bidets. Popular with visiting art directors and other creative types, the desks in the rooms are large and will easily let you spread out your portfolio. More than 100 originally commissioned Robert Mapplethorpe photographs of flowers crisply accent the public spaces. $$$

W Chicago City Center

172 W. Adams St., Loop/Downtown, 312-332-1200 / 800-621-2360
www.whotel.com

In a building that's long been a hotel under a variety of names in the heart of Chicago's financial district, the W City Center is its latest incarnation. And the old dowager has been emboldened by the innovative makeover, which takes the grand spaces and gives them pizzazz through whimsical design touches (look at how the names of various restaurants and bars are worked into the lamp shades, for instance) and mod yet slightly understated decor. The Living Room is the bar-cum-restaurant-cum-lobby on the main floor and entices guests to linger with various pleasures that include comfy sofas, games, stiff drinks, and a DJ spinning tunes nightly. It's actually transcended lobby status and attracts a large local crowd. Rooms enjoy traditional amenities and have rock-solid walls decorated in whites and blues with touches of blue and purple. $$$

W Chicago Lakeshore

644 N. Lake Shore Dr., Near North, 312-943-9200 / 888-625-5144
www.whotel.com

This edifice overlooking the lake was first a Holiday Inn and then demoted to a lowly Days Inn, but the W Lakeshore has raised it from the near dead thanks to the energetic efforts of this trendy arm of the Starwood lodging empire. Hip is worn on the sleeve—and everywhere else—in this radically made-over 1960s vintage tower. Water-polished creek stones line the floors of the hallways, and the rooms feature an array of touches not found in the hotel's previous incarnations, including bathrooms that open out to the rest of the room for those needing companionship, and bold black and red accents. Scrabble-style word games on the desks allow guests to create their own sophomoric puns. Although the views of Lake Michigan on the east side of the building are expansive, don't hope for the gentle noise of lapping water to drown out the cries of noisy neighbors through the still-thin walls. The top-floor Whiskey Sky nightclub has stellar views—and attitude to match. $$$

Hot & Cool Chicago:
The Restaurants

Atwood Café
1 W. Washington St., Loop/Downtown, 312-368-1900

State Street rarely looks better than it does through the windows of this classic American cafe on the ground floor of the historic Hotel Burnham building in the Loop. The menu is studded with American comfort foods, from the oozing omelets at breakfast and the soaring burgers at lunch to the more complex entrées at dinner. The Atwood does a big business with business folk and shoppers during the day and with the theatre crowd at night. *Open Mon.–Fri. 7 a.m.–10 p.m., Sat.–Sun. 8 a.m.–10 p.m.* $$

Ben Pao
52 W. Illinois St., River North, 312-222-1888

It figures that this Lettuce Entertain You Enterprises version of a Chinese restaurant would feature waterfalls and beautiful high-drama decor, given the company's winning history with the dinner-as-theatre concept. But as with all its places, the food holds its own even amid the red-lacquered pillars and gold statues. The menu is a blend of four great Chinese regional cuisines, Cantonese, Mongolian, Shanghai, and Szechuan, and dishes like the signature black-peppered sea scallops or "cherry bomb" shrimp keep the crowds coming to this bustling hot spot. *Open Mon.–Thurs. 11:30 a.m.–10 p.m., Fri. 11:30 a.m.–11 p.m., Sat. 11 a.m.–3 p.m. and 5 p.m.–11 p.m., Sun. 11 a.m.–3 p.m. and 4 p.m.–10 p.m.* $$

Bin 36
339 N. Dearborn St., River North, 312-755-9463

Bin 36 combines a restaurant, bar, and shop in one big celebration of all things grape. The menu brims with choices that cry out for a pairing with one of the more than 50 wines available by the glass. Crab salad with avocado, watercress, fennel, pistachios, and a citrus vinaigrette and an open-faced monkfish po' boy are among the imaginative choices. The interior is light, crisp, and clean, like a good sauvignon blanc. *Open for breakfast Mon.–Fri. 6:30–10 a.m., Sat.–Sun. 7 a.m.–noon; for lunch 11 a.m.–2 p.m.; dinner and tavern Mon.–Sat. 2 p.m.–1:30 a.m., Sun. 2 p.m.–10 p.m.* $$

Brasserie Jo
59 W. Hubbard St., River North, 312-595-0800

Yet another Lettuce Entertain You Enterprises buzzy megahit. This time, they've teamed up with chef Jean Joho (of Everest fame) to create a lively, casual brasserie that transports you to 1940s Paris with its zinc bar and Art Nouveau murals. The menu is unfancy French, with all the standards here done brilliantly: salad lyonnaise or niçoise, steak tartare or frites, coq au vin, and choucroute, plus "tartes flambées," Alsatian takes on pizza, and seafood and daily specials. *Open Sun.–Thurs. 5–10 p.m., Fri.–Sat. 5–11 p.m.* $$–$$$

Café des Architectes
Sofitel Hotel, 20 E. Chestnut St., Gold Coast, 312-324-4063

Given the kudos the Sofitel Chicago Water Tower has received for its daring architecture, it's fitting that the in-house restaurant should be named the Café des Architectes. You'll increase your hipness quotient by 20% just by sitting down. In summer the large sidewalk cafe opens up and you can sit outside, an excellent option. The menu is fusion French, with classics like onion soup complemented by decadent options like a lobster BLT. *Open for breakfast daily 6–11:30 a.m.; brunch Sat.–Sun. 11:30 a.m.–5 p.m.; lunch daily 11:30 a.m.–2:30 p.m.; dinner daily 5:30–11:30 p.m.* $$$

Carmine's
1043 N. Rush St., Gold Coast, 312-988-7676

What keeps this place on the A-list is the large, hip, and loyal following of owner Alex Dana, who also runs the local Rosebud restaurants, and it's abuzz nightly with beautiful people and local celebs. The menu focuses on the classic southern Italian flavors of tomatoes and garlic in the many pasta sauces. Fresh seafood is a specialty, with clams in particular prepared in many forms. Be forewarned that this scene requires reservations, although lunch is more accessible than dinner. On nice days, go for the sidewalk tables. *Open Sun.–Thurs. 11:30 a.m.–10 p.m., Fri.–Sat. 11:30 a.m.–11 p.m.* $$$

Hillary's Urban Eatery
1500 W. Division St., Wicker Park, 773-235-4327

An updated urban diner, Hillary's Urban Eatery ("Hue" to regulars) offers everything you need for the morning: great coffee, fresh baked goods, and a fun menu that might just put a smile on your still-grumpy face. Think diner classics like corned beef hash, only better, because here the homemade hash is sensational and does its humble roots proud. Besides American classics, look for Mexican staples such as huevos rancheros. Everything is fresh, and on one of those much-longed-for warm early-spring mornings, the fresh air in the serene back patio is a perfect accompaniment. *Open Mon.–Thurs. 7 a.m.–10 p.m., Fri.–Sat. 7 a.m.–11 p.m., Sun. 7 a.m.–8 p.m.* $

Ina's
1235 W. Randolph St., West Loop, 312-226-8227

Ina Pinkney's motto is "I can't wait to feed you," and believe us, you'll want her to at this stylish all-day restaurant, which serves a range of comfort classics. Breakfasts come with baskets of fresh breads and muffins, washed down with carafes of coffee. Scrapple (not the scary old Pennsylvania Dutch variety, but rather a fresh combination of Mexican flavors) is a standout. Whole-wheat pancakes are healthy and filling, while the omelets have a variety of fillings you pick yourself. Sidewalk tables have a good vantage on the trendy old Randolph Street Market area. Lunch and dinner menus offer classics with flair. *Open Mon.–Thurs. 7 a.m.– 9 p.m., Fri. 7 a.m.–10 p.m., Sat. 8 a.m.–10 p.m., Sun. 8 a.m.–2 p.m.* $$

Kevin
9 W. Hubbard St., River North, 312-595-0055

Named for chef/owner Kevin Shikami, this fusion restaurant manages to continually top itself. Menus change daily, and the spectrum of global influences shows in the fact that one night the salmon is cooked with Thai spices and served with jasmine rice while another night it's grilled crispy and served with garlic mashed potatoes. At least half the menu features seafood at any given time, but don't overlook meats such as beef tenderloin, lamb, and rabbit. Service wins raves for managing the delicate balance of being polished yet casual. This style extends to the decor, which is clean and modern with Asian accents throughout. In warm weather the front is opened up to the River North breezes. *Open for lunch Mon.–Fri. 11:30 a.m.–2 p.m.; dinner Mon.–Thurs. 5:30–10 p.m., Fri.–Sat. 5:30–11 p.m.* $$$

Le Colonial
937 N. Rush St., Gold Coast, 312-255-0088

Chicago has plenty of neighborhood Vietnamese restaurants, but only one Le Colonial, which takes the delicate flavors of the cuisine and serves them up in a movie-set–like tableau that transports you to early 1950s Saigon. Menu highlights include a whole red snapper filleted at the table and an authentic French bouillabaisse. In summer, the tall windows in the atmospheric bar upstairs (good anytime for just a drink) open out to a balcony where you can observe the Rush Street vibe below. *Open for lunch daily noon–2:30 p.m.; dinner Mon.–Fri. 5–11 p.m., Sat. 5 p.m.–midnight, Sun. 5–10 p.m.* $$

Mirai
2020 W. Division St., Ukrainian Village, 773-862-850

The front of this old church now boasts two-story-high windows, and creations by chef Jun Ichikawa are set off by a collection of ceramic, bamboo, and porcelain trays, and china that would be at home in a Tokyo designer's showroom. Though all the fish is ultrafresh, there's no doubting it when you watch it get plucked from one of the three large tanks and filleted on the spot. Imaginative dishes like a delicate salad featuring seared scallops are among the cooked items. Upstairs, a dark DJed lounge throbs techno into the night. *Open Sun.–Wed. 5:30–10:30 p.m., Thurs.–Sat. 5:30–11:30 p.m.* $$$

MK
868 N. Franklin St., River North, 312-482-9179

Michael Kornick has a string of hot restaurants behind him, but this is his most personal and arguably his best. MK has won raves for Kornick's inventive cuisine using North American ingredients. Although simple, the flavors are bold in the dishes on the constantly changing menu, which always features Alaskan seafood, Maine lobster, top-quality steaks, and roasts. Many preparations are grounded in French traditions but look to Asian influences as well. The old paint factory's skylights remain, but everything else in the decor takes its cues from the food itself: well-defined modern American. The lunch menu is simple, featuring sandwiches (although that word does little justice to the sublime lobster club). Book in advance and ask about the chance of eating at the kitchen table on the upper level, where you'll have the chance to graze the menu of the night. *Open Sun.–Thurs. 5:30–9:30 p.m., Fri.–Sat. 5:30–10:30 p.m.* $$$

Nacional 27
325 W. Huron St., River North, 312-664-2727

Rich Melman's Lettuce Entertain You restaurants have always been about fun, but also about good food, and Nacional 27 certainly scores on both points. The menu salutes the 27 nations of Latin America and the Caribbean region. The many tropical fruits and vegetables of equatorial America are featured in delightful and tasty combinations. Look for yucca, plantains, mangos, passion fruit, and much more. The waitstaff is casual and competent and can add to the sense of fun, with the many delightful libations from the bar lubricating things nicely. After 10 p.m., the middle of the room is cleared and a DJ starts spinning salsa hits. *Open Mon.–Thurs. 5:30–9:30 p.m., Fri.–Sat. 5:30 p.m.–11 p.m.; bar Mon.–Thurs. 5 p.m.–midnight, Fri. 5 p.m.–2 a.m., Sat. 5 p.m.–3 a.m.* $$$

HOT & COOL CHICAGO

Nine
440 W. Randolph St., West Loop, 312-575-9900

Nine is the age at which owners Michael Morton and Scott DeGraff met and became pals. Their friendship has spawned a string of event-of-the-moment hot spots in Chicago. The dark sleek interior with its cool blues, purples, and brushed metal is a good backdrop for the chic patrons who have made this one of the city's hottest restaurants. The food is classic surf and turf with huge steaks, lobster tails, and shellfish. Portions are such that if you're not taking a doggie bag, you can forget about fitting into your tailored frock next time. Starters include fun little items from the caviar-and-champagne bar. Perhaps in a nod to the owners' childhoods, you can make your own s'mores or suck up a root beer float for dessert. Upstairs, Ghost bar goes late and attracts the beautiful souls from below. *Open for lunch Mon.–Fri. 11:30 a.m.–2 p.m.; dinner Mon.–Wed. 5:30–10 p.m., Thurs. 5:30–11 p.m., Fri.–Sat. 5 p.m.–midnight; bar Thurs.–Fri. 9 p.m.–2 a.m., Sat. 9 p.m.–3 a.m.* $$$

one sixtyblue
160 N. Loomis St., West Loop, 312-850-0303

This is another one of those restaurants that have helped give Chicago a deservedly vaunted culinary reputation of late. The name combines the immediately obvious (the address) with what won't be obvious until you get there (the decor). But boy, will it be obvious then. Hot designer Adam Tihany has turned an old pickle factory into an indigo dream. Credited with returning the Pump Room to glory a few years ago, current chef Martial Noguier works wonders with the ingredients of the day. But the food is the restaurant's raison d'être. Staples like grilled chicken are done to perfection, and sides of fresh vegetables carry complex seasonings that are indicative of the kitchen's attention to detail. The staff also gets raves for its attention to detail, with points awarded for smoothly professional service and deep knowledge of the lengthy wine list. If possible, save yourself for the much-heralded and incomparable cheese course. *Open Mon.–Thurs. 5–10 p.m., Fri.–Sat. 5–10:30 p.m.* $$$

Orange
3231 N. Clark St., Lakeview, 773-549-4400

With an interior as bright and cheery as the center of a sunny-side-up egg, Orange has won a massive following of folks willing to travel a fair distance for its excellent breakfasts. Take the Dr. Seuss classic *Green Eggs and Ham.* As defined at Orange, it includes pesto and pancetta. Other items unlikely to be found at Denny's include brochettes of little French toast squares with fresh strawberries. The crates of oranges you see are destined for the busy juicers, and you can mix and match your drink with a bevy of other squeezables and juice-ables. *Open daily 8 a.m.–3 p.m.* $

Pierrot Gourmet
108 E. Superior St., Near North, 312-573-6749

The high qualities of the Peninsula Hotel are literally brought down to earth at this corner cafe in the building. Everything is French, and you might be forgiven if in a morning blur you thought for a moment that you were actually at a classic cafe in the Sixth—but the friendly staff will quickly disabuse you of that notion. Pastries baked onsite are superb (try any Danish), as is the coffee. At lunch you can't go wrong with classics such as Alsatian *flammenkuchen* (one of the great underappreciated street foods, with its garlicky cheese, onions, and ham) or niçoise salad. *Open Tues.–Sat. 7 a.m.–9 p.m., Sun.–Mon. 7 a.m.–7 p.m.* $$

RL
115 E. Chicago Ave., Near North, 312-475-1100

Ralph Lauren has made his name through his interpretation of classic American style, and the restaurant bearing his initials continues this theme. The walls in this clublike refuge from the bustle of North Michigan Avenue are lined with portraits and other classic works. Below are sumptuous booths covered in buttery velvet, and as you'd expect, the bar knows how to pour a proper martini. Lauren's personal touch extends to the menu—the beef comes from his ranch. At lunch there are staples like Cobb and Caesar salads, a fun little egg-salad-and-caviar sandwich, or steaks—plenty of steaks. Book in advance. *Open Mon.–Thurs. 11:30 a.m.–10 p.m., Fri.–Sat. 11:30 a.m.–11 p.m., Sun. 11 a.m.–10 p.m.* $$$

SushiSamba Rio
504 N. Wells St., River North, 312-595-2300

This is where the *Sex in the City* crowd has been drowning its sorrows since the last episode. The interior of this high-concept restaurant that started in New York is bold, beautiful, and multilevel. The bar is quite a sight, with backlit glass blocks, although on most nights you'll be hard pressed to notice given the crowds who throng the place waiting—and waiting—for tables (be sure to book). A busy sushi bar is nearby with a couple dozen stools for those who want to get close to the fish. Beyond the dramatic hangings of silver beads, the lucky ones with tables graze from a menu that combines Brazilian food (marinated steaks) with Peruvian (heavenly potatoes) and Japanese (sushi, fish, and more). It all works, and as an added bonus, the staff will happily ply you with a variety of caipirinhas, sakes, and other libations. There's also a great rooftop deck in summer. *Open Mon.–Thurs. 11:45 a.m.–1 a.m., Fri.–Sat. 11:45 a.m.–2 a.m., Sun. 11:45 a.m.–midnight.* $$$

Trotter's To Go
1337 W. Fullerton Ave., Lincoln Park, 773-868-6510

Charlie Trotter is probably Chicago's most famous chef, and among foodies his eponymous restaurant is true legend (see Luxe Chicago). But enjoying Trotter fare wasn't something you could do every day (there's those prices and those reservations) until he opened this storefront deli, grocery, and food emporium. Ready-made fare ranges from exquisite sandwiches to entire meals. Staff know their food—it's like they're auditioning for *The Restaurant*—and will guide you through the myriad of choices in the stark white display cases. Tell them you're going on a picnic and they'll have a ball. *Open Mon.–Sat. 10 a.m.–8 p.m., Sun. 10 a.m.–6 p.m.* $$

Vong's Thai Kitchen
6 W. Hubbard St., River North, 312-644-8664

Yet another Lettuce Entertain You restaurant concept, Vong's is chef Jean-George Vongerchten's more casual spinoff of his Vong restaurant in New York. The dining room is stylish and sumptuous, with red-lacquered walls and bamboo accents. The interpretation of what's Thai is flexible (it's now meant to be Thai-inspired French dining), and plenty of other Asian regions influence the menu as well—the Peking duck roll is superb and spicy. Sesame duck stir-fried with pineapple rice has a nice underpinning of tamarind. There's a sense of light-hearted fun to go with the fresh flavors: the mai tai here is called the Thai tai and bursts with fresh fruit. *Open for lunch Mon.–Fri. 11:30 a.m.–2 p.m.; dinner Mon.–Thurs. 5:30–9:30 p.m., Fri. 5:30–11 p.m., Sat. 5–11 p.m., Sun. 5–9 p.m.* $$$

Wave
W Hotel, 644 N. Lake Shore Dr., Near North, 312-255-4460

The W Hotel group tends to make a splash wherever it lands, and it's no exception here. Its signature hip and sleek design aesthetic here provides a sparkling backdrop for chef David Murphy's Mediterranean-accented seafood (he spent time cooking in Beirut, so he has a savvy for spice). The main room offers three- and four-course prix fixe options along with à la carte ordering, and the scene-y Ice Bar "living-room bar and lounge" offers its own menu, putting a mod spin on the classic raw-bar concept. *Open for breakfast daily 6 a.m.–11 a.m.; lunch daily 11 a.m.–2 p.m.; dinner daily 5–11 p.m.* $$–$$$$

Hot & Cool Chicago: The Nightlife

Back Room
1007 N. Rush St., Gold Coast, 312-751-2433

If it hadn't been here so long, you'd think the Back Room was a parody, but it ain't. It's the real deal, right down to the grungy alley leading to the sign that reads "Live Jazz." Over the years, the club has consistently booked the best local and touring jazz acts seven nights a week, which has given it a peerless reputation and keeps it among the Gold Coast's "musts." You'll have to choose between the two levels: ground floor near the stage, or in the loft with your own bar and bird's-eye view? *Open Sun.–Fri. 8 p.m.–2 a.m., Sat. 8 p.m.–3 a.m.* $

Berlin
954 W. Belmont Ave., Lakeview, 773-348-4975

Berlin is a total anomaly. It's a neighborhood place, it's free of attitude, it's neither entirely gay nor straight, and it's totally unpredictable. That's probably why it continues to be one of Chicago's trendsetters for late-night frolicking and dance. *Rolling Stone* called it the best dance club in Chicago, and it was right on the money. Check for theme nights, or just show up and get carried away. *Open Mon. 8 p.m.–4 a.m., Tues.–Fri. 5 p.m.–4 a.m., Sat. 5 p.m.–5 a.m., Sun. 8 p.m.–4 a.m.* $

BUtterfield 8
713 N. Wells St., River North, 312-327-0940

In the evening BUtterfield 8 (for whatever reason, it takes its name from an Elizabeth Taylor movie in which she plays a hooker) is a dinner joint with attitude. Later, it becomes a nightclub with attitude for a trendoid crowd who have made it one of the most popular stops on the late-night circuit. The floor by the bar is reminiscent of the illuminated one in *Saturday Night Fever,* although it's much more laid-back. The decor is goofy and will definitely get goofier as the specialty vodka drinks go down. After midnight, the less public upstairs lounge is the place to go for a kiss. *Open Mon.–Fri. 5 p.m.–2 a.m., Sat. 5 p.m.–3 a.m.* $$

ComedySportz
2851 N. Halsted St., Lakeview, 773-549-8080

The competition here is all about comedy—improv comedy of the kind that has become iconic for Chicago. ComedySportz offers an array of classes in improv, and the most promising students are formed into teams, which compete nightly for audience attention and laughter. Some of the stuff is forgettable, but there are also moments of brilliance (shout out your own comic suggestion for the team to react to), and you'll see why agents and scouts regularly pepper the audience. For libations it's BYOB. *Open Tues.–Sun. 7 p.m.–1 a.m. $$*

Crobar
1543 N. Kingsbury St., Old Town, 312-266-1900

The name comes from a time when the club was all retro-industrial grunge. Now it's all South Beach sunshine, which seems to have added new vigor to the always crowded and always frenetic dance floor. Upper-level booths allow for canoodling. The night of choice for those in the know is Saturday, when DJ Teri Bristol rules the house with an aggressive mix. A glass-enclosed VIP booth allows two-way viewing, and those who've been ensconced there say it's at the top of the local A-list thanks to its private bathrooms. Go totally over the top with your attire since getting in can get competitive. *Open Thurs.–Fri., Sun. 9 p.m.–4 a.m., Sat. 9 p.m.–5 a.m. $$*

Ghost
440 W. Randolph St., West Loop, 312-575-9900

The owners of the hypertrendy Nine restaurant have a ghost in their attic—this even more hypertrendy bar, complete with a face check that assures a distractingly attractive (if slightly *arriviste*) crowd. Famous folk and wannabes flock to the glow of the green backlit bar like moths, or slouch in the egg-shaped chairs at the bar or in the low chairs and sofas. Favorite drinks include the white chocolate raspberry martini and the signature glow-in-the-dark Ghostini, complete with Casper swizzle stick. This bar is ultraexclusive, so look good and arrive early (well, not desperately early) or, better yet, book downstairs to assure a spot here—diners at Nine are given priority if it's crowded. *Open Thurs.–Fri., 9 p.m.–2 a.m., Sat. 9 p.m.–3 a.m. $$*

Improv Olympic
3541 N. Clark St., Wrigleyville, 773-880-0199

Slightly less frenetic than ComedySportz, teams at Improv Olympic work the crowd for laughs, but the improvisational comedy runs longer—some bits based on audience suggestion manage to go for 30 minutes or more. There are also solo acts and other features. Improvisational guru Del Close is one of the principals here, and don't be surprised if you see some famous Second City alum lurking in the crowd. *Shows Tues.–Thurs. 8 and 10:30 p.m., Fri.–Sat. 8, 10:30, and midnight, Sun. 8 p.m., Mon. 8:30 p.m.* $

Le Bar
Sofitel Chicago, 20 E. Chestnut, 312-324-4000

This buzzy little bar attracts a trendy mix of business-luxe and fashion-forward types with its cool fiber-optic lighting, long zinc bar, and pulsing club-music soundtrack. Continuing the hotel's architectural theme, there's a small library at the entrance with books on architecture and comfy chairs and sofas. In the main bar, a time theme predominates (an oversize clock over the bar, clocks set to times around the world, time-themed drink names). Little niceties like martinis poured tableside, a good selection of Armagnacs, cognacs, and champagnes and wines by the glass, and great views out its large windows make this a swell spot to drink and people-watch. *Open Sun.–Wed. 3 p.m.–midnight, Thurs. 3 p.m.–1 a.m., Fri.–Sat. 3 p.m.–2 a.m.*

Lookingglass Theatre
821 N. Michigan Ave., Near North, 312-337-0665

It's not in the Loop Theatre District or along the Halsted Strip—two havens for local theater—but the Lookingglass Theatre has found a perfect home in newly renovated space in the old Water Tower Pumping Station (the large building across from the more famous tower). The troupe was founded by a bunch of Northwestern University grads, some of whom, like David Schwimmer of *Friends* and Tony Award-winner Mary Zimmerman, have since gone on to greater fame (though both are still part of the Lookingglass ensemble). Productions are generally among the best in town and often feature original works with physically dramatic and literally theatrical staging. *Call for shows and performance times.* $$$

HOT & COOL CHICAGO

Ontourage
157 W. Ontario St., River North, 312-573-1470

When you're in the blue cone that surrounds the stairs between the two floors of this huge River North club, you have to decide between the main floor with its cavernous dance floor and pulsating lights, or the far more intimate upper floor with cozy nooks and dark corners. Better yet, just get in the groove with the DJs, who play a range from house to hip-hop, and just wander. *Open Thurs.–Fri. 10 p.m.–4 a.m., Sat. 10 p.m.–5 a.m.* $$

Rednofive
440 N. Halsted St., West Loop, 312-733-6699

This retro-chic club eschews the glitz of competing clubs like Crobar and Ontourage and instead draws crowds with its pure dance-floor energy. Interestingly, given its unadorned vibe, it attracts a lot of famous folks, both locals and those passing through. Maybe they like the sinuous dark couches and lack of pretension. Anyway, on weekends it's maxed out by 2 a.m., so get there in plenty of time. *Open Mon.–Fri. 10 p.m.–4 a.m., Sat. 10 p.m.–5 a.m.* $

Steppenwolf Theatre Company
1650 N. Halsted St., Old Town, 312-335-1650

For many stage buffs, Steppenwolf is *the* Chicago theatre company, or maybe even the American theatre company—its success is now known worldwide, and it's a stranger neither to Broadway or London's West End. Certainly its artistic success has made possible its impressive three-stage theatre complex. Ensemble members include founders John Malkovich, Gary Sinese, Joan Allen, Glenne Headley, Laurie Metcalf, and John Mahoney, among others. Of the many noteworthy shows staged through the years, the premiere of David Mamet's *Glengarry Glen Ross* remains a breathtaking experience. $$$$+

Tini Martini
2169 N. Milwaukee Ave., Bucktown, 773-269-2900

You knew the once dubious Logan Square neighborhood had arrived when this club put up the velvet ropes out on the Milwaukee Avenue sidewalk. It's exclusive not only because of the intimate size, but also thanks to the fashionistas elbowing mere mortals out of the way. Intimate booths conceal a multitude of sins while the DJs spin tunes from salsa to hip-hop. *Open Sun.–Fri. 4 p.m.–2 a.m., Sat. 4 p.m.–3 a.m.* $

Whiskey Sky

644 N. Lakeshore Dr., Near North, 312-943-9200

On the top floor of the W Lakeshore hotel, this bar boasts stellar views, but also comes with a mortal dose of attitude. If you're famous (or just think you are), you can slip right in to one of the comfy leather loungers. Otherwise, get ready to be intimidated as your arrival is greeted by heads turning in unison to see who's just come in. Impresario Rande Gerber has a reputation for cool that stretches to New York City, and his latest effort in Chicago is packing 'em in. *Open daily 4 p.m.–2 a.m.* $

Y/Sound-Bar

224–226 W. Ontario St., River North, 312-274-1880

These two very upscale clubs in River North have distinctly different personalities. Y is all about sitting, sharing, and relaxing at little tables served by the oodles of waitstaff. Bottles of chilled vodka for $200 raise nary an eyebrow, maybe because the swanky patrons are too busy with the pricey caviar. Next door, Sound-Bar is all about dance in one of the city's largest spaces, some 20,000 feet on two levels. Nine bars quench thirst brought on by the driving house music. Service levels and prices are high: at both Sound-Bar and Y you can drop $3,000 on a bottle of champagne—albeit a good one—with the pop of a cork. *Open Thurs.–Fri. 9 p.m.–2 a.m., Sat. 9 p.m.–3 a.m.* $$

Zentra

923 W. Weed St., Old Town, 312-787-0400

The slightly funky feel here is Middle Eastern, and there's mood aplenty, with the little red lanterns hanging here and there, the chain-mail–draped private booths, and the hookah pipes on offer, complete with fruit-flavored tobacco. Like any good party venue, this one offers a backyard where you can cool off from the action. The crowd exudes fashion sense and is quite diverse. Among the DJs is local legend DJ Psycho Bitch who draws mobs on Saturday nights. *Open Sun.–Fri. 10 p.m.–4 a.m., Sat. 10 p.m.–5 a.m.* $

HOT & COOL CHICAGO

Hot & Cool Chicago:
The Attractions

Art on the Move
Various locations, 847-432-6265

Scheduled and custom tours are offered of Chicago art museums, galleries, artists' studios, even collectors' homes—if there's a particular type of work you'd like to see, these folks are a good bet since they can sort through the hundreds of local options and steer you to those matching your interest. $$

Bike and Roll
North Avenue Beach, Lincoln Park, 773-327-2706
Navy Pier, 600 E. Grand Ave., Near North, 312-595-9600

This friendly shop rents various bikes and Rollerblades from April through October at its Navy Pier location, only from June to August at North Avenue. It also offers tours and maps of Chicago's very bikeable lakefront and parks. $$

Chicago Board of Trade
141 W. Jackson Blvd., 5th Floor, Loop/Downtown, 312-435-3590

It started by trading the commodities grown by Midwestern farmers, but its scope has grown to include pretty much anything that has a fluctuating price. The Chicago Board of Trade is really legalized gambling on a multibillion-dollar level, where investors bet on the future price of the commodities in question. Farmers use the board to protect themselves from future price drops, while producers protect themselves from price raises. All this makes for some remarkably manic commerce, and the trading floors where contracts are bought and sold are famously anarchic, with pencils, hands, cards, and sometimes fists flying. Board of Trade tours offer a bird's-eye view of the action. *Tours Mon.–Fri. 9:15 a.m.–12:30 p.m.* $

Chicago Mercantile Exchange
20 S. Wacker Dr., Loop/Downtown, 312-930-2390

The city's other great local trading organization, the CME leans away from actual commodities like wheat and instead specializes in trading futures in currencies, interest rates, and other ephemeral entities that exist only in theory. The manic trading floors here are being supplanted by electronic markets, and the new visitor center does a great job of explaining the seemingly unexplainable. *Open Mon.–Fri. 8:15 a.m.–3:30 p.m.* $

Harborside International Golf Center
11001 S. Doty Ave. E., South Side, 312-782-7837

Chicago's most popular top-level public course has been built on restored industrial lands on the far southeast side of the city near the lake. Two courses, Port and Starboard, offer 36 holes of challenging golf. Numerous PGA events have been held here. Try your luck on the par 3 sixth hole on the Port course—that's where Bill Clinton scored a hole-in-one in 2002, the club's first. Opening hours vary but are generally good for daylight hours. Opening dates vary by the weather. $$$$

Holmes Place
355 E. Grand Ave., Near North, 312-467-1111

A posh import from London, Holmes Place does everything for its clients but the actual workout. The decor is sleek, exercise machines are state-of-the-art, and there are numerous niceties such as the heated floors in the changing rooms. But the real marvel is the swimming pool, which is lined with stainless steel and boasts an ozone filtration system that eliminates the need for chlorine. There's also an onsite spa and a healthy cafe. *Open Mon.–Thu. 5:30 a.m.–11 p.m., Fri. 5:30 a.m.–9 p.m., Sat.–Sun. 8 a.m.–8 p.m.* $$$

Honey Child Salon and Spa
735 N. LaSalle St., River North, 312-573-1300

One of the city's most popular spas, Honey Child describes every service as a "treat." The joys range from massage to treatments for your various body parts, plus complete salon services to ensure that you look your best after you emerge from the stylish shop. Avoid having to choose, and go for the "taste of honey" treatment, which combines a honey rock massage with a facial, pedicure, and manicure. *Open Tues.–Wed. 10 a.m.–6 p.m., Thurs.–Fri. 10 a.m.–9 p.m., Sat. 9 a.m.–5 p.m., Sun. 11 a.m.–5 p.m.* $$$$+

Jane Hamill
1117 W. Armitage Ave., Lincoln Park, 773-665-1102

This light and airy boutique is where you'll find that light and airy sundress designed by Jane herself. There's also a good range of little black dresses for your nighttime affairs. A Chicago native, Jane has found a strong following among Lincoln Park's young women who want flair with their casual clothes. The designs are simple and flattering (and as the store notes, "cut for real women"). All the clothes are produced right in Chicago and besides dresses include hats, coats, sweaters, purses, and more. *Open Tues.–Fri. 11 a.m.–7 p.m., Sat. 10:30 a.m.–6 p.m., Sun. noon–5 p.m.*

HOT & COOL CHICAGO

Lori's
824 W. Armitage, Lincoln Park, 773-281-5655

Shoe addicts know that Lori's is the place to go for their fix (some women travelers cab it straight from the airport to make it their first stop). Lori Andre herself travels twice a year to Europe to ensure she always has the edgiest fashions in shoes, handbags, and accessories. Her little Armitage Avenue shop, only 500 square feet when it opened in 1983, has grown tenfold and now showcases thousands of shoes. *Open Mon.–Thurs. 11 a.m.–7 p.m., Fri. 11 a.m.–6 p.m., Sat. 10 a.m.–6 p.m., Sun. noon–5 p.m.*

Mexican Fine Arts Center Museum
1852 W. 19th St., Pilsen, 312-738-1503

Recently expanded, this museum is a showplace of the energetic Latino arts community in Chicago. A number of noted artists live in town, many more in the surrounding community of Pilsen, and their works can be found here. Special exhibits are often ambitious, combining history, sociology. and other disciplines with art. The museum and adjoining park come alive for annual Day of the Dead celebrations each November 1. *Open Tues.–Sun. 10 a.m.–5 p.m. $*

Millennium Park

It cost half a billion dollars (give or take a few million) and came in four years after the actual millennium, but Chicago's newest park is a showplace. Built over a commuter rail yard, Millennium Park fills the last hole in the park structure downtown. Local boosters got solidly behind the project and it blossomed from being planned as a relatively simple arrangement of flowers and grass over a parking garage to a surprising showplace for architecture, art, and just plain fun. It's comprised of the following components:

Pritzker Pavilion A stunning Frank Gehry–designed bandshell with the architect's trademark sinuous stainless steel. The lawn behind the seats is larger than two football fields and there is a state-of-the-art sound system for concerts.

Ice Rink at McCormick Tribune Plaza Opened in 2003, this mechanically refrigerated open-air ice rink was wildly popular from the start. You can rent skates and glide across the ice from early until late, fall to spring.

Sculpture The as yet unnamed sculpture by London artist Anish Kapoor weighs 110 tons, is 33 feet high, and looks something like a Godzilla-size chrome jelly bean. You can walk right underneath it.

Fountain Another yet unnamed work, this time by Spanish artist Jaume Plensa, it features two 50-foot towers that combine fountains of water with huge video images of Chicagoans.

Joan W. and Irving B. Harris Music and Dance Theatre
205 East Randolph Dr., 312-334-7777

The entrance is at the north end of the park and the theatres are underground at this long-awaited home for many of the city's previously homeless dance and music groups, including Hubbard Street Dance Chicago and Joffrey Ballet of Chicago.

Oak Street Beach

Top of the A-list of the many beaches lining Chicago's lakefront, Oak Street is where beautiful people go to look beautiful. On weekdays there's a big rush at lunch as workers pop down from office buildings on the Mag Mile for a quick dose of vitamin D before heading back to their cubicle gloom. You can also get a drink, a snack, or a meal at Oak Street Beachstro, where you can sit and watch the parade go by.

Sears Tower
233 S. Wacker Dr., Loop/Downtown, 312-875-9696

The city's tallest building, at 110 stories and 1,454 feet, jousts with the Petronas Towers in Kuala Lumpur over the semantics of what constitutes the world's tallest building (something about the antennae). Regardless, this simple dark form based on nine interlocking square tubes of varying heights is emblematic of the Chicago's self-professed "can-do" spirit. The observation deck near the top floor boasts views of three states, although whether you scale the summit here or at the John Hancock Center should really be a matter of which neighborhood you're in when you're ready to catch a ride up into the atmosphere. (One aspect that argues for the Hancock is the sappy film that patrons have to sit through here before they ascend.) *Open daily 10 a.m.–8 p.m., summer until 10 p.m.* $

HOT & COOL CHICAGO

Luxe Chicago

Though Chicago is generally not a place that's about ostentatious consumption, that doesn't mean you can't enjoy luxury, comfort, and unparalleled services here. The Chicago dining scene's reputation grows each year and may soon reach the point where the breadth of dining experiences, quality of foods, and talent in the kitchen is unmatched. At night you'll have plenty of chances to flaunt it at clubs where the champagne lists are almost as long as the playlists and the service shines brighter than the jewels flashed by the crowds. Shopping here is storied, and rightly so. And for personal attention, what can beat touring the Art Institute's collections with a curator? You can enjoy the skyline from a plane you're piloting or from a yacht under your command on the lake. If you know how to live, Chicago offers innumerable opportunities to prove it.

Luxe Chicago: The Itinerary
Three Great Days and Nights

Your hotel: **The Peninsula Chicago**

Morning: There's no need to go far for your first breakfast in Chicago. **The Lobby** has the grandest public space along the Mag Mile and serves a varied and scrumptious lineup of breakfast items. If you must go out, toddle to the gastronomic playpen that is **Fox & Obel**, *Chicago's best food store*, and enjoy one of its rare coffees and sinful pastries.

For some, there's no better way to begin a day than some intensive shopping. *Oak Street* is Chicago's ritziest street for boutiques, with all the established names, including Barney's New York (No. 25), Prada (No. 30), Colin of London (No. 50), Luca Luca (No. 59), Kate Spade (No. 101), and Hermès (No. 110)—in all, there are more than 30 top-end shops, salons, and boutiques in one tree-shaded block.

But why see Chicago from the ground when you can see it from the air? **Sun Aero Helicopter**s can customize a helicopter tour for you along with *guide-to-the-stars* **Rolph Achilles**, who can show you Chicago in all its glory (or coordinate almost any other kind of tour that you'd like him to guide).

Afternoon: For lunch, dine like a celebrity at **Grill on the Alley**, which brings its honest food like Cobb salads to Chicago from the original power-lunch place in Beverly Hills. Or go one better and *dine like royalty* at **Erawan**, where the exquisite Thai food is served in a sumptuous teak-and-gold setting worthy of kings and queens.

The glories of the **Art Institute of Chicago** are vast, and fully appreciating them can be hard work. So let someone else do the heavy lifting—arrange a tour with your own personal guide. Nothing compares to the depth of knowledge and context that an expert can provide (especially if you can get the exhibit's curator herself). To *arrange a personal guide*, contact the **Chicago Tour Guides Institute**, the Art Institute, or your concierge (or, again, Rolph Achilles). The Museum of Contemporary Art also offers a similar service.

LUXE CHICAGO

Afterward, avail yourself of art of a different kind. **The Peninsula Spa** has found a loyal following for its practice of the art of *luxury treatments and therapies*. The pool is half Olympic size, and there's a sun deck so you can foster a glow. The **Four Seasons Spa** is equally plush and has an elixir paraffin wrap found nowhere else. Wherever you've indulged yourself, go ahead and indulge a little further: have a happy-hour drink at the Peninsula's swell hotel bar, **The Bar**.

Evening: The only challenge your first dinner in Chicago presents is deciding where to go. For a meal where the setting is as transcendent as the cuisine, try one of these: **Tru** takes the dinner-as-theatre concept to dramatic heights in its *luminescent dining room*, and **Zealous** takes exquisite ingredients and gives them a global whirl in a stunning converted vintage auto showroom with its own bamboo forest and a wall of some 6,000 wines. For something very refined but no less stylish, **NoMI** in the Park Hyatt serves up of-the-moment fusion cuisine in a beautiful setting overlooking the Water Tower.

Follow your outstanding meal with the dynamic dancing of the **Joffrey Ballet Chicago**. The world-renowned troupe performs classic and cutting-edge works at its new home in Millennium Park. For a schmoozier evening, join the fashion models at **Whiskey Bar**, Rande Gerber's *clubby hip spot* in the heart of the Gold Coast.

Late at night, it doesn't get much swankier than **Le Passage**, which has a late-night dance club that coddles guests with service in a palm-fringed underground setting. You'd expect something wilder at **Syn**—and you'd get it. This club, with its *cool mix of dance music*, has one of the best local VIP rooms, where the champagne flows like water.

Day 2

Morning: Charge into your second day with a *stylish French breakfast* at **Fuse**, which has a sunny location on the Chicago River in the Hotel 71. Or join the city's business elites at one of their favorite early-meeting spots, **Lloyd's Chicago**, which takes its name and interior-design inspiration from Frank Lloyd Wright.

The Chicago area has some superlative golf courses, so if you're a golfer, you've got your morning cut out for you. The private **Butler National Golf Club** and the **Chicago Golf Club** are memorable if you can arrange a tee time (and you have the connections necessary to get in to these *private clubs*). Have your concierge arrange a limo to transport you and your irons.

Off the links, there are oodles of antique and design stores awaiting your inspection. Begin your hunt at **The Golden Triangle**, which specializes in Asian artifacts, and continue by exploring this neighborhood and its wealth of *high-end shops* and galleries. Or stop in at the mammoth **Merchandise Mart**, where you can browse home-design showrooms for as long as you can last.

Afternoon: Avoid the midday doldrums with some of Carrie Nahabedian's bold Mediterranean food at **Naha**. Lunch here offers everything from superb sandwiches to complex entrées, served in a spare indigo-colored dining room. If you want to zero in on Italy for your lunch, swanky **Café Spiaggia** serves an acclaimed changing menu of Italian classics in a dining room that combines *knockout views* with an Italian villa motif.

This afternoon, you've several options. If you didn't see Chicago by helicopter (or, what the heck, even if you did), you should really *see it from the air* while flying your own plane. **Flight School Midway** offers onetime introductory flying lessons that include your own stint at the controls while you cruise the lakefront.

Much closer to earth, **Morlen Sinoway Atelier** is where you'll find the *amazing furniture creations* of local designer Sinoway. *Atelier* means "workshop," but this is really a gallery of fine woods, artworks, and complementary antiques. Afterward, check out the treasures on offer at **Leslie Hindman Auctions**, which handles famous estates and collections.

For a more entertaining option, see your concierge about scoring tickets for a taping of *Oprah*. Normally these ducats are snapped up months in advance, but where there's a will there may be a way. And whatever you do, prior to your big night out, prepare for the fun ahead with a facial at Mila Bravi's **Face & Facial Co.** on Oak Street. Her magic has earned her a *celebrity-studded client list*.

Evening: Chicagoans have been putting together picnics with panache and making the trek up to the **Ravinia Festival** ("the Wolf Trap of the Midwest") for a century. Everyone who's anyone has performed at this *summer festival under the stars*, from George Gershwin to Janis Joplin. Ask your concierge to help outfit your picnic hamper (people really do it up here, with linens and silver), and arrange a limo take you. If you'd rather stay in town, you can still reach for the stars. **Charlie Trotter's** is arguably Chicago's most famous and respected chef. If you can, book (months in advance) for the kitchen table to watch the *master at work*. For a livelier time, **Boka** in Lincoln Park creates artful plates of seasonal cuisine in a fun and stylishly luxe setting. If these all seem too complicated, settle in at the Chicago steakhouse that's so hot, Beverly Hills has embraced it as its own—**Morton's**.

Après le diner, ensconce yourself in an appropriately alluring environment. **Base Bar** in the Hard Rock Hotel is dark, supercool, and at the top of the *A-list* for stylish places to have a drink after dinner. But if you prefer a place that revels in the excesses of wealth, **Domaine**'s the place for you. It's modeled on Versailles, so you can browse a menu of rare libations, enveloped in red velvet and under the reflected glow of gold-framed mirrors.

Wait—the evening isn't over. In fact, it's just getting started. ***Moda*** means "fashion" in Italian, and that's the modus operandi at this *très chic dance club* in River North. To come back to earth with a cushioned landing after your night on the town, **Harry's Velvet Room** has commodious booths that offer privacy while you're being soothed by romantic songs.

Day 3

Morning: It's so hard to live this way. You may need to stay in your room and have a spa breakfast served while luxuriating under the expert ministrations of an *in-room masseuse* this morning. But if you're up to it, **Seasons** in the Four Seasons Hotel combines an elegant setting with superb breakfasts, including many healthy selections.

After two days of enjoying the best Chicago has to offer, you might feel a need to *tone up*, and you should do it at the city's best health club, the

East Bank Club. The cavernous building contains every piece of equipment or personal service you could dream of, including four pools. Or head the other way on that slippery slope. It's calories be damned at the **French Pastry School**, where you can enjoy a few hours with the students of the renowned culinary program and sample their projects.

Afternoon: For a lunch that's as much an experience as a chance to eat, **Heat** offers *sushi without compromise*. Many choices are plucked live from tanks in the stark dining room, and even sushi veterans are astounded at some of the dishes prepared. The other option du jour is rustic Italian cuisine with California flair at Rick Gesh's **Caliterra**, with its showy open kitchen and daily menu emphasizing fresh ingredients and bold flavors.

Lake Michigan and Chicago's winds combine to provide a perfect sailing venue. This afternoon, enjoy a private lesson on a sailboat or yacht at Belmont Harbor's **Chicago Sailing Club**. If you'd rather skip the work, *charter a boat* and crew for an afternoon cruising the shoreline.

Or, if you haven't yet had too much pampering (is that even possible?), book an appointment at **Marilyn Miglin Salon**. The staff at this Oak Street institution can create a makeup look for you and teach you how to apply it, and they also craft custom perfumes. Afterward, laze away the afternoon by tasting fine wines at the **Randolph Wine Cellar**. There are more than 1,000 wines stocked and the staff can take you through *tastings of varietals*.

Evening: For your last night, settle into the luxurious arms of **Ambria**, a refined Lincoln Park fixture noted for its sensational Basque-inspired food (the wine list alone will wow you). Closer to your hotel, **Avenues** serves exceptional seafood in an elegant yet unstuffy room with a discreetly open kitchen. For a more elevated experience, ascend **Everest**, which serves fantastic French Alsatian food with *drop-dead views* in its dressy 40th floor dining room in the financial district.

Close out the night with classic jazz or crooning at **Green Dolphin Street**, an opulent venue that seems right out of a 1930s MGM musical. Later at night, you can wind down in one of the plush booths at hedonistic **Narcisse**, which is all about fine champagnes, mirrors, gold, and self-indulgence, or have your cake and shake it, too: order one of the sinful offerings at the ultrahip *late-night dessert-bar nightclub* **Sugar**.

LUXE CHICAGO

Luxe Chicago:
The Hotels

Fairmont Chicago
200 N. Columbus Dr., Loop/Downtown, 312-565-8000 / 800-257-7544
www.fairmont.com

Rising like a pink vision from the dubious architectural charms of the vast Illinois Center development, the Fairmont Chicago excels at pampering guests with special touches both big and small. Rooms are done in warm shades of rose and are larger than average even at this end of the spectrum. The equally commodious bathrooms have marble surfaces and separate showers and tubs. Views are good in most directions, either Grant Park and the Lake or the skyline north of the river. Twice-daily maid service ensures that you won't mess things up too much, and you'll enjoy small gestures like the little ribbons around the hand towels. The hotel is an easy stroll from all the action along the Magnificent Mile, at Millennium Park, and in the Art Institute. $$$

Four Seasons
120 E. Delaware Pl., Gold Coast, 312-280-8800 / 800-819-5053
www.fourseasons.com

It's long been one of the top hotels in town, and new competition has only spurred the Four Seasons to be even more on top of its game. High atop the 900 N. Michigan shopping and commercial center, the Four Seasons has justly popular public spaces including the noted Season restaurant, cafe, and lounge. Rooms offer a variety of color schemes, but all could easily be the focus of a photo shoot in *Architectural Digest*. Fabrics, furnishings, and colors are all rich and elegant. All rooms have sitting areas, and superior rooms have truly sensational views of the city and the lake. The one-bedroom suites have lovely sitting rooms with equally nice views. Executive rooms are good for those needing to do a little business—they have an array of built-in services, including fax machines and printers. The swimming pool is large and an attraction in itself, with Roman columns and views under a large domed skylight. $$$$

Le Meridien Hotel

521 N. Michigan Ave., Near North, 312-645-1500 / 800-543-4300
www.lemeridien.com

Hidden behind the preserved façade of the 1929 McGraw-Hill Building,
Le Meridien is part of the Nordstrom's development along the Mag Mile.
The moment you enter its quiet lobby, your blood pressure will go down a
few critical notches. The emphasis in the modern design is on serenity, and
this is most apparent in the rooms themselves. Although the façade is historic, the structure is new, which allowed for rooms without compromises.
Bathrooms are large and feature separate showers and tubs. The color
scheme is all creams and whites, which makes the rooms feel both calm
and radiant, even if Chicago is hunkering through a nasty winter day. Off
the lobby, a patio area is the perfect place for a restorative drink on a
sunny day. $$$

Park Hyatt Chicago

800 N. Michigan Ave., Near North, 312-335-1234 / 800-633-7313
www.park.hyatt.com

Just across from the Peninsula, these two top hotels could take potshots
at each other if they were not so genteel. The Park Hyatt opened in the
late 1990s and takes a classic twist on contemporary design. The public
spaces and rooms artfully combine elements of Le Corbusier, Mies van der
Rohe, and Frank Lloyd Wright. The rooms are quite astonishing, combining
an array of comforts with views of the lake and city through huge windows.
Eames chairs, window seating areas, and DVD players are just some of
the details. Bathrooms are decked in rose granite with cherrywood accents
for a warm and luxurious feel. The soaking tubs in many rooms have wood
panels that open so you can enjoy the views while you relax. Candles are
provided to set the mood. There is a 7,000-square-foot health club with a
lap pool. The main restaurant, NoMI, has some of Chicago's most sought-
after tables. $$$$

The Peninsula Chicago

108 E. Superior St., Near North, 312-337-2888 / 866-288-8889
www.chicago.peninsula.com

The Peninsula is the current winner of the best-place-to-stay-in-Chicago sweepstakes, which is all the more impressive given the fact that the competition is pretty intense. It was just named the second-best hotel in the country by *Travel & Leisure* (after the Peninsula Beverly Hills). Here the fun begins with the fifth-floor public spaces. The Bar is a clubby retreat popular with locals (always an accolade for a hotel bar). The Lobby and Avenues restaurants are standouts (see separate listings in this chapter). Behind the concierge desk, a large mural by French artist Gerard Coltat celebrates the city in deeply textured gold, silver, and copper leaf combined with colorful oils. Upstairs in the rooms, luxuries include flat-screen TVs, both wired and wireless high-speed internet connections, fax, bedside control panels for all the room's lights and other features, and more. The amazing bathrooms feature soaking tubs with steam-free TVs and speakerphones that cancel out water noise so you can cut a deal while covered in suds. All this technology is artfully integrated into the room's traditional cream-colored decor. If possible, go for one of the suites—you won't move out. The spa has a devoted local following (see separate listing) and includes a long pool with huge windows overlooking the Magnificent Mile and a sun deck. $$$$

Ritz-Carlton Chicago

160 E. Pearson St., Near North, 312-266-1000 / 800-819-5053
www.fourseasons.com/chicagorc

Somewhat confusingly, the Ritz-Carlton Chicago is not part of the chain of the same name but rather is owned and operated by Four Seasons. Of course, given that chain's levels of service, that's not a bad thing after all. High atop the Water Tower Place shopping complex, the Ritz was one of Chicago's first luxury hotels of the modern age when it opened in 1979. The sizable rooms are traditionally decorated in Queen Anne style with plush velvets and brocades. The window treatments are thick and ornate. Marble bathrooms are also sizable, and rooms superior-level and above have walk-in closets and dressing areas. Try to book a corner suite, with views of the lake and the city. There is a full health spa, and the lap pool has four lanes and is more than 50 feet long. $$$$

Luxe Chicago: The Restaurants

Ambria

2300 N. Lincoln Park West, Lincoln Park, 773-472-5959

The Basque region of France and Spain is too often only in the news for the outrages of separatists—a great shame, given its rich and distinct culture. At Ambria, the cuisine of the region is the basis for an excellent menu served in one of the most gracious rooms in Lincoln Park. The dishes, like the Basque region, combine French and Spanish elements. Typical is the seared diver scallops with oyster mushrooms and a jamon serrano chive vinaigrette. Summer might see exquisite gazpacho, while in winter you might find a confit of squab. The many-paged menu changes often, and possibly the best way to traverse it is to place yourself in Ambria's hands and enjoy one of the many degustations. Desserts are of the standard you'd expect; don't be shy, have the chocolate degustation. The wine list includes rare choices at rarified prices. *Open Mon.–Thurs. 6–9:30 p.m., Fri. 6–10:30 p.m., Sat. 5–10:30 p.m. $$$$*

Avenues

108 E. Superior St., Near North, 312-573-6754

The premier restaurant in the Peninsula Hotel is a gem, and turns out some exquisite meals under chef David Hayden. The kitchen is open to view, but in keeping with the refined service it's not the center of attention. Rather, it's a place where you're aware something amazing is going on. As in the rest of the hotel, the colors are light and woody, and the tables are spaced far apart. Seafood is the specialty, and preparations of the familiar are surprising (no clam chowder compares to that here with its lush creaminess) and of the unfamiliar, superb (wild sea bass comes with candied garlic). Service is of the highest order (linen napkins are replaced using tongs). *Open for brunch Sun. 10:30 a.m.–2:30 p.m.; dinner Tues.–Sat., 6–10:30 p.m. $$$$*

LUXE CHICAGO

Boka
1729 N. Halsted St., Lincoln Park, 312-337-6070

A stylish restaurant near the always-hot Steppenwolf Theatre in Lincoln Park, Boka is posh without being pretentious. Guests are greeted by a foyer with river rocks, bamboo, and a fountain, and in the dining room, the sizable booths are deep and comfortable. The bar area is alive every night with well-off denizens of the neighborhood enjoying the finely poured cocktails. The wine list is long, and there are many choices by the glass. At the tables, chef Giuseppe Scurato has created a menu of simple yet satisfying dishes based on seasonal ingredients. Presentation is superb and the artful design of the dishes (many are small to encourage grazing) is highlighted by the complex lighting. One item that has been drawing raves from the neighborhood swells is the thick pork chop with apple compote and blue cheese—it may stay on the menu year-round. *Open Sun.–Wed. 5–10:30 p.m., Thurs.–Sat. 5–11:30 p.m.* $$$

Café Spiaggia
980 N. Michigan Ave., Gold Coast, 312-280-2750

A casual sibling of the swanky Spiaggia restaurant, Café Spiaggia does a roaring lunch business with fresh interpretations of classic Italian cooking. Seafood starters are boldly seasoned, while the pastas are all homemade and many, such as the perciatelli (thin, hollow tubes), will test your knowledge. There are always several roasted meats on the menu, each—like a strip steak in a spicy garlic crust—redolent with seasonings. Save room for the house-made ice creams that explode with the sweet flavors of a Tuscan summer. Murals are copies of those in a 15th-century villa and contrast nicely with the Mag Mile and lake views. *Open for brunch Sun. 11:30 a.m.–2:30 p.m.; lunch Mon.–Sat. 11:30 a.m.–2:30 p.m.; dinner Sun.–Thurs. 5:30–9 p.m., Fri.–Sat. 5:30–10:30 p.m.* $$$

Caliterra
633 N. Saint Clair St., Near North, 312-274-4444

Rustic Italian cuisine gets a dash of California flair at Caliterra, a twist on a winemakers' phrase for wines from the Golden State made with Italian varietals. It's easy to see this cuisine take shape at the large and dramatic open kitchen that occupies one corner of the simple yet elegant dining room. Chef Rick Gresh favors bold flavors. Good examples of this can be found in his rotating Soup Trilogy, which recently included squash with ginger, cream of semolina in brown butter and white truffle oil, and a rich toasted almond.

Pasta dishes change regularly and are available in small and main sizes so you can try more than one. Spicy artichokes with perciatelli come with accents of lobster. Main dishes include sautéed wild salmon with an artichoke and mushroom ragout and garlic vinaigrette. If you order the cheese course, Gresh himself is likely to lead you through the choices. The entire room is nonsmoking. *Open Sun.–Thurs. 7 a.m.–10 p.m., Fri.–Sat. 7 a.m.– 10:30 p.m. $$$*

Charlie Trotter's
816 W. Armitage Ave., Lincoln Park, 773-248-6228

People fly to Chicago just to eat at Charlie Trotter's. People book the kitchen table months in advance to see the master at work. People can recall what was served at a meal they enjoyed five years before. Superlatives beget superlatives at Chicago's finest restaurant. Prepare yourself for a gastronomic tour de force as Trotter magically combines foods from the more than 90 organic suppliers he's personally picked worldwide. Each night, three degustation menus are offered: grand, vegetable, and one for the lucky few at the kitchen table. Here are some highlights from a recent eight-course grand menu: warm organic egg with cold smoked sturgeon, purple Peruvian potato, chervil, and citrus crème fraîche; Alaskan halibut with crispy veal sweetbreads, celery, and fennel-infused apple vinaigrette; and rhubarb sorbet with spring onion marmalade and manni olive oil. Service matches the aspirations of the food, and you'll do well to put yourself in the hands of the sommelier. *Open Tues.–Sat. 5:30 p.m.–11 p.m. $$$$*

Erawan
729 N. Clark St., River North, 312-642-6888

Royal Thai cuisine differs from the boldly flavored standards you'd get from a street vendor in Bangkok or a storefront in Chicago by virtue of its costly ingredients, subtlety of spices, and artistry of presentation. Erawan features the talents of noted Thai chef Art Lee, who truly prepares dishes worthy of kings and queens. An early sign that you're in for a memorable experience is the snowbird dumplings, which consist of delicately seasoned chicken in little rice pouches carefully arranged on the porcelain plate like a flock of swans. Main dishes such as lobster in a turmeric cream and lamb Mussaman (a braised shank in a turmeric curry) are superb. The room is sumptuous in carved teak accented with gold leaf. *Open for lunch Mon.–Fri. 11:30 a.m.– 2:30 p.m., dinner Sun.–Thurs. 5–10 p.m., Fri.–Sat. 5–10:30 p.m. $$$*

Everest
440 S. LaSalle St., 40th Floor, Loop/Downtown, 312-663-8920

The well-respected critics of *Chicago* magazine recently named Everest the best restaurant in Chicago (knocking Charlie Trotter's to number two in what many see as a mischievous move). So the restaurant's name reflects not only its preeminent position atop the competition but also its place on the 40th floor of its building. The views are superb, and although you can't see all the way to chef Jean Joho's homeland in Alsace, the food will certainly take you there. One of the richest cuisines of France, Alsatian food is grounded in classic traditions accented with bold flavors from neighboring Germany. Joho's signature lobster roasted in Gewurztraminer-and-ginger-flavored butter is a must-order. Desserts include the widest selection of soufflés in town and should not be missed. The wine list includes a tremendous selection of Alsatian vintages. Service is par excellence. Joho is known for sending out surprise courses to tables so you may get a treat. *Open Tues.– Thurs. 5:30–9 p.m., Fri.–Sat. 5:30–10 p.m.* $$$$

Fox & Obel
401 E. Illinois St., River North, 312-410-7301

Chicago's highest-end food emporium, Fox & Obel operates a cafe where you can sample some of the range of dishes prepared daily by its chefs. All are fresh and you can work up your appetite by browsing the store and taking in some of its offerings—sniffing your way through the more than 350 cheeses is an expedition in itself. The pastries are much coveted. Outside mealtimes, the cafe is the scene for cooking demonstrations and cookbook signings, so you may want to stick around. *Open daily 7 a.m.–9 p.m.* $$

Fuse
71 E. Wacker Dr., Loop/Downtown, 312-462-7071

Located in the renovated Hotel 71, Fuse is a French restaurant helmed by the hot young chef Eric Aubriot. The menu is an ever-changing lineup of modern French creations. At breakfast, things are a bit more familiar, but this is where power breakfasters come to enjoy their eggs with élan—leather booths and dramatically sculpted ceilings add style you don't often get with an omelet. The eclectic menu rewards with quality. As you'd expect, brioches and croissants are up to snuff, and so are the other dishes on the menu, many of which feature seasonal fruits. Selections at lunch and dinner are playful variations on French classics. *Open daily for breakfast 6–10:30 a.m.; lunch daily 11:30 a.m.–2:30 p.m.; dinner Sun.–Thurs. 5:30–10:30 p.m., Fri.–Sat. 5:30–11:30 p.m.* $$

Grill on the Alley

909 N. Michigan Ave., Gold Coast, 312-255-9009

An offshoot of the well-known Beverly Hills classic, the Chicago edition has brought new life to the once nearly moribund ground level of the Westin Hotel on the Mag Mile. The large menu here is filled with dishes that you'd expect (steaks, seafood, salads, etc.) but that surprise for their depth of quality. Actually, they shouldn't surprise since the honest food at the original has been a favorite accompaniment to dishonest deals by Hollywood agents for years. Feel like an agent yourself and order the huge Cobb salad, which combines cheeses and meats of the first order. The crab Louie groans under the weight of all the shelled crustaceans. Steaks and seafood are also top quality. In season, don't miss the strawberry shortcake. Adding class to the swank scene are the efficient waiters in white jackets. *Open Mon.–Thurs. 6:30 a.m.–midnight, Fri.–Sat. 6:30 a.m.–2 a.m., Sun. 6:30 a.m.–9 p.m.* $$$

Heat

1507 N. Sedgwick St., Old Town, 312-397-9818

Three fish tanks at Heat ensure that the sushi is the freshest possible—it's killed as you order. A veritable oceanarium of treats awaits, from eels and prawns to puffer fish and more. There are just a few tables here and one long sushi bar, so the waitstaff has little to distract it from serving an amazing procession of dishes. Unless you have firm convictions, letting the chefs decide what to serve and with which wines and sakes to pair each course is the way to go. Although much attention focuses on the live fish (some still alive when they reach your table), many of the daily offerings aren't actually plucked from the tank, although their freshness is never in question. Beautiful floral displays add accent to the stark space. *Open for lunch Wed.–Mon. 11:30 a.m.–2 p.m.; dinner Mon.–Sat. 5–10 p.m.* $$$$

Lloyd's Chicago

200 W. Madison St., Loop/Downtown, 312-407-6900

Lloyd's could have just as easily been named Frank's or Wright's, given that the large clubby space takes its inspiration from the Prairie-style work of Frank Lloyd Wright. Certainly there are only a couple of other Loop locations where you can enjoy breakfast surrounded by this much style. The two-level space is done nicely in wood, and in summer the patio is a wonderful spot for the first coffee of the day. The breakfast menu is straightforward. Omelets are excellent, and a real sleeper is the muesli with fresh fruit. At other times, Lloyd's serves classic fare like steaks, pasta, and upscale sandwiches. *Open Mon.–Fri. 7:30 a.m.–7 p.m.* $$

LUXE CHICAGO

The Lobby
The Peninsula Chicago, 108 E. Superior St., Near North, 312-573-6760

This grand room off the lobby in the Peninsula is one of the most spectacular places along the Mag Mile. Floor-to-ceiling windows let the light pour in from the east. Tremendous meals are served throughout the day, starting with a breakfast that holds many surprises. Choices range from decadent treats from the bakery to healthy dishes featuring unusual fresh fruits. This place also knows how to do eggs Benedict. The daily afternoon tea gives the pastry chef another chance to show her chops and features a tea service loyal to the Peninsula's Hong Kong roots. At other times, the menu reflects influences from Asia, Europe, and the Americas, both casual and complex. On weekends there's a deadly chocolate buffet. *Open daily 7 a.m.–1 a.m.* $$

Morton's
1050 N. State St., River North, 312-266-4820

This anchor of Rush Street nightlife boasts a bar where the ardor of the more mature patrons for making new friends puts bars with younger and supposedly more energetic clientele to shame. Actually you may want to make friends before you dine since everything—from the lobsters and steaks to the desserts—is huge. The dining room is frenetic as solid members of Chicago's see-and-be-seen elite air-kiss and schmooze with abandon. *Open for lunch Fri.–Sun. 11:30 a.m.–3 p.m.; for dinner daily 4 p.m.–midnight; bar food daily 3 p.m.–1 a.m.* $$$$

Naha
500 N. Clark St., River North, 312-321-6242

The interior of Naha is a vision in blue, provided by the indigo window shades screening diners from busy Clark Street. Other decoration is muted, which means there's little to compete with chef Carrie Nahabedian's bold Mediterranean cooking. The lunch menu is one of the best in River North, combining casual ingredients in ways that stimulate the palate but won't weigh you down for the afternoon ahead. Everything changes seasonally, but recent choices included grilled scallops with marinated fennel and rhubarb to start. Main courses are solid, with standouts being the roast chicken with potato Caesar salad and grilled steak brushed with garlic, herbs, and sea salt accompanied by a Greek salad and frites. You might opt for simplicity and order the open-face Prosciutto sandwich with gorgonzola and figs on walnut bread. The interesting wine list features many choices by the glass. At dinner the menu is much more complex. *Open for lunch Mon.–Fri. 11:30 a.m.–2 p.m.; dinner Mon.–Sat. 5:30–10 p.m.* $$$

NoMI

800 N. Michigan Ave., Near North, 312-239-4030

Sitting at one of NoMI's coveted seventh-floor window tables on a snowy night with flakes filtering down around the Water Tower is the most romantic experience in the city, if not the world. Chef Sandro Gamba leads a restaurant that is easily among Chicago's best any time of year. The cooking is that form of modern fusion that incorporates flavors and techniques from cultures worldwide while keeping things harmonized with a classic French underpinning. Presentation is everything, and even the preparation of a classic dish like rack of lamb can change dramatically from one visit to the next. The design is richly elegant in a minimalist sort of way—lots of rubbed woods and dark accents. There are a range of options here that start with breakfast, where a rich hot chocolate is the true star. In summer, the open-air patio is probably the finest fresh-air dining venue in town. *Open for breakfast Mon.–Fri. 6:30–10:30 a.m., Sat. 7–11 a.m., Sun. 7–10:30 a.m.; brunch Sun. 10:30 a.m.–2:30 p.m.; lunch Mon.–Fri. 11:30 a.m.–2:30 p.m., Sat. noon–2:30 p.m.; dinner daily 5:30–10 p.m.* $$$$

Seasons

Four Seasons Hotel, 120 E. Delaware Pl., Gold Coast, 312-649-2349

Rich wood paneling, plush carpet, shaded windows, and awesome floral arrangements make Seasons a lavish and appealing setting for a meal any time of day. Breakfasts are unparalleled for quality. Try the seasonal berries with whole grain pancakes. The Sunday brunch is bounteous. At lunch, a warm goat-cheese salad makes a good starter, followed by one of the serious sandwiches (the Atlantic salmon on a potato-dill roll is a winner) or entrée specials. For dinner, the restaurant hops to the beat of chef Robert Sulatycky's imaginative and complex cooking. Adjoining the restaurant, the Seasons Lounge celebrates the views of the Mag Mile, Oak Street Beach, and the lake, and is an ideal spot for the lavish tea service or a late-afternoon drink. *Open for breakfast Mon.–Sat. 6:30–10 a.m., Sun. 6:30–9 a.m.; brunch Sun. 10:30 a.m.–2 p.m.; lunch Mon.–Sat. 11:30 a.m.–2 p.m.; dinner Mon.–Sat. 6–10 p.m.; lounge open Mon.–Fri. 11:30 a.m.–1 a.m., Sat. 11:30 a.m.–2 a.m., Sun. 10:30 a.m.–midnight; high tea Mon.–Sat. 3–5 p.m.* $$–$$$$

LUXE CHICAGO

Tru

676 N. St. Clair St., Near North, 312-202-0001

The courses just keep coming at Tru, easily the town's most surprising and entertaining high-end restaurant. The entrance is dark, which adds to the drama when you enter the luminescent dining room with its array of muted pastels and bold blue banquettes. The bar features a dramatically blue statue of the torso of a woman. Meals are by fixed courses or degustations, which gives the kitchen under Rick Tramonto a chance to wow you over and over again. Each dish is staged like a theatrical show. One of the best-known is the caviar service, which comes arrayed on a glass staircase. A vegetable dish might have two dozen or more tastings of tiny vegetables (try naming that many). A first course may have four little bites in one setting, from a mushroom terrine with truffle vinaigrette to the ethereal tomato foam with basil oil. Desserts by Gale Gand are the stuff of legend—expect a boffo close to the evening's culinary entertainment. Jackets are required for men. *Open Mon.–Thurs. 5:30–10 p.m., Fri.–Sat. 5:30–10:30 p.m.* $$$$

Zealous

419 W. Superior St., River North, 312-475-9112

An old brick automobile showroom has been transformed into a magical and minimalist work of art. Zealous describes chef/owner Michael Taus's attention to detail, and it's apparent throughout. The stark dining room is done in muted colors that bring out the drama of a live bamboo forest growing beneath the original skylights. Nearby, a huge redwood wine rack rises to the high ceiling behind a wall of glass. The 6,000 bottles can be found listed on the 750-item wine list that garners awards year after year. Servers are dressed in Donna Karan. The food is true to Taus's roots as a protégé of Charlie Trotter. Influences are global, and ingredients are valued for their purity and individual flavor. Salads might be lemon shrimp with lima beans or Hawaiian greens with macadamia nuts and hearts of palm. Main courses run the gamut on the long menu. And although the lineup is always changing, sesame-crusted Chilean sea bass with noodles and curry sauce is a signature dish that has a devoted following. Desserts show the same fusion sensibilities. *Open for lunch Tues.–Fri. 11:30 a.m.–2 p.m.; dinner Tues.–Thurs. 5–10 p.m., Fri.–Sat. 5–11 p.m.* $$$$

Luxe Chicago:
The Nightlife

The Bar

The Peninsula Chicago, 108 E. Superior St., Near North, 312-573-6766

This warmly chic update of the classic hotel bar draws a crowd of stylistas, worldly travelers, and metrofessionals to its warm-hued and comfortable space. Attentive service and top-shelf bar selections ensure that you'll be well taken care of, and modern art and lively trip-hoppy music give the otherwise laid-back lounge some zip. *Open Mon.–Thurs. 3 p.m.–1 a.m., Fri. 3 p.m.–2 a.m., Sat. noon–2 a.m., Sun. noon–1 a.m.* No cover.

Base Bar

Hard Rock Hotel, 230 N. Michigan Ave., Loop/Downtown, 312-345-1000

The bar on the ground floor of the Hard Rock Hotel has nothing to do with the popular and ubiquitous cafes related to the hotel that are dotted around the globe, and, it's fair to say, neither would the ultratrendy patrons here. The couches are low, the lighting is dim, and the music is house at this stylish and minimalist lounge with a long drink list. Until somebody tops it, this is the hippest place for a drink in the Loop. *Open Sun.–Fri. 5 p.m.–2 a.m., Sat. 5 p.m.–3 a.m.* No cover.

Domaine

1045 N. Rush St., Gold Coast, 312-397-1045

Versailles comes to Rush Street. There's no record that French royalty had any sense of humor (although that cake line was good), and neither does this palace of stylish excess. The decor is all mirrors and gold in a nod to the palace. Sadly Marie's perfumed sheep aren't in evidence, despite there being plenty of perfume here. The chairs and couches are mostly covered in red velvet, with some bearing fabrics that are a nod to famous Chanel ensembles. Drinks are served by people as gorgeous as the models who hang out here. In a further nod to Eurotrash, the euro is accepted (not a bad deal, given the weakness of the dollar of late). Private rooms feature direct lines to the bar. To really fit in, spend your day in the clothing boutiques along Oak and Rush Streets. *Open Sun.–Fri. 5 p.m.–4 a.m., Sat. 5 p.m.–5 a.m.* $$

LUXE CHICAGO

Green Dolphin Street
2200 N. Ashland Ave., Lincoln Park, 773-395-0066

Easily the swankiest jazz club in town, Green Dolphin Street is hard by
the Chicago River and not far from Chicago's major remaining foundry. This
adds some industrial chic to this large club that features a long bar staffed
by talented bartenders who make good use of the floor-to-ceiling display
of liquors. The main performance venue is large and has lots of little candlelit tables that, combined with the neon lights, give the room a 1940s
feel. Major touring acts from swing or big band to Latin and cabaret are
booked nightly. The onsite restaurant is noted for good seafood. *Club open
Tues.–Thurs. 9 p.m.–2 a.m., Fri.–Sat. 8 p.m.–3 a.m., Sun. 8 p.m.–midnight
(Sundays spring and summer only). $$*

Harry's Velvet Room
56 W. Illinois St., River North, 312-527-5600

The middle name tells you what you need to know about this plush little
place in the heart of River North. The furnishings are lavish and the couches
and booths commodious. Drinks are well-poured and the sounds veer away
from the hard edges of many clubs with a groovy mix of house, disco, and
jazz. Candles provide romantic heat you can stoke with the many cham-
pagnes available by the glass. *Open Mon.–Wed. 6 p.m.–4 a.m., Thurs.–Fri. 5
p.m.–4 a.m., Sat. 8 p.m.–5 a.m., Sun. 9 p.m.–4 a.m. $*

Joffrey Ballet Chicago
Auditorium Theatre, 50 E. Congress Pkwy., Loop/Downtown, 312-902-1500

Chicago's dance scene got a major boost when the Joffrey Ballet left New
York for the Windy City. Since then the group has thrived, performing its
vision of a classically based cutting edge company. The local season runs
from October through May. Look for the company to be moving to the new
Joan W. and Irving B. Harris Theater for Music and Dance in Millennium
Park. $$$$+

Le Passage
937 N. Rush St., Gold Coast, 312-255-0022

This high-concept club by nighttime impresario Billy Dec is down a flight of
stairs just off Rush Street. The staff manages to avoid copping attitudes,
even though this is very much a place for beautiful people and the beautiful
people who serve them. The central VIP area is roped in velvet—good if
you're a VIP and you want to be close to the masses, bad if you'd rather the
masses were massed farther away. The music is a mixture of tunes one

would euphemistically call "hits of the '70s, '80s, and '90s." The decor is vaguely Egyptian, possibly from when Napoleon was wandering about, but this is an easy place to hang for a while, so you'll have time to figure it out. There's a restaurant serving French fare until about 10 p.m., but really the big deal here is the club. *Open Wed.–Fri. 7 p.m.–4 a.m., Sat. 7 p.m.–5 a.m.* $$

Moda
25 W. Hubbard St., River North, 312-670-2200

Not dressed fashionably? Hit the road, 'cause Moda won't be letting you through the doors. (*Moda* in fact means "fashion" in Italian.) Things are low-key on both levels of the club. The music runs toward the mellower end of the current club range. Video screens show loops of fashion shows, and the employees can be seen casting an envious glance at the monitors now and then. Huge red leaves climb the walls and dark velvet sofas invite lounging. *Open Thurs.–Fri. 8 p.m.–2 a.m., Sat. 8 p.m.–3 a.m.* $$

Narcisse
710 N. Clark St., River North, 312-787-2675

Poor Narcissus, he'd probably go mental what with all the mirrors at Narcisse, but that's the idea, isn't it? In what's possibly the most lavishly decorated club in Chicago, the golds, brocades, and velvets pile one on top of the other in a stunning display of excess. Booths are deep and secluded, all the better for working your way through the menu of caviar and champagne. There are 11 choices by the glass of the latter and more than 100 choices by the bottle, including a few topping $1,000. Recently the kitchen has gotten more serious about food (it doesn't take much to open a jar of caviar) and the menu has plumped out with plenty of French classics. You can order some tasty nibbles until near closing. *Open Mon.–Fri. 5 p.m.–2 a.m., Sat. 5 p.m.–3 a.m., Sun. 7 p.m.–2 a.m.* $$

Sugar
108 W. Kinzie St., River North, 312-822-9999

It's a wild fantasy scene! Sugar combines a hip club with a dessert bar for folks looking for something sinful to put in their mouths late at night. The decor is pure confectionary, with the lights, tables, and booths all sharing a candy motif. Given the perfection of the clientele, it's obvious that the only thing they've eaten all day is one of the desserts here, which are truly rich and scrumptious. Music is house and fairly quiet compared to other clubs, which lets you whisper sweet nothings that much easier while you sip some dessert-friendly ports, liqueurs, and various dessert wines. *Open Sun.–Fri. 5 p.m.–2 a.m., Sat. 5 p.m.–3 a.m.* $$

Syn
1009 N. Rush St., Gold Coast, 312-664-0009

Don't waste your time with mere mortals, head straight for the champagne VIP room—if you can afford it and if you're a VIP. The decor is futuristic in a lime-green-plastic sort of way. The crowd is among the more beautiful of the beautiful Gold Coast and is serious about dancing—the floor is always packed. Music starts in the '70s and moves forward. On many nights the DJs take requests, so if you've got a hankering for that special tune, here's your chance. *Open Sun.–Fri. 5 p.m.–4 a.m., Sat. 5 p.m.–5 a.m.* $$

Whiskey Bar
1015 N. Rush St., Gold Coast, 312-475-0300

The ceilings are low and the decor is dark, woody, and leathery: the effect here at the Whiskey Bar in the Sutton Place Hotel is that of a classic high-end bar. In keeping with the name, just about every whiskey on the planet is stocked, making this not the best place to demand a fuzzy navel. However, what keeps this place from being a salesman-and-cigar place might just be the owner, Mr. Cindy Crawford (a.k.a. Rande Gerber), who has created a vibe that attracts hipsters galore, crowding the place at night, drinking, schmoozing, and otherwise creating a genuine scene. *Open Sun.–Fri. 5 p.m.–2 a.m., Sat. 5 p.m.–3 a.m.* No cover.

Luxe Chicago:
The Attractions

Art Institute of Chicago
111 S. Michigan Ave., Loop/Downtown, 312-443-3600

The star of local cultural institutions, the world-renowned Art Institute collection covers a range of ancient to modern works from a range of cultures. Besides the fabulous Impressionist paintings, there are many other famous pieces that can be found throughout the galleries. With a guide you can plunge deep into the vast collection and plumb rooms far from the crowds. The Chinese collection is among the best anywhere and contains treasures from a string of dynasties. Also notable are the works from Korea and Japan, including stunning 12th-century pottery from the former and prints from the latter. The American collection is also strong, and besides the paintings, the galleries of decorative arts have examples of furniture and other crafts that will cause you to pause and marvel at the exquisite craftsmanship. *Open Mon.–Fri. 10:30 a.m.–4:30 p.m. (until 8 p.m. Tues.), Sat.–Sun. 10 a.m.– 5 p.m. $*

Butler National Golf Club
2616 York Rd., Oak Brook, IL, 630-990-3333

The former home of the Western Open (until pressure was brought to move it from this all-men's club), Butler is probably the best course in the Chicago area, with one punishing array of 18 holes. The club is private, so you will need a connection or reciprocal rights to gain entrance. Opening hours vary but are generally good for daylight hours. *Opening dates vary by the weather. $$$$*

Chicago Golf Club
25 W. Warrenville Rd., Wheaton, IL, 630-665-2988

This very exclusive club first opened in 1895. The 18 holes are challenging and a bit of a throwback due to their open nature—trees are at a minimum. Located in the genteel western suburbs, the club has a Who's Who list of local members, including Michael Jordan. This is another private club, so you'll need a connection or reciprocal rights to gain entrance. Opening hours vary but are generally good for daylight hours. *Opening dates vary by the weather. $$$$*

LUXE CHICAGO

Chicago Sailing Club
North end of Belmont Harbor, Dock B, Lakeview, 773-871-7245

Lots of wind, lots of water, convenient harbors: Chicago's patch of Lake Michigan is an ideal place for sailing. The Chicago Sailing Club at lovely Belmont Harbor offers popular sailing classes to all levels of students. But you can escape the hordes and arrange private lessons on any boat in the fleet. Beginners may prefer the sporty 22-foot boats, but there's no reason you can't learn to take command of a 47-foot yacht. The instruction can be customized in a myriad of ways. If you'd rather let the crew do the work while you recline in splendor, you can charter any of the boats complete with a crew and enjoy the lake without homework. *Open daily summer 9 a.m.–8:30 p.m. $$–$$$$*

Chicago Tour Guides Institute
27 N. Wacker Dr., Ste. 400, Loop/Downtown, 773-276-6683

This firm has a network of guides with all areas of expertise, including museums, architecture, shopping, and other aspects of city life. You can set up a tour in advance or work through your concierge. Some tour ideas include being met at the airport by a guide and a limousine who can start your education of the city while you roll in luxurious splendor to the center; custom walks focusing on architecture, the parks, museums, and more; and special itineraries—including shopping trips—in a limo once you are in town. $$$$+

East Bank Club
500 N. Kingsbury St., River North, 312-527-5800

You'll need your hotel to arrange your visit unless you know a member or have reciprocal arrangements, but a visit to the East Bank Club is not just healthy, it's fun. The vast club on the river exudes superlatives: four pools, hundreds of machines, spas, racquetball, squash, aerobics, restaurant and bar, and just about every other way you can think of to engage your body in an activity. It's said that more business deals have been cut over the EBC's bike machines than at power lunches. *Open Mon.–Fri. 5:15 a.m.–11 p.m., Sat. 6:45 a.m.–9 p.m., Sun. 7:30 a.m.–8:30 p.m. $$$$*

Face & Facial Co.
104 E. Oak St., Gold Coast, 312-951-5151

During her two decades on Oak Street, Mila Bravi has built up a following that's not just loyal, they're also largely famous. Cindy Crawford, Goldie Hawn, and Oprah are some of the notables who have turned their complexions over to the amazing ministrations of Bravi. Famous Chicago fashion photographer Victor Skrebneski has an account—he sends his models here first before clicking the shutter release. The salon uses Bravi's own line of products and techniques she herself has developed. Other services include pedicures, manicures, and waxing. Focusing on results, the atmosphere is more about the business at hand than it is about pampering. *Open Tues. 10 a.m.–7 p.m., Wed.–Fri. 10 a.m.–6 p.m., Sat. 9 a.m.–6 p.m.* $$$$+

Flight School Midway
4943 63rd. St., South Side, 773-767-8100

What better way to see Chicago than from the vantage point of a pilot? Flight School Midway lets you do just that in just a couple hours. A 90-minute program introduces you to the preflight checks of a small single-engine plane. After learning about the systems, you taxi out to the runway and take off at the dual controls with an instructor at your side. Once in the air, you try a few basic turns and maneuvers while flying along the lakefront for 40 minutes. Alternately, you can try a three-hour program that includes a 90-minute flight and landing at another airport up to 50 miles away before returning to Midway. This is an exciting way to see Chicago—the first time the instructor hands the controls over to you and you feel the plane respond to your commands, it's unforgettable. *Call to make an appointment.* $$$$+

Four Seasons Spa
120 E. Delaware Pl., Gold Coast, 312-280-8800

The Four Seasons Spa embodies the standards of service and comfort the hotel is known for. There's a complete range of therapies. Two that are special to the Four Seasons are the elixir paraffin wrap, which starts with an exfoliation using ground olive stones and follows with a wrap of juniper berries, lavender, and grapefruit, and the Four Seasons in One Treatment, which includes a body scrub, hydration, massage, body wrap, scalp therapy, and more. *Open daily 8 a.m.–8 p.m.* $$$$+

LUXE CHICAGO

French Pastry School
226 W. Jackson Blvd., Loop/Downtown, 312-726-2419

This Harvard of the flaky-crust set is renowned for its intensive eight-week courses in the art of pastry. You can join one for a day and get a thorough tutorial in the business of creating extravagant items. The kitchens here are works of art in themselves, with gleaming copper pots hanging in rows, and enough specialized tools of the trade on display to send kitchen-gadget freaks into a form of shock. Depending on the day you visit, you may be part of a class learning cakes, tarts, specialty desserts, candy, or other sweets. $$

The Golden Triangle
72 W. Hubbard St., River North, 312-755-1266

In a neighborhood filled with top-end antique stores and shops, the Golden Triangle is a standout. The collection of rare Asian artifacts is presented in a setting worthy of Angkor, with carved details giving the goods on sale a lavish backdrop. Look for ancient works such as Tang Dynasty (AD 600) ceramic burial statues. Somewhat more modern is the large collection of classic Chinese pieces of furniture dating from the period roughly from 1000 through the 1800s. Careful and ingenious design has made these items timeless—many feature rare woods and pearl inlays, while pieces from the 1800s are often finished in much-coveted black lacquer. *Open Mon.–Wed., Fri. 10 a.m.–6 p.m., Thurs. 10 a.m.–7 p.m., Sat. 10 a.m.–5 p.m.*

Leslie Hindman Auctions
122 N. Aberdeen St., West Loop, 312-491-9522

The biggest auction firm locally, with auctions taking place frequently and running the gamut of items. Look for auctions focused on artwork from various periods, antique furniture, entire estates, collectibles including timepieces, books, vintage photographs, and sports memorabilia, plus other valuable items. Auctions are held in Hindman's recently rebuilt facilities, which are excellent venues for browsing the goods on offer. Many of the catalogues produced for the sales are themselves works of art. $$$$

Marilyn Miglin Salon
112 E. Oak St., Gold Coast, 312-943-1120

Completely custom makeup consultations are the specialty here; the staff will first work with you to design a look and then teach you how to re-create it each day. Products are all in-house formulas from Miglin's line. The namesake herself is a local legend, having been in business since 1963. In fact, Oak Street has the honorary name of Marilyn Miglin Way. A recent expansion includes a custom perfume salon, where you can get one of several unique scents that are geared to your own chemistry. Most popular is the "Pheromone." Limited spa services are available, but they don't do hair. *Open Mon.–Fri. 10 a.m.–6 p.m., Sat. 10 a.m.–5 p.m.* $$$$+

Merchandise Mart
222 Merchandise Mart Plaza, River North, 312-527-7990

The largest commercial building in the world at four million square feet, the 1931 Mart is a sight itself, perched proudly across from the Loop on the north bank of the Chicago River. It is home to hundreds of wholesale showrooms for the trade. You can ignore giftwares and office goods and instead focus on home design. Here the displays—all open to the dark and quiet corridors through plate-glass windows—are like ads out of the pages of *Architectural Digest* come to life. Although only commercial buyers can technically do business here, there's nothing stopping you from getting an advance look at next year's designs and getting inspiration for plans and dreams you can share with your own designers, and there are occasional sample sales open to the public. *Open Mon.–Fri. 9 a.m.–6 p.m., Sat. 10 a.m.–5 p.m.*

Morlen Sinoway Atelier
1052 W. Fulton Market, West Loop, 312-432-0100

A local boy made good, Morlen Sinoway graduated from the School of the Art Institute in 1975. His custom furniture creations are now sought after worldwide. At his showplace showroom in the Randolph Street market district, Sinoway displays not only examples of his furniture creations and other artwork, but also fine antiques and works of art he has collected for sale. For most browsers, the store will be more of a museum and an education in boldly executed design using premium materials. *Open Mon.–Sat. noon–5 p.m.*

The Peninsula Spa
The Peninsula Chicago, 108 E. Superior St., Near North, 312-337-2888

Chicago's best hotel has a very fine spa, as you'd expect. The pool's half the length of an Olympic-size swimming pool and is one of the city's best, with huge picture windows letting in the light. Services run the gamut from massage and skin care to an array of body treatments such as green-tea body therapy. Among available programs is the Sanctuary for the Senses, a 2-1/2-hour series of therapies that includes a range of substances that in other forms would make pretty good juice. There's a lemon sugar body polish; detoxifiers made from mango, papaya, and pineapple; and a full body massage with citrus cream. *Open Mon.–Fri. 6 a.m.–10 p.m., Sat.–Sun. 7 a.m.–8 p.m.* $$$$+

Randolph Wine Cellar
1415 W. Randolph St., West Loop, 312-942-1212

More than a thousand different wines are stocked in this elegant shop on the hot Randolph Street corridor. Temperature and humidity are controlled year-round and staff are ready to guide you through the process of selecting just the right bottle. Better, on Saturday afternoons there are extensive tastings that are as informative as they are fun. *Open Mon.–Fri. 11 a.m.–8 p.m., Sat. 10 a.m.–8 p.m., Sun. 1–6 p.m.*

Ravinia Festival
Ravinia Park Rd., Highland Park, IL, 847-266-5100

Celebrating its 100th anniversary in 2004, the Ravinia Festival is the oldest outdoor music festival in North America. Not only is this the summer home of the renowned Chicago Symphony Orchestra, it also presents jazz, pop, rock, dance, opera, theatre, and cabaret, and hosts some 150 events during its three-month summer season. Practically everyone has appeared here at one time or another: George Gershwin, Ella Fitzgerald, Dave Brubeck, Yo-Yo Ma, Luciano Pavarotti—even Janis Joplin, and music directors have included Seiji Ozawa, James Levine, and Christoph Eschenbach. But for Chicagoans of a certain stripe, the real event is putting on a show of one's own: picnicking here is a competitive sport, and folks bring the good linen and silver to enhance their alfresco experience. You can, of course, sit in seats in the pavilion or rent chairs for the lawn, and if you don't want to be saddled with silverware, you can dine at one of the onsite restaurants or have them arrange a picnic for you (lavish or simple). *Park opens Mon.–Sat. at 5 p.m., Sun. at 4 p.m., with some exceptions, and show times vary; box office hours Mon.–Sat. 10 a.m.–6 p.m., Sun. 1–6 p.m.* $$$$+

Rolph Achilles, Personal Guide
773-477-8138

Achilles has both architectural and artistic training, which he puts to good use as a guide extraordinaire. Whether by helicopter, limo, or foot, Rolph can put together an itinerary that matches your interest. How good is he? This is the person that the city's tourism office uses to show VIPs around. $$$$+

Sun Aero Helicopters
Lansing Municipal Airport, Lansing, IL, 708-895-8958

Based south of the city in Lansing, IL, Sun Aero can pick you up in downtown Chicago. Flight-seeing itineraries are fully customizable, but you can't go wrong starting with the lakefront, parks, and architect/city planner Daniel Burnham's grand boulevards. The fleet handles between one and four passengers, depending on which helicopter you charter. Internal communications on headsets mean you can hear your guide and the pilot. $$$$+

Hipster Chicago

"Hip" is a subjective term, so what's hip in one town won't necessarily be in another. In Chicago, hipsters know that "hip" doesn't have to be trendy. Rather, it's like the Supreme Court's definition of pornography—it's hard to define but you know it when you see it. It's about the places that make us feel great to be living here. Whether it's a breakfast place that breaks with tradition, a bar with idiosyncratic personality (and crowd), a blues joint better than any cliché, a restaurant with an assured sense of style, or a magnificent new park no other city in the world would try to build—all these things make Chicago hip. And the really cool thing is, you don't need to actually live here to enjoy them.

Hipster Chicago: The Itinerary

Three Great Days and Nights

Day 1

Your Hotel: **House of Blues**

Morning: What hipper way to start your visit to Chicago than at one of Oprah's favorite restaurants? She loves the corn muffins at **Wishbone**, and you will too. Even if she isn't there, you're sure to be joining some of her staff and guests (her studio is across the street) in enjoying the great *Southern cooking*. Another option is **LT's Grill**, where you'll find fresh-squeezed orange juice and surprising standards like the Porky Pig hash.

After breakfast, head out to the current *cradle of creative cool*. The West Loop has a number of contemporary shops and galleries where you can see what's happening with artwork, furniture, and crafts. Focus on the 1000 block of West Fulton Market, the 100 block of North Peoria, and the 900 block of West Lake Street. For a more energetic and unusual introduction to the city, rent a canoe or kayak from **Chicago River Canoe & Kayak** and paddle the Chicago River—the North Branch is clean, the views are great, and you'll see lots of wildlife.

Afternoon: Lunch options offer a study in contrasts. **Sushi Wabi** is one of the city's most popular purveyors of sushi. The setting is minimalist, but the scene is hip and the soundtrack is house. Those in the know head for the long sushi bar and follow the chef's recommendations. The only thing raw at **Twisted Spoke** is the language of the patrons —it's a biker bar. But it has panache, and its talented kitchen turns out the *best burgers in town*.

Chicago is home to a large community of world-class photographers, and you can see their work along with works of the masters at the **Museum of Contemporary Photography**, which also mounts regular special exhibits. Continuing your *culture tour*, a short stroll up Michigan Avenue brings you to **Gallery 37** a showcase for the work of people enrolled in the city's art programs.

HIPSTER CHICAGO

Evening: Unlike the local baseball teams, Chicago's restaurant scene keeps hitting 'em out of the ballpark year after year. The selection of great places for dinner is long. **Blackbird** is one of *Gourmet* magazine's 50 best U.S. restaurants, thanks to its razor-sharp skill at taking regional ingredients and making them shine. At **Red Light**, Jackie Shen hits home runs for her Asian cooking done with flair in a flaming open kitchen; the food is as appealing as the beautiful *Asian Art Nouveau* dining room. At **Marche**, French technique is combined with flawless ingredients to produce memorable dishes in a boisterous and happy converted produce warehouse.

If it's good enough for the Rolling Stones, it's good enough for you—your first-choice after-dinner venue is the **Double Door**, a classic and intimate *rock venue* in Wicker Park. For a larger venue (but not necessarily bigger bands), try **Metro**, a huge old theatre in Wrigleyville that put the Smashing Pumpkins and many others on the map.

After midnight, you always have choices in Chicago. Tonight try the always fun, always cool **Funky Buddha Lounge**. Music may be house, soul, reggae, or anything else, and that's just fine with the crowds—including many a celeb—who love the unpretentious scene. If you liked Metro, you'll love the **Smart Bar** downstairs, which is open way late and plays *cutting-edge dance music* for people who are serious about busting a move. For just hanging, it doesn't get much more relaxed than the **Rainbo**, with its good drinks and comfy booths.

Day 2

Morning: Start the day at one of the city's breakfast institutions: the **Melrose Diner** offers plate-filling omelets oozing with your choice of good stuff and *sunny sidewalk seating* to welcome a bleary "god-was-I-up-late" crowd. Or make like a kid at **Leo's Lunchroom** in Wicker Park, where the decor is rumpus room and the food is familiar and tasty.

If you're ready for a morning with a little edge, prepare for your nights in Chicago's coolest clubs by getting a tattoo or piercing—or both—at Uptown's **Tattoo Factory**. On your way back, stop off at one of the two

Reckless Records for a selection of indie music you won't find at Best Buy. Find out what bands are in town while you're there. Then walk the sidewalks of *Lakeview*, specifically the triangle of Belmont Avenue and Clark and Halsted Streets. Always funky, Lakeview is home to a mix of young urban professionals and creative types. Start by seeing everything Goth at the Alley, the anchor for an eclectic collection of stores. Then cheer yourself up with a trip to **Uncle Fun**, a veritable *funhouse for adults* with vintage and new toys, games, and *tchotchkes* that make you feel like a kid again (come here if you're looking to replace that old Twister or Family Feud game).

Afternoon: Prepare for this afternoon's highlight by dining on modern fusion cuisine at **Puck's** (as in Wolfgang) in the Museum of Contemporary Art. If the day is nice, don't prevaricate—sit outside on *the city's best patio*. Or head around the corner to one of North Michigan Avenue's institutions, the always-cool **Bistro 110**. Enjoy the country French cooking and save room for the crème brûlée.

This afternoon you have a chance to bring your *art appreciation* into the 21st century. The **Museum of Contemporary Art** wins praise for its collection as well as for its efforts to contextualize the works on display for visitors in its home in the revamped Chicago Armory.

Evening: Cool dinners take many forms. **Japonais** has gorgeously fresh fusion Japanese cuisine in a setting worthy of a fashion shoot. (You'll want to check out the moody lounge downstairs, which opens out onto a wildly popular deck right on the Chicago River.) For an even more overtly *fashionable dinner*, try the Northern Italian classics at **Follia**, which shares owners with a fashion agency that also supplies the servers. For a romantic hideaway, find the tables hidden in the vaults at **Opera**, an otherwise bustling Asian place located in a colorfully restored old film warehouse. Latin food makes an appearance at **Vermilion**, but with a twist—it's paired with Indian flavors to fulfill the culinary vision of chef Maneet Chauhan.

After dinner, have your change ready and hit the best jukebox in the city at **Betty's Blue Star Lounge** on the West Side. The booths and sofas are dreamy, and you can also let the DJs in the back room do the playing for you. If you'd rather get a little exercise, Friday nights are the time for art *gallery openings* in the River North Gallery District. Prowl the blocks around the intersections of Franklin, Wells, Superior, and Huron Streets and Chicago Avenue, and see what you find. Or head to one of the city's liveliest neighborhood bars, the **Hideout**.

Late night, go for the *punk vibe* at the no-holds-barred **Exit**, or let Marie work her drink wonders at the ever-charming **Marie's Rip Tide Lounge**, a mellow haven open until 4 a.m. and possibly beyond.

Day 3

Morning: Start the day by seeing what the surprises are on the **Bongo Room**'s creative and ever-changing breakfast menu. You won't get simple French toast, but instead one pegged to the season (pumpkin spice, perhaps) or cook's whim (*cherries jubilee*, anyone?). For a more refined experience, **La Tache** serves a Saturday brunch that would do any French bistro proud.

Scene-y *Wicker Park* provides a cool walk any time of year, so start your day here. Milwaukee and Damen Avenues are lined with a mixture of ebullient, creative shops (stop in **p.45**, one of Chicago's best boutiques, hailed by mags like *Lucky* and *Wallpaper* for championing hot young designers). The rhyming residential streets of Hoyne and LeMoyne are lined with funky old mansions in various states of restoration, and you can view novelist Nelson Algren's home at 1958 W. Evergreen Ave. (don't knock, people still live there). Later on, stop to recaffeinate at **Caffe Deluca**, a classic Italian coffee bar.

For a morning farther afield, you can sniff, squeeze, and chew your way through Chicago's great *melting pot* of diversity on the **Ethnic Grocery Tour**, which takes you to classic purveyors for a myriad of cuisines. If you're more in the mood for a journey inward this morning, you can take one of the yoga classes at Bucktown's groovy **Chi Healing Center**.

Afternoon: "Classic comfort food and cocktails" is the motto at the comfy retro-diner **Silver Cloud** in Bucktown, and it offers the latest brunch in the city if you're getting a slower start to your day. (If you're feeling rough, maybe its *signature s'more-tini* will perk you up.) Or see how far the definition of Japanese food can be stretched at Wicker Park's dark and romantic **Ohba**, where brie tempura fondue is a signature dish.

Spend the afternoon exploring the alternative scene in Wicker Park's cool next-door neighborhood, *Bucktown*. Armitage and Damen Avenues have some of the city's most exciting boutiques, many run by hot young designers. Go west on Armitage from Damen or north on Damen from Armitage. At the six-way intersection of Damen, North, and Milwaukee, look for some of Chicago's edgiest galleries, displaying works by people destined to make it big—or work as waiters for the rest of their lives, you decide.

If shopping's not your forte, check out the **Chopping Block**, just west of Lincoln Park. It offers intimate *cooking courses* specializing in Midwestern cuisine and ingredients.

Evening: For dinner, **Frontera Grill** is maybe as cool as it gets. Chef Rick Bayless has made an art of exploring the wonders of regional Mexican cuisine at this *wildly colorful*, very busy cafe that has a reputation far beyond Illinois. (If you want the ultimate Bayless experience, you'll want to reserve well in advance for his fine dining establishment, the adjoining **Topolobampo**.) For Italian, try **Gioco** in the South Loop, which takes classic Italian, prepares it in an open kitchen, and makes it trendy. Or zoom into the future and try the boutique-supplier sourced cuisine at **Mod**, where modern American cuisine is served in a *space-age setting* à la Jetsons, complete with bright Jell-O colors.

After dinner, groove to the global music on offer at the **HotHouse**, a *rough-cool* nonprofit club with a different lineup of musicians and music styles every night. To hear simply good rock in a simple setting, it doesn't get any sweatier or more honest than the **Empty Bottle**, which gets big names despite its diminutive size. For something completely different, catch the female impersonators in all their flamboyant glory at **The Baton**. Surprisingly, this club is a Chicago institution, and even more popular with straights than gays.

Close out your night at **Sonotheque**, a *high-concept* DJ-driven lounge that doesn't cater to attitude or pretension. If you'd like to get more horizontal than you would on a dance floor, there's **Iggy's**, a laid-back bar with plenty of couches and sheltering drapes.

HIPSTER CHICAGO

Hipster Chicago:
The Hotels

Hotel Allegro

171 W. Randolph St., Loop/Downtown, 312-236-0123 / 800-643-1500
www.allegrochicago.com

For a good part of the 20th century, the Hotel Allegro was known as
the Bismark Hotel and it was a haven for Chicago's political machine.
Shenanigans galore transpired in its smoke-filled halls. Now rehabbed into
one of the best hotels in the Loop, the Allegro boasts a bright and colorful
interior that looks good day or night. The second-floor lobby with its tall
windows is a good place to relax or have a drink. Rooms feature various
appetite-inspiring shades of chocolate, salmon, honey, and cream. There's
conveniences aplenty, including flat-screen TVs and free wireless internet.
There's also the same sense of fun that can be found throughout the
Kimpton Group boutique hotels—bowls of Tootsie Rolls are everywhere
and the spacious suites have Mr. Bubble dispensers to go with the
Jacuzzi tubs. $$

Hotel Burnham

1 W. Washington St., Loop/Downtown, 312-782-1111 / 877-294-9712
www.burnhamhotel.com

It's fair to say that few hotels have been more carefully watched during
their development than the Kimpton Group's Hotel Burnham, which is
based in the landmark Reliance Building. Built in 1891, the Reliance is
easily one of the most important buildings still surviving in the Loop. It is
the prototype for today's glass-and-steel skyscrapers. The façade is covered
in luminescent terra-cotta tiles, while the design itself harks back to the
Gothic era in its drive to use as much glass as possible. Despite the build-
ing's premier status, by the 1990s it had fallen on hard times—the small
floors were poorly suited to commercial use. But small floors were perfect
for this hotel, named after pioneer architect Daniel Burnham, whose firm
designed the building. Worried fans of architecture were calmed by the
careful restoration. The luxurious rooms have traditional furnishings in plush
golds and blues. The public spaces are suitably lavish, and the restaurant,
Atwood Café, is one of the Loop's best. $$$

Hotel Monaco
225 N. Wabash Ave., Loop/Downtown, 312-960-8500 / 800-546-7866
www.hotelmonaco.com

Lonely at night? If you're looking for a little companionship that respects all the current social norms, the Hotel Monaco provides it—in the form of your own goldfish. Shortly after checking in, there will be a knock at the door and a large fishbowl with a spry little fellow will be placed in your room. Another whimsical property in the Kimpton Group, the hotel is in a classic old building with massive thick walls. Rooms have lively color schemes to match the fish, and those facing north have good views out over the Chicago River. Luxuries include mahogany writing desks. Inquire into the "Party Like a Rock Star Suite." It has famous concert photographs, real gold records, and handwritten John Lennon song lyrics on the walls, a fully loaded digital jukebox in the living area as well as a 52-disc CD player in the bedroom, an electric guitar and amp for you to riff on, and a two-person Jacuzzi tub. $$

House of Blues Hotel
333 N. Dearborn St., River North, 312-245-0333 / 800-235-6397
www.loewshotels.com/hotels/chicago

The House of Blues chain, which includes the original Blues Brother Dan Ackroyd among its owners, has opened a hotel in Chicago. In the still-mod Marina City complex, the hotel is managed by the luxury Loews chain. It's too bad that they don't give tours of the rooms, since each is both a spectacle and a work of art. Primitive artworks abound, and the colors, fabrics, and details can best be described as wild. But the results are very cool and might give you some ideas for a major redecoration once you get home. Among the amenities are a full-scale health club with all the latest in machines and fitness gizmos. If you are staying Saturday night, reserve a table for the Sunday morning House of Blues gospel brunch, a wildly popular weekly musical event that you can get in to thanks to your hotel patronage. The adjoining blues club has a much more predictable rural Mississippi theme. $$

HIPSTER CHICAGO

Hipster Chicago: The Restaurants

Bistro 110
110 E. Pearson St., Gold Coast, 312-266-3110

For 20 years this casual bistro has been serving up tasty French classics right off Michigan Avenue. The signature roasted garlic that comes with the bread will chase the demons away. Soups, salads, and roasted meats are all delicious. The various coffees work well to help you regroup in the middle of the day. Eat light or somehow save room for the superlative crème brûlée at dessert. *Open Mon.–Wed. 11:30 a.m.–10 p.m., Thurs.–Sat. 11:30 a.m.–11 p.m., Sun. 11 a.m.–10 p.m.* $$

Blackbird
619 W. Randolph St., West Loop, 312-715-0708

One of the cornerstones of Chicago's fine dining scene, Blackbird emphasizes visual perfection and clarity of taste in its modern preparations. Chef Paul Kahan takes French influences and molds them into dishes that have kept the simple dining room packed since 1998. Look for classics like pâté and seasonal seafoods to start. Mains are meaty with quail, lamb, duck, and other traditional meats much in evidence. *Gourmet* has recognized the kitchen's skill and named it one of America's 50 best restaurants. To close, you'll be forgiven if you get a little giddy at pastry chef Elissa Narow's creations, which, like the rest of the offerings, are simply perfect. Avec, the neighboring wine bar, serves up some of Blackbird's classic starters in a casual setting. *Open for lunch Mon.–Fri. 11:30 a.m.–2 p.m.; dinner Mon.–Thurs. 5:30–10:30 p.m., Fri.–Sat. 5:30–11:30 p.m.* $$$$

Bongo Room
1470 N. Milwaukee Ave., Wicker Park, 773-489-0690

Pancakes and French toast: been there, done that, right? Well, at the Bongo Room you're wrong. Here the pancakes may be Black Forest cherry or the French toast may be mango. Surprising flavors abound in the old classics, and the selection changes daily. Omelets are equally good, and on weekends you can get eggs Benedict. Driving music teams with the coffee to wake you up. *Open Mon.–Fri. 8 a.m.–2:30 p.m., Sat.–Sun. 9:30 a.m.–2:30 p.m.* $$

Caffé Deluca

1721 N. Damen Ave., Wicker Park, 773-342-6000

Caffé Deluca thrives on a loyal coterie of customers who delight in the misty fog of memories of a place that evokes the rough-edged charms of postwar Europe. Is that a spy over there in the corner? Anyway, the coffee will be familiar to anyone who's swooned over a similar offering at a cafe in Rome, and for many, the fresh pastries are even better. Throughout the day Caffé Deluca also serves panini, pastas, and salads. *Open Mon.–Fri. 6 a.m.–11 p.m., Sat.–Sun. 7 a.m.–2 a.m.* $$

Follia

953 W. Fulton Ave., West Loop, 312-243-2888

The haute couture–draped mannequins in the windows at Follia are just the start of a truly fashionable experience. If the servers look like models, it's no coincidence: the owners also run a modeling agency. In keeping with the theme, the food is sort of what you'd expect to find in Milan after a day watching the runways. Classic northern Italian cuisine is prepared with fresh ingredients flown in by Alitalia daily. The caprese salad is everything you could hope for, with tomatoes, basil, fresh mozzarella, and rich olive oil that each burst with flavor. Thin-crust pizzas are the real (Italian) deal and nothing like the bomber-size variations created elsewhere in town. Entrées change nightly but usually feature a few fresh pastas. *Open Sun.–Thurs. 5–11 p.m., Fri.–Sat. 5 p.m.–1 a.m.* $$$

Frontera Grill

445 N. Clark St., River North, 312-661-1434

Rick Bayless has become a cooking legend, thanks to this temple of regional Mexican food. For almost 20 years Bayless has celebrated the myriad of variations of ingredients, subtle flavors, and fiery sauces possible with Mexican food. Roasted meats and peppers, citrus-marinated seafood, and deep, complex sauces are some of the components found in the frequently changing menu, all served up with freshly made corn tortillas. It's all a revelation, which explains why waits in the no-reservation room can exceed 90 minutes. Come early or late (early if you want to snag an order of the limited-quantity chiles rellenos), or be prepared to settle in with the signature margaritas (several types, all better than most anywhere). The adjoining Topolobampo is Bayless' fine dining extension, where the ingredients are more unusual, the creations more daring, and the prices much higher (see separate listing). *Open for lunch Tues.–Fri. 11:30 a.m.– 2:30 p.m., Sat. 10:30 a.m.– 2:30 p.m., dinner Tues.–Thurs. 5–10 p.m., Fri.–Sat. 5–11 p.m.* $$

HIPSTER CHICAGO

Gioco

1312 S. Wabash Ave., South Loop, 312-939-3870

Classic Italian seafood and meat dishes star at this anchor of the booming South Loop restaurant scene. A huge open kitchen dominates the rustic beamed dining space, which sprawls over several levels. The menu changes often and there are numerous seasonal variations. The roasted Brussels sprouts are a fall and winter classic that have gone from being a mere side to a menu item in their own right. If you're ready for an alternative to inventive little plates, then hearty mains like saltimbocca pork chop or the oven-roasted striped bass will please. Fried calamari—another of Chicago's favorite dishes—is moist, tender, and has a herbed crispy crust. There are always several boldly flavored vegetarian dishes, many based on eggplant. *Open Sun.–Wed. 5:30–10 p.m., Thurs. 5:30–11 p.m., Fri.–Sat. 5:30 p.m– midnight.* $$$

Iggy's

700 N. Milwaukee Ave., Wicker Park, 312-829-4449

Iggy's is a great place to end an evening. Not a club but a late-night bar and restaurant, it has many of the comforts of a club—lots of low couches, shielding velvet drapes, attentive drink servers—but it's also very laid-back, which means you can settle back and enjoy whomever you're with. Don't worry about club clothes either; everything from T-shirts to Prada is here. Food is fairly basic, from burgers to pasta. Late, more people drink than eat. *Open Sun.–Fri. 7 p.m.–4 a.m., Sat. 7 p.m.–5 a.m.* $

Japonais

600 W. Chicago Ave., River North, 312-822-9600

Japonais melds two other trendy and popular restaurants, Mirai Sushi and Ohba. Influences of both can be found in the kitchen here: sushi and other raw items from the former and inventive modern Japanese dishes from the latter. Look for stunningly fresh unagi rolls and fusion items like a spring roll with soft-shell crab and chutney. Adventuresome diners will find much to explore on the long menu; there's also a long and interesting selection of wines. Choices extend to two dark and sensual dining rooms. The red room has accents of the namesake color while the green room sizzles with an unusual triple fireplace. Like so many Chicago-cool places these days, Japonais has a stylish lounge downstairs with deeply secluded sofas and a great view of the Chicago River, and it also spills out onto a fabulous patio in the summer. *Open for lunch Mon.–Fri. noon–2:30 p.m.; dinner Mon.–Thurs. 5–11 p.m., Fri.–Sat. 5–11:30 p.m., Sun. 5–10 p.m.* $$$

La Tache
1475 W. Balmoral Ave., Andersonville, 773-334-7168

La Tache is the kind of French bistro you fly to Paris to enjoy. Located on a quiet side street in hot Andersonville, the dining room is très perfect, with dark mahogany wainscoting and little linen curtains on the windows. The bar up front has the de rigeur zinc, and there's a good list of French wines by the glass. The menu scores for authenticity as well. Rich and tender beef bourguignonne is an ideal comfort on a cold Chicago night. The steak frites provides fun with the flavor as you can choose both your cut of meat and the sauce. Deserts include a sinful crème caramel and at times a puckery and rich tarte au citron. The bar stays open for desserts and drinks until at least 1 a.m. on weekends. *Open for brunch Sat.–Sun. 10:30 a.m.–2:30 p.m.; dinner Sun.–Wed. 5:30–10 p.m., Thurs.–Sat. 5:30–11 p.m.; Thurs.–Sat. appetizers and desserts until 2 a.m.* $$$

Leo's Lunchroom
1809 W. Division St., Ukrainian Village, 773-276-6509

Not everyone can afford the pricey offerings of the city's hottest restaurants, but that doesn't mean they don't want to dine with style and enjoy food with flair. At Leo's, a tiny space near Wicker Park, the style is best described as rumpus room—or at least this is how you would have decorated the basement if your parents had let you. Instead of old comic books, however, this rumpus room comes equipped with good cookbooks. Breakfasts include sweet corn cakes with butter and syrup, flavored pancakes, and various egg dishes. Things get more adventuresome later in the day, and the changing menu often features salmon and pastas. Staff can be friendly or exude attitude, possibly thanks to the lack of decaf coffee. The back patio is an urban refuge. *Open Tues.–Sun. 8 a.m.–10 p.m.* $

LT's Grill
1800 W. Grand Ave., West Loop, 312-997-2400

Another of Chicago's takes on classic breakfast diners, LT's has a familiar menu that packs a few surprises. Swedish pancakes rolled in a berry sauce are great, as is the Porky Pig hash (lots of smoked pork and potatoes, fried crispy). The room is simple and so is the service, but the orange juice is fresh. *Open Mon.–Fri. 7:30 a.m.–2:30 p.m., Sat.–Sun. 8 a.m.– 3 p.m.* $

HIPSTER CHICAGO

Marche

833 W. Randolph St., West Loop, 312-226-8399

How does a cool restaurant stay cool over time? In Marche's case, it's by serving rock-solid food that draws crowds while not being afraid to shake things up from time to time. One of the earliest outposts in the Randolph Street dining district, Marche has been popular for more than ten years thanks to an entertaining open kitchen, a see-and-be-seen vibe, servers with character, and top-notch food. Recently Corcoran O'Connor took over as chef and shook things up by giving the menu a total overhaul. His new line-up (look for nightly changes) emphasizes fresh ingredients with bold flavors. A grilled pear exudes a woody charm and a pork tenderloin comes with a hearty accompaniment of sausage, potatoes, and savoy cabbage, under a mustard-y sauce. The bar has a long list of specialty drinks, fueling the good cheer that reverberates throughout the large space. *Open for lunch Mon.–Fri. 11:30 a.m.–2 p.m.; dinner Sun.–Wed. 5:30–10 p.m., Thurs. 5:30–11 p.m., Fri.–Sat. 5:30 p.m.–midnight.* $$$

Melrose Diner

3233 N. Broadway St., Lakeview, 773-327-2060

This Lakeview haven bustles around-the-clock, and the servers could easily write a book about the sights they've witnessed after the bars and clubs close and the zombies come staggering in. Breakfasts are always good, and in a town where several places vie to produce the best omelets, Melrose is always in the running. The tables outside along the side of the restaurant are always in demand in summer, and for good reason: you have your choice of sun or shade, and the open air makes the fresh-squeezed orange juice taste that much better. *Open daily 24 hours.* $

Mod

1520 N. Damen Ave., Wicker Park, 773-252-1500

"Mod" doesn't even begin to describe this culinary and design marvel that embraces both scenesters and foodies. The decor is ultramod, with Jetsons furnishings in Jell-O colors, scoopy egg-shaped chairs, inflatable lamps, and more. The menu goes in the other direction, getting back to basics and emphasizing fresh organic foods, preferably sourced from local growers and artisanal producers. But this doesn't mean the menu is simplistic. The food is modern American cuisine, which means the "Texas truck stop" rib eye has chanterelle mushrooms, a Stilton fondue, and Vidalia onions, your basic pork chop comes with decadent mascarpone mac 'n' cheese, and you might be served gazpacho with Kumamoto oysters. Desserts are knockouts, from the mini chocolate trio (mini choco-cherry soda, mini crème brûlée, mini chocolate cake à la mode) to the complimentary little dishes of cotton candy. *Open for dinner Mon.–Thurs. 5–10:30 p.m., Fri.–Sat. 5–11:30 p.m., Sun. 5–10 p.m.; Sunday brunch 10 a.m.–2 p.m.* $$–$$$

Ohba
2049 W. Division St., Ukrainian Village, 773-772-2727

Modern Japanese dining is part of the experience at Ohba, a very happening place in Wicker Park. But the menu also bears many other influences. How else to describe the brie fondue with tempura vegetables for dipping? Rather than trying to classify things, sit back and enjoy unique items like the wildly popular signature ohba chips, which are lightly battered and fried minty ohba leaves. Most of the food comes on small plates for sharing and grazing. You'll need a sense of adventure since the dark romantic lighting (if you can call it lighting) means that your first clue about your food will be from your tongue rather than your eyes. Desserts are worth a flashlight, especially the PB and J that combines fried bananas, a dollop of peanut butter, and a spot of blueberry jelly ice cream. Ohba also has a hip lounge and well-stocked sake bar. *Open for lunch Tues.–Sun. 11:30 a.m.–2:30 p.m.; dinner Sun., Tues.–Wed. 5:30–10:30 p.m., Thurs.–Sat. 5:30–11 p.m.* $$$

Opera
1301 S. Wabash Ave., South Loop, 312-461-0161

An old Paramount Pictures film distribution warehouse has been turned into Opera, a Chinese restaurant that pushes the boundaries of the cuisine. Brought to you by the same folks behind neighboring Gioco, Opera boasts a whimsical interior that is reminiscent of *The Wizard of Oz* (an MGM release). Although seemingly one open space cleverly broken up by a stair-case to nowhere (literally), in the back of the restaurant are six tables hidden away in Paramount's old film vaults. Each has a rich color scheme and is sheltered by the thick walls and heavy curtains. It's hard to imagine a better spot for a tête-à-tête—these are among the most romantic tables in Chicago; book in advance. The menu is long. Ask the server for advice, although the dumplings are delicate and delicious and anything with shrimp

HIPSTER CHICAGO

is a success. Signature dishes include fiery Sichuan green beans and a full-blown Peking duck served in three courses. Save room for the passion-fruit cheesecake. *Open Sun.–Wed. 5–10 p.m., Thurs. 5–11 p.m., Fri.–Sat. 5 p.m.–midnight.* $$$

Puck's
220 E. Chicago Ave., River North, 312-397-4034

Wolfgang Puck's Chicago edition of Spago croaked amid the tough local com-petition, but he retains a beachhead—and a tasty one at that—in the Museum of Contemporary Art. Serving lunch only (except Tuesdays when the museum is open late), the food is the nicely seasoned fusion fare that has made Puck his fortune. Asian dishes like satays share the menus with an all-American burger and Puck's signature wood-fired pizzas. Artwork changes regularly and is drawn from the museum's collection. The restaurant really shines in summer, when the huge patio is set with umbrella-shaded tables. *Open Tues.–Fri. 11 a.m.–3 p.m., Tues. 4:30–7:30 p.m., Sat.–Sun. 10 a.m.– 3 p.m.* $$

Red Light
820 W. Randolph St., West Loop, 312-733-8880

The little red tea lights in the trees outside this nationally recognized restaurant draw you in to one of Chicago's most inviting spaces. Organic ironwork forms a sensuous structure that supports a captivating sculptural Thai Buddha head. All this stays in character with chef Jackie Shen's explo-sive Asian cooking in the large open kitchen. Many of the dishes are Thai-inspired. The spicy ribs sound pedestrian but pack a punch and are tender. Grilled beef and green papaya salad has the same kick you'd get at Pataya Beach. The Penang beef curry is simply superb. Desserts include an item Shen has made famous through her many TV appearances: a dark chocolate "bag" filled with a fruit-laced white chocolate mousse. *Open for lunch Mon.–Fri. 11:30 a.m.–2 p.m.; dinner Sun.–Wed. 5:30–10 p.m., Thurs. 5:30–11 p.m., Fri.–Sat. 5:30 p.m.–midnight.* $$$

Silver Cloud
1700 N. Damen, Bucktown, 773-489-6212

This retro diner and lounge serves up tasty comfort food and whimsical cocktails to a hip but mellow crowd, especially on weekends, when its "hangover helper" brunch specials are popular with those who were over-served last night. There's also a lengthy martini menu that offers variations ranging from the tiny tini (for lightweights) to the award-winning s'moretini, complete with graham cracker crust and a toasted marshmallow. If that sounds way too complicated, stick to the simple, hearty menu items including mac 'n' cheese, sloppy joes, and chicken pot pie, or be more adventurous and go for the Frito pie or jerk chicken skewers. At night the lounge part of its personality predominates and folks gather more for cocktails. *Open Sun. 10 a.m.–midnight, Mon.– Fri. 10 a.m.–2 a.m., Sat. 10 a.m.–3 a.m.* $$

Sushi Wabi

842 W. Randolph St., West Loop, 312-563-1224

Twenty years ago going out for fish in Chicago meant a bowl of clam chowder. Sushi Wabi is riding the current wave of popularity for Japanese food, and to many locals it is the city's best purveyor of sushi. The focus is on the fish, and the art-free walls, understated yet knowledgeable servers, and subtle lighting minimize distractions (although the atmosphere is charged thanks to the pulsing house music). Sushi favorites like tuna are of course all here, but for an experience worthy of the place, try sitting at the long sushi bar and let the chefs take you on a voyage. Just be sure it includes the succulent sea urchin. *Open Mon.–Thurs. 11:30 a.m.–2 p.m. and 5–11 p.m., Fri. 11:30 a.m.–2 p.m. and 5 p.m.–midnight, Sat. noon–midnight, Sun. 5–11 p.m.* $$$

Topolobampo

445 N. Clark St., River North, 312-661-1434

Rick Bayless' Mexican Mecca, Frontera Grill, has a chichi sister, the incomparable Topolobampo. Though the food at Frontera is terrific, this is where Bayless really gets to show off, using organic and custom-grown ingredients to create Mexican festival foods and little-known regional specialties. The menu changes every other week, but look for dishes like almond soup with crab, sweet corn, and serrano chiles, creamy tamal with braised duck and *tlatonile* (red chile–sesame sauce), or fresh fish with pecan-thickened tomatillo sauce infused with wine and fennel and served with crispy sticky rice. The stellar wine list includes many unusual varietals chosen especially to complement the spicy flavors here, and the super sommelier is always willing to help you choose among them. Reservations are essential, and they recommend booking *at least* two weeks in advance. *Open for lunch Tues. 11:45 a.m.–2 p.m., Wed.–Fri. 11:30 a.m.–2 p.m.; dinner Tues.–Thurs. 5:30–9:30 p.m., Fri.–Sat. 5:30–10:30 p.m.* $$

Twisted Spoke

501 N. Ogden Ave., West Loop, 312-666-1500

The skeleton atop the sign tells you that this ain't the Olive Garden. It's a biker bar with a twist. Although everything Harley is honored and there are more tattoos than cell phones among the patrons, the Twisted Spoke really has a gentrified heart, with a talented kitchen turning out what are among the best burgers in town—juicy and redolent with seasoning. The slab of mighty fine meat loaf comes atop garlic Texas toast, and the onion rings are the best north of Texas. The huge patio is hard to beat on nice days. Thirsty? Besides beer, Jim Beam is on tap. *Open Sun.–Fri. 11 a.m.–2 a.m., Sat. 11 a.m.–3 a.m. $*

Vermilion
10 W. Hubbard St., River North, 312-527-4060

Chef Maneet Chauhan opened this inviting space in early 2004, and from the start the crowds flocked to it, which really says something since there's intense competition on this block. The dishes combine elements of Indian and Peruvian food with delightful results. Ceviche comes atop a beguiling Chardonnay jelly, while Malabar crab cakes are redolent with subcontinent spices not found in the Maryland version. The menu is long on small plates, which is good for this part of town, where people like to hop around during the course of an evening. Chauhan also serves up a few Indian standards; visiting Brits will want to take her back to Blighty after tasting the sublime chicken tikka masala. The name shows up in the red accents in the otherwise starkly decorated dining room. *Open Tues.–Thurs., Sun. 5 p.m.–midnight, Fri.–Sat. 5 p.m.–2 a.m. $$$*

Wishbone
1001 W. Washington Blvd., West Loop, 312-850-2663

Oprah eats here. Her Harpo Studios are right across the street, and after you've enjoyed the terrific Southern cooking here you'll understand why sometimes you don't just get Oprah, you get Big Oprah. The perfect corn muffins are part of a breakfast that certainly screams "Welcome to Chicago!" albeit with a friendly drawl. Weekends are mobbed, so it's best to grab your grits on a weekday. The crispy French toast is a wonder and the homemade sausage an integral part of the biscuits and gravy. The place is large, with a patio that's great when the sun is shining. Later in the day, look for top-notch renditions of good-ol'-boy standards like chicken-fried steak. *Open for breakfast Mon.–Fri. 7–11 a.m.; brunch Sat.–Sun. 8 a.m.–2:30 p.m.; lunch Mon.–Fri. 11 a.m.–3 p.m.; dinner Tues.–Sat. 5–10 p.m. $*

Hipster Chicago: The Nightlife

The Baton

436 N. Clark St., River North, 312-644-5269

A third generation of female impersonators is bumping and grinding at this Chicago institution. Talent ranges from um, enthusiastic to truly remarkable, with acts ranging from homemade to carefully crafted celebrity impersonations (the Whitney Houston is better than the real thing). Make reservations and get there early for a good seat, or avoid the packed-in little tables by sitting at the bar. *Showtimes Wed.–Sun. 8:30 and 10:30 p.m. and 12:30 a.m.* $$

Betty's Blue Star Lounge

1600 W. Grand Ave., West Loop, 312-243-1699

One of the best jukeboxes in the city awaits your dollars at this unpretentious bar and dance club on the booming West Side. A little blue neon sign beckons you in, and a variety of booths and sofas make you comfortable. The front bar area is separated from the back room by a curtain. After ten o'clock things heat up considerably, with DJs spinning a range of dance music. Betty's is big with service-industry folks who unwind after they flee their shifts elsewhere. Some Thursday nights feature live bands. *Open Sun.–Fri. 7 p.m.–4 a.m., Sat. 7 p.m.–5 a.m.* No cover.

Double Door

1572 N. Milwaukee Ave., Wicker Park, 773-489-3160

One of the best places to hear bands in Chicago is in the heart of Wicker Park. The gritty old building has an entrance on Damen Ave. for customers. Inside, it's nothing fancy, although the mural of fulsome nudes behind the bar has plenty of fans. The space is fairly small, which means the feel is intimate whether the group playing is a touring acid-jazz act or a major act like the Rolling Stones (yes, they've been here). *Open Sun.–Fri. 8 p.m.–2 a.m., Sat. 8 p.m.–3 a.m.* $$

HIPSTER CHICAGO

Empty Bottle
1035 N. Western Ave., Ukrainian Village, 773-276-3600

It's mostly rock at the Empty Bottle, and unadorned rock at that. A small club known for booking big acts; don't expect much in the way of extras except for generally excellent music. Also expect smoky air, a line for bottles of beer, and big crowds. People take their music seriously here, which engenders a delightful sense of camaraderie. *Open Mon.–Wed. 5 p.m.–2 a.m., Thurs.–Fri. 3 p.m.–2 a.m., Sat. noon–3 a.m., Sun. noon–2 a.m.* $

Exit
1315 W. North Ave., Wicker Park, 773-395-2700

Chicago's best punk bar has the best punk jukebox in the Midwest. DJs are legendary, and there is no accommodation made for those not ready to dive right into the scene—literally. But that doesn't prevent Exit from being a remarkably friendly place. Thursdays are fetish nights, weekends are classic '80s punk, while Sundays are devoted to death metal and Brit rock. *Open Sun.–Fri. 5 p.m.–4 a.m., Sat. 5 p.m.–5 a.m.* $$

Funky Buddha Lounge
728 W. Grand Ave., River North, 312-666-1695

Away from the glitzy clubs of River North, the Funky Buddha Lounge may be Chicago's coolest. Not far from the river in a dump of a building, the club lives up to its name with a pastiche of interior details drawn from cultures from Morocco to Thailand. Look for the Buddhas stashed here, there, and everywhere. Music varies nightly but usually is some combination of hip-hop, house, soul, reggae, and dance classics. The place is one of the more welcoming clubs in town, and it draws a large and mixed crowd, including a fair number of celebs who avail themselves of the various VIP rooms. *Open Mon.–Fri. 9 p.m.–2 a.m., Sat. 9 p.m.–3 a.m.* $$

Hideout
1354 W. Wabansia Ave., Wicker Park, 773-227-4433

A glowing Old Style sign hangs out front. Inside it's a classic friendly local bar filled with pals hanging out and tossing a back few. But as with Chicago's best neighborhood bars, there are a few twists on this classic formula. There's often a bluegrass band playing in the back room, and on some nights there's a classic or foreign movie playing. *Open Mon. 8 p.m.–2 a.m., Tues.–Fri. 4 p.m.–2 a.m., Sat. 7 p.m.–3 a.m.* No cover.

HotHouse

31 E. Balbo Dr., Loop/Downtown, 312-362-9707

How many cool bars are also nonprofits? The HotHouse is the ambassador for an organization that promotes cultural awareness largely through music—world music, to be exact, and during the course of a month you can hear local and touring bands playing styles of music from around the globe. Celtic, Cuban, African, and much more are on offer in the simple space. And fear not, Hothouse isn't filled with a bunch of tea-sipping lefties. The bar has a selection of draft beers and other libations. *Open Mon.–Thurs. 6 p.m.–1 a.m., Fri. 6 p.m.–2 a.m., Sat. 6 p.m.–3 a.m., Sun. 6 p.m.–midnight.* $

Marie's Rip Tide Lounge

1745 W. Armitage Ave., Bucktown, 773-278-7317

Once Marie's was filled with Polish immigrant workers. But as the neighborhood has changed, so has Marie's. Now crowds of the hip and not-so-hip flock here for the late liquor license and a friendly scene that feels timeless. Also timeless is Marie herself, who has been making nice almost every night since the joint opened in 1961. She stopped adding to the jukebox years ago, but that just means that it's full of Rat Pack classics and other time-tested tunes. *Open Sun.–Fri. 8 p.m.–4 a.m., Sat. 8 p.m.– 5 a.m.* No cover.

Metro

3730 N. Clark St., Wrigleyville, 773-549-0203

A converted movie palace, Metro has been booking top national acts since way before this neighborhood in the shadow of Wrigley Field was dubbed "Wrigleyville" by gentrifying yuppies. The seats (and any leftover gum on their bottoms) are long gone, which leaves a venue with good sight lines that's also fairly small. This is the place where the Smashing Pumpkins and other local acts made it big. The basement Smart Bar is open every night (see below). *Call for show times.* $$$$

Rainbo

1150 N. Damen Ave., Wicker Park, 773-489-5999

The bartenders here also double DJs who take pride in their selection of indie rock sensations (and those about to become sensations). Booths are primo seating, but the rest of the place is comfortable although crowded, with a crowd that varies between somewhere south of 25 and north of 40. It's a friendly place for people of all persuasions, and if the famous photo booth was connected to a website, it'd make a fortune. *Open Sun.–Fri. 4 p.m.–2 a.m., Sat. 4 p.m.–3 a.m.* No cover.

HIPSTER CHICAGO

Smart Bar

3730 N. Clark St., Wrigleyville, 773-549-4140

Bands on tour play in Metro upstairs. DJs on tour play at Smart Bar, which has been the place for serious dance music for more than 20 years. Most of the current styles can be heard one night or another, but know that this is not a place to lounge around, this is a place to dance. *Open Sun.–Fri. 9 p.m.–4 a.m., Sat. 9 p.m.–5 a.m.* $$

Sonotheque

1444 W. Chicago Ave., Wicker Park, 312-226-7600

The antidote for clubbers who have seen one too many $20 covers and $15 martinis, Sonotheque eschews pretension and attitude. The space is high-concept, a sort of industrial high-tech gray, but it is also fairly unadorned. It's given over to booths and couches and one heck of a large dance floor. The owners, veterans of other clubs and restaurants, attract top local DJs, who do their thing from a commodious booth. Dress here is less of an issue than at other places; wear what you like. *Open Tues.–Fri. 8 p.m.–2 a.m., Sat. 8 p.m.–3 a.m.* $

Hipster Chicago: The Attractions

Chi Healing Center
1733 N. Milwaukee Ave., Wicker Park, 773-278-8494

It's fitting that ever-cool Bucktown is home to Chicago's coolest place for yoga and other spiritual enlightenment. Chi's name is derived from "Create, Heal, Inspire," and this large and airy space has six therapy rooms as well as an art gallery displaying the works of patrons and locals. There is a range of yoga workouts and classes, plus therapies using massage, acupuncture, and other holistic methods. Reiki healing is a specialty. And to give your body a glow to match your inner one, you can choose from various wraps and treatments to cleanse your skin. *Open Mon.–Fri. noon–9 p.m., Sat. 10 a.m.–6 p.m., Sun. noon–6 p.m.* $$$

Chicago River Canoe & Kayak
3400 N. Rockwell St., west of Lakeview, 773-252-3307

The North Branch of the Chicago River winds through the city and is a surprising urban oasis. Herons and scores of other birds nest along its banks. One advantage of having been ignored for so long is that in many places the river's banks are undisturbed and here's wildlife in abundance. Paddling is easy and it makes for a very delightful couple of hours floating along. The rental kayaks and canoes are in good shape and the staff cheerfully give recommendations on where to go. *Open April–Oct.* $$$

Chopping Block
1324 W. Webster Ave., Lincoln Park, 773-472-6700

This intimate school offers daily courses in everything from cooking basics to advanced techniques, plus special events like Girls' Night: Dipping Party (girls making and eating various dips) and Guys' Night: Make It Spicy (guys eating spicy food and drinking microbrews), plus holiday and theme classes. The hands-on courses using Midwestern ingredients and focusing on regional cuisine are very popular. There's a second location in Lincoln Square. *Open Mon.–Fri. 11 a.m.–9 p.m., Sat. 10 a.m.–9 p.m., Sun. noon–6 p.m.* $$$

Ethnic Grocery Tour
2010 W. Chase Ave., west of Andersonville, 773-465-8064

Chicago's scores of ethnic neighborhoods are a vital part of the city's vibrant diversity. Each is filled with stores selling goods that conjure its homeland, and many of these same stores are regularly prowled by chefs looking for new inspiration and ingredients. Evelyn Thompson knows where to find the most authentic and out-of-the-way markets, from Jamaican to Southeast Asian, Russian, and Middle Eastern. Her personal tours of these foodie heavens offer a wealth of knowledge plus tastings galore. *Exact schedules vary; tours run about three to four hours in length, Wed., Thurs., Fri. at 1 p.m., plus alternate weekends a.m. or p.m. start times; phone to customize a tour.* $$$$

Gallery 37
66 E. Randolph St., Loop/Downtown, 312-744-7274

A city-run cultural center for the people, Gallery 37 has a store up front selling the best works created by students in the center's many art classes. There is also a 100-seat theatre where experimental works are performed. There's a captivating energy to the place, and it's always worth a look to see what's happening. *Open Mon.–Sat. 10 a.m.–6 p.m.*

Museum of Contemporary Art
220 E. Chicago Ave., Near North, 312-280-2660

The four-story aluminum-clad building by Berlin architect Josef Paul Kleihues off Michigan Avenue has a large collection of works in all media. The permanent collection includes Magritte, Duchamp, Miro, and of course Warhol. There are spaces on the top floor for performance art and other unusual installations. The museum also presents rotating exhibits of modern art and has been lauded for its efforts to make some of the more esoteric works accessible through interpretive text. *Open Wed.–Sun. 10 a.m.–5 p.m., Tues. 10 a.m.–8 p.m.* $

Museum of Contemporary Photography
600 S. Michigan Ave., South Loop, 312-663-5554

A solid permanent collection and talented curators make this an exciting place to visit year-round. The museum regularly presents shows of the best in current photography as well as retrospectives by the greats. *Open Mon.–Wed., Fri. 10 a.m.– 5 p.m., Thurs. 10 a.m.–8 p.m., Sat. noon–5 p.m.* $

p.45
1643 N. Damen Ave., Wicker Park, 773-862-4523

If ever there was a boutique to put Chicago on the fashion-world map, p.45 is it. Jessica Darrow and Trisha Tunstall opened p.45 in 1997 with one goal in mind: to find and nurture exciting new designers from Chicago and beyond. Expect to find chic, streamlined pieces from LoyandFord, Susana Monaco, and Splendid. Expect, also, to find the chic, streamlined Chicago fashionistas who wear them. *Open Mon.–Sat. 11 a.m.–7 p.m., Sun. noon–5 p.m.*

Reckless Records
3161 N. Broadway St., Lakeview, 773-404-5080

The best source for independent music in the Midwest. Not just a place for new and used CDs, tapes, and albums, Reckless is also a de facto cultural center where you can browse a myriad of band postings and find out who's playing where. *Open Mon.–Fri. 10 a.m.–10 p.m., Sat.–Sun. 10 a.m.–8 p.m.*

Tattoo Factory
4408 N. Broadway St., Uptown, 773-989-4077

Since 1976, this Uptown institution has been decorating customers' bodies with permanent art and exotic piercings. The gallery of artwork is immense, and the experienced employees are good at custom jobs. A simple heart— always popular—runs a mere $20. *Open daily noon–midnight.*

Uncle Fun
1338 W. Belmont, Lakeview, 773-477-8223

This eccentric toy store is for kids kind of the way Pee Wee Herman is for kids—there's a lot of weirdness and double entendre, so adults get a lot more out of it, and among the robots, stink bombs, fart powder, and holographic Jesus postcards and such, you're also likely to find stuff from your childhood, whenever that was (looking for a JFK tapestry or a Church Lady doll?). *Open Tues.–Fri. noon–7 p.m., Sat. 11 a.m.–7 p.m., Sun. noon–5 p.m.*

HIPSTER CHICAGO

Neighborhood Chicago

Every election, politicians utter the old chestnut "Chicago is a city of neighborhoods," and well they should, for to forget the city's distinctive neighborhoods and their diverse denizens is to lose touch with its basic character. To find the real Chicago, you've gotta get outta downtown. Though Chicago's neighborhoods used to be distinct ethnic enclaves, today each defies easy categorization. Ukrainian Village and Bucktown are now home to chic fashionistas, nouveau bohemians, grunge bands and their fans, blue-collar workers, and gentrifying yuppies as well as actual Ukrainians. Lincoln Park was dodgy 40 years ago but today is one of the most sought-after places to live. The lifeblood of the best neighborhoods is change, and few areas of the city remain static from one decade to the next. What's exciting is that as new groups arrive they add their own vibrancy. You'll find some of the city's most creative restaurants and clubs, most accessible culture, and most interesting shops out in the 'hoods, so hop a cab and get going.

Neighborhood Chicago: The Itinerary

Three Great Days and Nights

Your hotel: **The Belden-Stratford**

Morning: Begin your day at the **Argo Tea Café**, a current local favorite for its surprising teas and yummy baked goods. After your breakfast, enjoy the pleasures of Lincoln Park, which is both a trendy neighborhood and a bucolic park. The neighborhood offers beautiful vistas, charming tree-shaded streets lined with historic homes, and interesting and *eclectic boutiques* and shops along Clark and Halsted Streets and Lincoln Avenue. **Lincoln Park** is Chicago's great North Side park. Its miles of green space welcome walking, running, biking, or rollerblading (on a great path along the lakefront), or even pedal-boating on one of its two lakes. The **Lincoln Park Conservatory** brings together plants from all over the world in stately 1894 greenhouses and the **Lincoln Park Zoo** is a nice urban zoo with a great location; look for the new Regenstein Center for African Apes and its notable gorilla groups. If you want a walk on the less-wild side, the **Chicago Historical Society**, at the south end of the park, has a vast collection of items relating to Chicago's past.

Afternoon: Across from the park, history was made. **RJ Grunts** is where local über-restaurateur Rich Melman got his start 30 years ago, serving up great burgers, backed up by what was arguably the first salad bar in the mainland U.S. (he says he got the idea from a very small-scale version he saw in Hawaii and expanded the concept to include all the fixin's we're now used to). Step back into *the swingin' '70s* for a classic Lincoln Park lunch.

Spend some time this afternoon exploring another neighborhood named Lincoln. *Lincoln Square* was once the center of Chicago's German community, but today it's a thriving neighborhood where old ethnic delis and shops coexist with trendy new boutiques in and around Milwaukee, Western, and Lawrence Avenues. The El Brown Line stops right here, so jump on and cruise around this new groovy Mecca. One lively place to stop is the **Old Town School of Folk Music**, which migrated here from Old Town a number of years ago and has daily performances by musicians from around the world. You can *blow your own horn*—or something else—at one of the many two-hour introductory lessons the school offers. After a grueling music lesson, be sure to stop at **Lutz Café & Konditorei** around teatime and have one of its restoratively decadent Old World pastries.

Afterward, head north to the old Swedish neighborhood of *Andersonville*, which is now a lively mix of writers and artists, gays and lesbians, young professionals with strollers, and more. Wander along Clark Street north of Foster to sample a vibrant mix of shops and cafes. If you need an activity fix, get a day pass at **Cheetah Gym**, where fountains flow into koi ponds as people *pump iron* or take yoga and Pilates classes.

Evening: Tonight, finding dinner is easy. For your first option, you need go no farther than your hotel lobby—**Mon Ami Gabi** is a *swellegant update of a Parisian bistro*, and a tasty and tasteful scene, both inside and on the patio facing the park. Or how about a trip to Little Italy, just southwest of the Loop, for a romantic Italian dinner—sans clichés—at the hip **La Vita**? At the opposite end of the atmospheric spectrum, order flaming saganaki served to the cries of "*Opahhh!*" at **Pegasus** in Greek Town before enjoying the kinds of seafood that will make you feel like you're vacationing in Mykonos.

For your night's entertainment, it's hard to top the quality of the dramas at Lincoln Park's award-winning **Victory Gardens Theater**. Many of the plays are written by Chicago playwrights. Or hear *classic Hollywood celebs* (well, *fabulous* facsimiles) serenade you at the Chicago branch of Puerto Vallarta's gender-bending **Kit Kat Lounge and Supper Club**.

You could also stay in Little Italy to hang out at the lush **Beviamo**, a stylish lounge that attests to the neighborhood's resurgence as a Mecca for more than manicotti. For something more lively (and unusual), try **Big Wig** for dancing and entertainment in a *retro beauty-parlor setting*.

Late night is the best time to trek west to *Chicago's best blues bar*, **Rosa's Lounge**—it doesn't get any more honest than this gritty, friendly club. For high-end cocktails in, well, a matchbox setting, squeeze into the buzzy confines of **Matchbox** and enjoy one of its rare whiskies, or order a mojito and rest assured that it's prepared with fresh mint—this bar takes its tending seriously.

Day 2

Morning: Start your day in Hyde Park (another area of leafy charms) at **Valois**, the breakfast spot of choice for the masses, including half a dozen Nobel Prize winners, from the nearby *University of Chicago*.

Then begin your tour of Hyde Park in earnest at the moving and informative **Du Sable Museum of Afro-American History**. Check out the photo of a pouting Jane Byrne watching her successor Harold Washington sworn in as Chicago's first black mayor. The **Museum of Science and Industry** also calls Hyde Park home, and you could easily spend the better part of a day lost in the joys of its *interactive exhibits*.

Afternoon: For lunch, rub elbows with the professorial types at **La Petite Folie**, Hyde Park's upmarket French bistro. After lunch, continue with a poke around the **University of Chicago**. Look for the campus maps posted on street kiosks and visit neo-Gothic buildings such as the 1925 Rockefeller Memorial Chapel and the cloistered 1926 Joseph Bond Chapel. In the **Oriental Institute** you'll think you've stepped into an Indiana Jones movie as you view one of the world's finest collections of *ancient Persian treasures*. Next to the campus you'll find Frank Lloyd Wright's perfectly conceived **Robie House**. Afterward, head south to Jackson Park and catch your breath in the serene setting of the **Osaka Garden**.

Evening: After your day afield, come back to one of the beauties of Lincoln Park, **North Pond**, named for the pond whose shoreline it graces. Its menu is drawn from fresh Midwestern ingredients used in dishes created by chef Bruce Sherman. For French, head to the *red-hot Lincoln Square* neighborhood and **Tournesol**, a postcard-perfect bistro. Or let **Atlantique** wow you in Andersonville with its fresh global-fusion seafood dishes.

Tonight, hang out for a while in one of the many mellow but happening neighborhood bars that make this city so great. The **Black Beetle Bar and Grill** has something for everyone in *a happily hip eatery* that draws crowds from all over the city, while the **Map Room** is the choice for people who are serious about beer but don't want to be serious while drinking it.

NEIGHBORHOOD CHICAGO

Late at night up in Andersonville, laugh yourself silly during the rapid-fire wit of *Too Much Light Makes the Baby Go Blind*, where you'll see 30 plays in 60 manic minutes. In Lincoln Park, lay back with the well-heeled natives (and the occasional celeb) at **Katacomb**, with its colorful heiroglyphics, leopard-print chairs and comfy banquettes, and *chic cavelike setting* (courtesy of New York's Bogdanow Partners restaurant and hotel designers). At **Liar's Club** near Bucktown you'll drive yourself to drink trying to label the crowd (don't bother—just join the lawyers, hippies, bikers, and others dancing and drinking in this high-energy late-night haven). Over on Halsted Street in Boystown, the sidewalks will be crowded as thirsty gay denizens start off at the scene-y video bar **SideTrack** and go in search of more exotic pleasures at clubs like **Spin**, with its *notorious dance contests*.

Day 3

Morning: One of Lakeview's most venerable breakfast institutions calls for your attention this morning: **Ann Sather** serves *legendary cinnamon rolls* and foods with Swedish flair to the crowds who flock here daily.

Spend the morning getting to know one of the city's cool neighborhoods on board one of the superb city-run **Chicago Neighborhood Tours**, which employ local residents to explore the fabric of different areas of the city. Golfers will want to have arranged a tee time at the city's only in-town course, the **Sydney R. Marovitz Golf Course** (still known and loved by its old name, Waveland, to most locals) *a par 3 gem* right on the lakefront.

Afternoon: For lunch, get hooked on **Penny's Noodle Shop**, a Wrigleyville neighborhood favorite that serves the pad Thai and lad nar by which all others may be judged. Then take yourself out to the *ball game*. Few pleasures can compare to the joys of afternoon baseball, and with the **Chicago Cubs** and the **Chicago White Sox** both calling this home, one team likely will be in town, playing in the sunshine. The El goes to both parks.

Alternately, spend your last afternoon in style, in the Gold Coast. This posh neighborhood is *home to millionaires* and their mansions, and to the venerable **Newberry Library**. A research library that's a bibliophile's dream, the Newberry also houses some amazing rarities of interest to us plebes, like ancient illustrated manuscripts and important historic documents, and it also presents surprisingly interesting special exhibits. Reward yourself for such high-mindedness with a stop at **Urban Oasis,** which offers a full range of massages (including one with salt and infrared lighting).

Evening: Say "oui" to dinner out in tonight's neighborhoods. In Andersonville, Michael Roper's dream bar and authentic Belgian restaurant **Hop Leaf** will leave you dreaming of coming back. The city's best selection of beer is up front and mussels and frites are out back. Over in Bucktown, **Café Matou** serves contemporary French food in a stylish room that draws inspiration from its name, which means "tomcat." For something more exotic, think **Spring**, an excellent place for dinner, with *award-winning Asian fusion* cuisine.

Spend your last night listening to *hot music* in style at one of two Uptown veteran venues, the **Aragon Ballroom** or the **Riviera Theatre**. Both are old movie palaces that book top local and national acts. For the kind of bar that reflects well on the city, pop in for a drink and a dance at **Big Chicks**, a straight-friendly gay bar owned by a lesbian, with a truly great art collection on the walls (like Lisette Model and Diane Arbus photos) and a mixed crowd of gays, lesbians, and straights, rich and poor, *grooving together*.

Close out your night and your adventures with the *laid-back hipsters* at **Simon's**, a happening bar that extols some of Andersonville's Swedish character, or stare into the red glow of the lava lamps at Ukrainian Village's **Lava Lounge**, where the music and the crowd defy categorization.

NEIGHBORHOOD CHICAGO

Neighborhood Chicago: The Hotels

The Belden-Stratford
2300 Lincoln Park West, Lincoln Park, 773-281-2900 / 800-800-8301
www.beldenstratford.com

Built in 1922 in classic Parisian boulevard style complete with Mansard roof and limestone façade, the Belden-Stratford has many things going for it. First, there's its unbeatable location. On Lincoln Park directly across from the conservatory and zoo, you're within walking distance of scores of clubs, restaurants, and shops, not to mention the park, the lake, and the neighborhood, all of which makes it very pleasant for strolling. A close second is the property itself. This beauty is actually an apartment hotel and most of its floors are rented long-term. This means that the guest rooms are generous to enormous (a one-bedroom suite is is a full-on apartment complete with a separate dining room), some with sweeping views, so you can get the feeling that you're actually living here for a while rather than just visiting. With a fitness center, a rooftop deck, valet service and valet parking, and a spa, market, and two great restaurants in the building, you can overlook the fact that the desk staff, though nice enough, aren't quite as professionally polished and service-oriented as in a full-on hotel. $$

Majestic Hotel
528 W. Brompton St., Lakeview, 773-404-3499 / 800-727-5108
www.cityinns.com

Another Neighborhood Inns of Chicago property, the Majestic is modeled on a quaint English B&B. It's on a leafy and fairly quiet street in Lakeview close to the lake, Wrigley Field, and Lincoln Park. Guests enjoy continental breakfast each morning. The large suites include butler pantries with microwaves, fridges, and wet bars. The decor is frilly as one would expect from an English inn, although there are good-size desks and work areas in all rooms. $$

The Whitehall Hotel
105 E. Delaware Pl., Gold Coast, 312-944-6300 / 800-948-4255
www.thewhitehallhotel.com

Modeled on small European luxury hotels, the Whitehall dates from 1928. It has 221 units and a high ratio of staff to guests. Want something odd at 3 a.m.? Somebody will run out and find it for you. Rooms have traditional decor and even the king-size beds have four posts. Upgrade yourself to a Pinnacle Room and you have access to a special lounge with drinks and snacks throughout the day. For a real treat, opt for one of the suites on the top floors, which are spacious and have views out over the Gold Coast. The lobby bar is rich with mahogany and is a good refuge from the clamor outside. $$$$

Willows Hotel
555 W. Surf St., Lakeview, 773-528-8400 / 800-787-3108
www.cityinns.com

Surf Street in Lakeview is lined with graystones that hover in the upper ranges of Chicago's real estate strata. The Willows Hotel is a converted large graystone residential apartment hotel that was built in the 1920s. Luxurious renovations have resulted in comfortable rooms that come with refrigerators and bathrooms with conveniences like makeup mirrors and thick robes. The hotel is very close to Lincoln Park, and the 30-minute walk south to the Gold Coast is one of Chicago's prettiest. The Willows is also operated by the Neighborhood Inns of Chicago. $$

Note: For an alternative to a hotel experience, check out the choice selection of luxurious properties offered by Bed and Breakfast Inns Chicago, www.chicago-bed-breakfast.com. Most of the properties are in the leafiest districts of Lincoln Park, one of Chicago's most genteel neighborhoods. Expect your own space with bedrooms, sitting areas, and often a kitchen area, in which you can enjoy comforts of the same level demanded by Chicago's most-discriminating residents. Typical of these properties is the Windy City Inn (773-248-7091), which has rooms in a vintage house and comfortable apartments in a quiet and shady coach house out back. $$–$$$

NEIGHBORHOOD CHICAGO

Neighborhood Chicago: The Restaurants

Ann Sather
929 W. Belmont Ave., Lakeview, 773-348-2378

This wildly popular coffee shop in Lakeview was serving up incredible cinnamon rolls long before they became a trendy staple of chain restaurants across the country. In keeping with its Swedish roots, Ann Sather's menu has items like the very good and thin Swedish pancakes, Swedish meatballs, potato sausage, and lingonberry pie, but also has fabled breakfasts and hearty lunches and dinners of the home-cooking-diner type. On cold days, the fireplace-warmed front-room is a perfect setting for your meal. As a side note, the current owner, who expanded the original diner and opened three more recent branches (Ann Sather sold the original to him a number of years ago), is Tom Tunney, Chicago's first openly gay alderman. *Open Sun.–Thurs. 7 a.m.–9 p.m., Fri.–Sat. 7 a.m.–10 p.m.* $$

Argo Tea Café
958 W. Armitage Ave., Lincoln Park, 773-388-1880

Move over, Starbuck's—this Lincoln Park cafe has become the hottest place for a morning drink along trend-setting Armitage Avenue. There are comfy chairs and couches as well as floor-to-ceiling windows for viewing the passing parade. But the teas are the real appeal and the menu lists more than three dozen varieties from around the world, all organic. One of the biggest sellers is a naturally fizzy tea. *Open Mon.–Fri. 6 a.m.–11 p.m., Sat.–Sun. 8 a.m.–10 p.m.* $

Atlantique
5101 N. Clark St., Andersonville, 773-275-9191

One of Chicago's best seafood restaurants is a neighborhood place up north in thriving Andersonville. You know you're in a seafood place from the moment you enter and see the large fish mounted over the bar. But this isn't a throwback place with schools of stuffed carp competing for your eye; most of the decorative accents come from an array of beautiful ceramic fish created by a local artist. What's on the plate is also beautiful—the changing lineup of fresh seafood is prepared using French, Italian, and Asian techniques. There's usually some form of lobster available, and you'll score it for much less here than at a River North joint. Servers will helpfully guide you through raw options like the many various oysters. There are a few meaty options for non-fishy folk. *Open Mon.–Thurs. 5:30–10 p.m., Fri.–Sat. 5:30–11 p.m., Sun. 5–9 p.m.* $$$

Café Matou
1846 N. Milwaukee Ave., Wicker Park, 773-384-8911

This outpost along a fast-gentrifying stretch of Milwaukee Avenue between Wicker Park and Logan Square serves fine French food in a contemporary setting. *Matou* means "tomcat" in French, and that's the design inspiration here, most notably in the clever ceiling lights. Look for French classics, from mussels to rack of lamb, on the daily menu. Chef Charlie Socher knows his way around the French regions, and offerings can include Basque escargots or a Nice bouillabaisse. Service is more formal than chatty, but, that said, you can leave any pretension at the door. *Open Tues.–Thurs. 5–10 p.m., Fri.–Sat. 5–11 p.m., Sun. 5–9 p.m.* $$$

Hop Leaf
5148 N. Clark St., Andersonville, 773-334-9851

Chicago's only true Belgian restaurant resides in a hip two-level space behind Chicago's best bar. For years, Michael Roper has run a great neighborhood bar with an unparalleled selection of Belgian and American beers. Now he's added a popular restaurant with mussels and frites, a very fine steak, tasty sandwiches, trout, and more. Service and atmosphere are casual and there are plenty of wines by the glass for those who don't care for beer. Best of all, before or after the meal you can hang out in the bar out front, enjoying the range of brews while contemplating the authentic old bar details, like the pressed-metal ceiling. *Bar open Mon.–Fri. 2 p.m.–2 a.m., Sat. 11 a.m.–3 a.m., Sun. 11 a.m.–2 a.m.; kitchen hours Mon.–Fri. 5 p.m.–12:30 a.m., Sat. noon–1:30 a.m., Sun. noon–12:30 a.m.* $$

La Petite Folie
1504 E. 55th St., Hyde Park, 773-493-1394

Possibly the best place for a meal in Hyde Park, La Petite Folie is the dream of Michael and Mary Mastricola, who have taken classic French training and translated it into a fine restaurant. Somewhat lost in the translation is the name, which literally translates as "the small madness" but which the owners would prefer you to think of as "the small extravagance." Certainly you won't be mad after tasting the extravagant food, where luxurious items such as foie gras and fresh wild seafood feature prominently. Service is refined. and the dining room is a luminous vision in various shades of white. *Open for lunch Tues.–Fri. 11:30 a.m.–2 p.m.; dinner Tues.–Sun. 5–10 p.m.* $$$

NEIGHBORHOOD CHICAGO

La Vita

1359 W. Taylor St., Little Italy, 312-491-1414

Food in the Little Italy neighborhood of Taylor Steet can tend to be ho-hum since many places are content simply to rest on the clichéd atmosphere of the place. This is not the case at La Vita, which boasts an upscale and stylish dining room done up in rich purples and maroons that accent a terra-cotta tile floor. The menu is far from static, and there are many specials each night. The lovely food, coupled with the dark and mood-setting decor, make La Vita popular with couples looking for a dose of romance with their modern Italian meal. *Open Mon.–Thurs. 11 a.m.–10 p.m., Fri. 11 a.m.–2 a.m., Sat. 5 p.m.–2 a.m., Sun. 11 a.m.–9 p.m.* $$$

Lutz Café and Konditorei

2458 W. Montrose, Lincoln Square, 773-478-7785

The Lutz family has been baking since the 1770s (though only since 1948 at this location), so it's no surprise that they have decadent Old World German cookies, cakes, tarts, and tortes down pat. They also have a tasty selection of ice cream desserts and handmade Swiss chocolates. *Cafe and pastry shop open Tues.–Thurs. and Sun. 8 a.m.–8 p.m., Fri.–Sat. 8 a.m.–10 p.m.; pastry shop also open Mon. 8 a.m.–8 p.m.* $

Mon Ami Gabi

2300 N. Lincoln Park West, Lincoln Park, 773-348-8886

Step back into late 1800s Paris in this posh bistro and bar in the Belden-Stratford Hotel in Lincoln Park, another of the dramatic creations in the Lettuce Entertain You Enterprises domain. Although absinthe can't be found on any menus these days, you can choose a more legal libation and settle back into the deep booths surrounded by brass fixtures and marble trimmings while enjoying the light streaming in from the huge windows facing the park. Better yet, take the air on the patio when the weather is nice. *Open Sun.–Thu. 5:30–10 p.m., Fri.–Sat. 5:30–11 p.m.* $$

North Pond

2610 N. Cannon Dr., Lincoln Park, 773-477-5845

A former warming shed has been beautifully restored and converted into a high-end restaurant right in the heart of Lincoln Park—not the neighborhood but in the park itself. Guests can revel in the Arts and Crafts interior while gazing out the windows at the North Pond of the park. Chef Bruce Sherman prepares a constantly changing menu that emphasizes organic ingredients from small craft-proprietors. A recent menu included oysters, goose, and langoustines on the first course list. Main courses featured venison, wild squab, and wild pheasant. Preparations are as uncomplicated as Sherman, who was named one of America's ten best new chefs for 2003 by *Food & Wine* magazine. He wants the primary flavors of the top-quality ingredients to come through. The side of the building opens up to the air on warm days, a real treat during the popular weekend brunches. *Open for brunch Sat.–Sun. 11 a.m.–2 p.m.; lunch (summer only) Tues.–Fri. 11:30 a.m.–2 p.m.; dinner Tues.–Sun. 5:30–10 p.m.* $$$

Pegasus
130 S. Halsted St., West Loop, 312-226-3377

Rhodes might not be on your schedule this year, but you can get some of the Greek island vibe at this Greek Town classic. The walls are bright with beach colors and the menu has a good selection of fresh fish as well as that Chicago standby, calamari. As at any good Greek Town joint, the waiters here are characters who equate job satisfaction with bantering with the diners. Of course there are near continuous cries of "Opahhh!" as another flaming plate of saganaki erupts on a waiter's tray. This stretch of Halsted is lined with classic spots that can always deliver a fun night out, but Pegasus does the competition one better by delivering the best food. *Open Mon.–Thurs. 11 a.m.–11 p.m., Fri. 11 a.m.–midnight, Sat. noon–1 a.m., Sun. noon–midnight.* $$

Penny's Noodle Shop
3400 N. Sheffield Ave., Lakeview, 773-281-8222

This cheap and cheerful Thai diner, with its clean and simple decor and photograph-gallery walls, puts together such tasty Thai noodle dishes that once you leave town you'll be jonesing for them back home. The key is a light touch—no gloppy sauces here. Appetizers like spring rolls and potstickers are simple and delicious, the pad Thai is fresh and bright, the lad nar noodles are crispy on their edges but soft in the middle and swim in a not-too-sweet bean sauce with loads of fresh broccoli and chicken, and soups are plentiful and soul-satisfying. What more can you ask? Oh, how about pint glasses of rich and sweet Thai iced coffee? They've got those too. BYO beer or wine. Two other locations are at 1542 N. Damen Ave. and 950 W. Diversey Pkwy. *Open Sun., Tues.–Thurs. 11 a.m.–10 p.m., Fri.–Sat. 11 a.m.–10:30 p.m.* $

RJ Grunts

2056 Lincoln Park West, Lincoln Park, 773-929-5363

Before going on to open some of the most popular restaurants in town (Ben Pao, Nacional 27, etc., etc.), local mega-restaurateur Rich Melman got his start at this little Lincoln Park eatery. A timeless combination of a lavish salad bar and excellent sandwiches and burgers ensures that RJ Grunts remains great. *Open Mon.–Thurs. 11 a.m.–10 p.m., Fri.–Sat. 11 a.m.–11 p.m., Sun. 10:30 a.m.–10 p.m. $$*

Spring

2039 W. North Ave., Wicker Park, 773-395-7100

Attention to detail is paramount at Spring, an Asian fusion restaurant that was recently named best new restaurant in America by the James Beard Foundation. Crowds flock here for its minimalist setting (you'd never guess this was once a Turkish bath) and because of that attention to detail. Tables zigzag through the dining room to make service less obtrusive, and a Zen garden adds calm to the entranceway. Dishes take their flavor inspirations from a swath of Asia extending from Japan to Thailand. Most everything is based on fresh fish, so the menu changes constantly. *Open Tues.–Thurs. 5:30–10 p.m., Fri.–Sat. 5:30–11 p.m., Sun. 5:30–9 p.m. $$$*

Tournesol

4343 N. Lincoln Ave., Lincoln Square, 773-477-8820

The name means "sunflower," and the dining room is perfumed with the smells of an array of flower arrangements year-round. Look for all the French classics like poached pears in port, a salad lyonnaise with killer croutons, braised leeks, escargots, onion tart, steak frites, roast chicken, roast cod, and more. Finish with the creamy chocolate mousse (you'll never want it to leave your tongue) or specials made with seasonal fruits. Service is classic as well—competent and helpful. You can wait for a table at the zinc-topped bar up front. *Open Sun.–Thurs. 5:30–9:30 p.m., Fri.–Sat. 5:30–11 p.m. $$$*

Valois

1518 E. 53rd St., Hyde Park, 773-667-0647

More than one Hyde Park novelist has set scenes in her book in this local institution, which has been ladling up classic fare for more than 70 years. Food is served cafeteria-style under a banner that reads "see your food." You'll like what you see. It's more than likely you'll find one of the University of Chicago's Nobel prize winners at the next table since Valois has a loyal following with longtime locals. *Open daily 5:30 a.m.–10 p.m. $*

Neighborhood Chicago: The Nightlife

Aragon Ballroom
1106 W. Lawrence Ave., Uptown, 773-561-9500

Once a venue for ballroom dancing, the Aragon is now home to the kind of big-name concerts that have no problem filling it to its 4,500-person capacity. While waiting for the music, look around at this veritable performance palace, which dates from 1926. Moorish details are laid on thick, from the turreted balconies to the statuary found throughout. The twinkling stars in the deep blue ceiling high overhead help transport snow-bound Chicagoans to warmer climes. Look for top touring and national acts and those just on the verge of making it really big.

Beviamo
1358 W. Taylor St., Little Italy, 312-455-8255

One of the best late-night haunts in Little Italy, Beviamo has more than 40 different wines by the glass and 80 choices overall. Flights of three tastings are fun ways to broaden your knowledge by comparing vintages. Those not looking for solace from the grape will enjoy the long list of large martinis. The decor is a sort of sumptuous Mediterranean, and there are plenty of plush surfaces for lounging. The crowd includes medical students from the nearby hospitals (those are the cross-eyed patrons in need of sleep), new residents to the newly trendy neighborhood, postdinner partiers, and those out cruising the city by night. *Open Mon.–Fri. 5 p.m.–2 a.m., Sat. 5 p.m.– 3 a.m.* No cover.

Big Chicks
5024 N. Sheridan Rd., Andersonville, 773-728-5511

Chicago has a lot of friendly bars, so it's always going to be an injustice to name any bar "the friendliest." But Big Chicks would always be a contender if such a contest were held. The crowd is a mixture of gay men, lesbians (the bar's name extends to the art on the wall), yuppies, straights, youngsters discovering new diversity, and old codgers from the neighborhood who like to snack on the occasional free weenies at weekend barbecues. Look for DJs on weekend nights spinning dance tunes, and at all times look for Michelle Fire, the mood-setting owner. *Open Mon.–Fri. 4 p.m.–2 a.m., Sat. 3 p.m.–3 a.m., Sun. 11 a.m.–2 p.m.* No cover.

Big Wig
1551 W. Division St., Ukrainian Village, 773-235-9100

The theme at this hip lounge and club in Wicker Park is a sort of beauty shop from the '50s, right down to the big ol' hair dryers where bouffants were cured under the helmet-like tops for hours. Today there are all sorts of glam lights and other posh touches to add to the nighttime mood, and DJs spin house, hip-hop, and more most nights. *Open Sun., Tue.–Fri. 9 p.m.–2 a.m., Sat. 9 p.m.–3 a.m.* $$

Black Beetle Bar and Grill
2532 W. Chicago Ave., Ukrainian Village, 773-384-0701

This Ukrainian Village neighborhood place has morphed into a hot spot thanks to the classic combination of qualities that make for good bars any-where in Chicago: a friendly vibe, right-priced drinks, a varied beer and wine selection, a cool guy manning the door, a great jukebox, DJs late at night, a fine menu of snacks, sandwiches, and salads, a sunny patio, and a roaring winter fireplace. Expect things to get increasingly busy as the night pro-gresses. *Open Sun.–Fri. 5 p.m.–2 a.m., Sat. 5 p.m.–3 a.m.* $$

Katacomb
1909 N. Lincoln Ave., Lincoln Park, 312-337-4040

Very popular with Lincoln Park scenesters and bar/restaurant industry types, this subterranean lounge offers a schmoozy, laid-back, groovin' scene, espe-cially late nights—it doesn't get going until after midnight, and lines form after 2 a.m. when other bars are closing. Its designer decor (courtesy of the creators of places like New York's Cub Room and Soho Grand) is a, well, catacomb-like affair; its swoopy ceilings and walls, decorated with hiero-glyphics and mottled with shadowy lighting, suitably showcase the well-heeled crowd. DJs spin on weekends, but it's not really a place for dancing. *Open Wed.–Fri. 8 p.m.–4 a.m., Sat. 8 p.m.–5 a.m.* $

Kit Kat Lounge and Supper Club
3700 N. Halsted St., Wrigleyville, 773-525-1111

This is the place to come if you've ever wanted to be serenaded by Rita Hayworth, or at least a reasonable facsimile therof—the chanteuses here are all glamorous female impersonators. A classic 1940s supper club is the model for this large restaurant and club, which is a branch of the Puerto Vallarta original. The decor is an always-chic retro off-white, which compli-ments not only the faux Rita but also the faux Marilyn, among other period icons. *Open daily 5:30 p.m.–1 a.m.* $

Lava Lounge
859 N. Damen Ave., Ukrainian Village, 773-772-3355

Lava lamps inspired the name of this Ukrainian Village hot spot, and there are plenty of them behind the bar. Besides the freeform blobs floating in the fixtures, there are red accents everywhere else as well. Bright red walls and fabrics bring the otherwise omnipresent black to life. The crowd is diverse—everybody from bike messengers to the secretly tattooed lawyers who receive their deliveries. DJs spin everything, and just watching the action on the worn wooden dance floor is worth the trip. *Open Sun.–Fri. 5 p.m.–2 a.m., Sat. 5 p.m.–3 a.m.* $

Liar's Club
1655 W. Fullerton Ave., Lincoln Park, 773-665-1110

You just never know whom you'll meet at the Liar's Club, and that's the idea. Easily one of the most diverse bars in the city, it has basic black decor, with no end of rock schmaltz providing accents (Elvis statues and the like). Everything coalesces toward midnight, when the crowds explode, the dance floor becomes an anything-goes free-for-all, and the bartenders pour drinks like they're possessed. Expect to see punks, Goths, frat-boys, bankers, joggers, and any other character you can conjure up. *Open Sun.–Fri. 5 p.m.–2 a.m., Sat. 5 p.m.–3 a.m.* No cover.

Map Room
1949 N. Hoyne Ave., Bucktown, 773-252-7636

Globes, maps, and guidebooks set the theme at this mellow but generally crowded bar in Bucktown. It's one of the best places in Chicago to try an unusual American microbrew. The bartenders know their brews and make recommendations; ask if they have any barley wines. Despite the beer emphasis, it's far from a guy's bar, and most times there are as many women as men. The decor is classic Chicago tavern, with large front windows so you can check out the passing parade of folks, many of whom pop in for a pint. On weekend nights there's live music in the cavernous rear of the building—usually jazz, blues, or rock. *Open Sun.–Fri. 10 a.m.–2 a.m., Sat. 10 a.m.–3 a.m.* No cover.

Matchbox
770 N. Milwaukee Ave., Wicker Park, 312-666-9292

Matchbox is a classy little place—really little. A well-heeled crowd shoe-horns into this tiny bar, which is ten feet wide at its widest. Rare whiskies, tequilas, and wines are the draws on the liquid front, but it's also the kind of place you can trust to have fresh mint on hand for mojitos. Look also for a rotating lineup of fine beers on tap. Artworks by local artists and candlelight add to the intimacy. There's a great outdoor area where you can grab some space and air. *Open Sun.–Fri. 5 p.m.–2 a.m., Sat. 5 p.m.–3 a.m.* No cover.

Riviera Theatre
4746 N. Racine Ave., Uptown, 773-275-6800

Part of a trio of huge old venues in Uptown (the Aragon Ballroom and the shuttered Uptown Theatre are the others), the Riviera, which attracts big-name punk and rock bands, dates from 1918 and was one of the first movie palaces built in Chicago. The seats are long gone, but vestiges of its opulence remain. Sight lines are good, especially from the bars in back.

Rosa's Lounge
3420 W. Armitage Ave., Bucktown, 773-342-0452

Chicago's best blues club is a haven for purists that scores because it welcomes everyone with open arms, even if you're just slumming and soaking up the atmosphere. In an otherwise unheralded section of the West Side, Rosa's is the personal vision of the Mangiullo family, led by blues drummer Tony, his mother Rosa, and other relatives. It really doesn't get any better than this, as scores of adoring fans will tell you. On weekends there are acts with national stature, on weekdays local regulars. There's no adornment of any kind—as one would expect from a true blues bar—and all seats face the stage. It's hot, smoky, and intimate. *Open Tues.–Fri. 8 p.m.–2 a.m., Sat. 8 p.m.–3 a.m.* $

SideTrack
3349 N. Halsted, Lakeview, 773-477-9189

This teemingly popular gay bar was the second video bar in the U.S., and you have to hand it to its owners for taking the idea and running—and running—with it. After numerous expansions, it's now Chicago's largest and most popular gay bar and is pretty much a mandatory stop on any North Halsted bar crawl. Some seven rooms (including a patio and grilling area), numerous bars (including a new indoor-outdoor one), and more than 20 TV screens throughout keep the guys and gals (though guys predominate) cruising, laughing, singing, and drinking. It's a fun, energetic place, and its theme nights (most popular: Monday show tunes, Thursday comedy) showcase the talents of the tireless VJs, who scour the world for videos and clips and mix them with real flair to always keep it entertaining. *Open Sun.–Fri. 3 p.m.–2 a.m., Sat. 3 p.m.–3 a.m.* No cover.

Simon's

5210 N. Clark St., Andersonville, 773-878-0894

An old Swedish codger bar has found new life as the favored haunt of Andersonville's trendy denizens. Little has changed from its classic 1950s neon-accented motif, and that's good. There's a long bar, or booths where you can settle in for the long lineup of cocktails that include seasonal glogg (hot spiced wine) in winter. Sprinkled among the crowd are a few old characters left over from the days when Simon's was filled with Swedes intent on high jinks. They still liven it up today. *Open daily 11 a.m.–2 a.m.* No cover.

Spin

800 W. Belmont Ave., Lakeview, 773-327-7711

A large gay dance club strategically located at the corner of Belmont and Halsted, Spin keeps busy with a series of popular weekly theme nights. Most notorious is the Friday night shower contest, during which patrons compete to see who can take the "hottest" shower. Monitors everywhere allow the DJs to be VJs as well. Wednesday night is dollar-drink night, which is all the gimmick needed to send a line snaking down the street. *Open Sun.–Fri. 4 p.m.–2 a.m., Sat. 4 p.m.–3 a.m.* $

Too Much Light Makes the Baby Go Blind

5153 N. Ashland Ave., Andersonville, 773-275-5255

This long-running show is theatrical Nirvana to those with short attention spans: the Neo-Futurists theatre company performs 30 plays in 60 minutes. If one skit doesn't quite work, it doesn't matter, because another has already begun. The results are raucous and hard-hitting as the actors blast through material that is better not contemplated. Each week new shows are added, and every month the entire lineup changes. *Shows Fri.–Sat. 11:30 p.m., Sun. 7 p.m.* $

Victory Gardens Theater

2257 N. Lincoln Ave., Lincoln Park, 773-871-3000

Serious new works are the hallmarks of this well-respected theatre. Winner of the Tony Award for regional theatre in 2001, Victory Gardens has built its superb reputation over 20 years by staging more world premieres than any other Chicago theatre. Plays are carefully staged and acted. Among the five or six new works each season, look for those by Chicago writers Claudia Allen, Jeffrey Sweet, and Lonnie Carter, among others. $$$$+

NEIGHBORHOOD CHICAGO

Neighborhood Chicago: The Attractions

Cheetah Gym
5248 N. Clark St., Andersonville, 773-728-7777

This gym manages to combine neighborliness with upscale flair, qualities that make it a very Chicago kind of place. Located in trendy Andersonville, Cheetah Gym is a full-service facility that has all the expected machines and other devices for exercise. Other options include massage, aerobics, yoga, and a variety of personal training regimes. There's a good juice bar and cafe where you can choose from healthy options that include high-protein drinks, smoothies, salads, and more. *Open Mon.–Thu. 5:30 a.m.–11 p.m., Fri. 5:30 a.m.–10 p.m., Sat.–Sun. 8 a.m.–9 p.m.*

Chicago Cubs
Wrigley Field, 1060 W. Addison St., Wrigleyville, 773-404-2827

"Lovable losers" is just one of the monikers pinned on the North Side's legendary baseball team (and nonfans—such as anyone living on Chicago's South Side—would skip the "lovable" part). The Cubs' baseball futility has lasted almost 100 years, but you'd never know it, given that just about every game these days is a sellout. Wrigley Field is a gem—one of the few great old ballparks still standing and the model for countless modern-day copies. The park is intimate and offers many screwy traditions, from the hordes that gather to party atop neighboring buildings or the anarchy of the bleachers to the fans waiting for homers on Waveland Avenue. The surrounding Wrigleyville neighborhood has one of the highest concentrations of bars and restaurants in the city. Whatever you do, go to the game via El—it's the true Chicagoan way to get there. $$$$+

Chicago Historical Society
1601 N. Clark St., Lincoln Park, 312-642-4600

Chicago celebrates its history openly and though it might sound musty, this well-funded Lincoln Park institution is a must-see sight on any itinerary. Permanent galleries trace the life of Abraham Lincoln, the destruction of the city by the Great Chicago Fire, its subsequent rebirth, and the racial struggles that divided the city and reached their culmination in the election of the city's first black mayor, Harold Washington, in 1983. There is always a range of worthwhile special exhibits. *Open Mon.–Sat. 9:30 a.m.– 4:30 p.m., Sun. 11 a.m.–5 p.m.* $

Chicago Neighborhood Tours
78 E. Washington St., Loop/Downtown, 312-742-1190

One of the coolest city projects in Chicago. Each week, Chicago Neighborhood Tours visits a different part of the vast and diverse city. Departing by luxury bus from the Chicago Cultural Center, the expeditions are limited to about 40 people and are led by experts in the particular neighborhood, usually people who have lived there much of their lives. Expect to learn about history, social habits, racial and ethnic relations, and much more. The bus stops at places of real significance and, depending on the tour, you may visit a cultural center, grocery store, art studio, or historical site, among others. Tours usually last about four hours. *Tours Sat. 10 a.m.* $$$$

Chicago White Sox
U.S. Cellular Field, 333 W. 35th St., South Side, 312-674-1000

Long the self-defined blue-collar alternative to the Cubs, the South Side's White Sox have been almost as bad a team. Unfortunately, it too maintains a history of futility that has only been aided by various Philistine owners. Typical of its hapless heritage is that it was the last team in baseball to build a sterile modern stadium before the current craze for fun-filled retro ballparks began. However, lately there's an effort under way to change this, and U.S. Cellular Field (formerly Comisky Park) has been given a rehab that brings in more bars and other fun features. The best part of seeing the Sox play is watching the fans, who are as tough-minded and as passionate about their team as any in baseball. $$$$+

Du Sable Museum of Afro-American History
740 E. 56th Pl., Hyde Park, 773-947-0600

Housed in a renovated and expanded 1910 administration building for the Chicago Park District, the Du Sable museum is named for Chicago's first resident, Jean Baptiste Point Du Sable, an Afro-Caribbean man. The museum provides a good overview of Black experience in Chicago, both the good and the bad. There are interesting exhibits on the Great Migration, when hundreds of thousands of blacks moved to Chicago from the South in search of jobs. A section of the museum is devoted to Harold Washington, the city's first black mayor, who brought great changes to Chicago from his election in 1983 to his death in 1987. *Open Mon.–Sat. 10 a.m.–5 p.m., Sun. noon–5 p.m.* $

NEIGHBORHOOD CHICAGO

Lincoln Park

600–5800 N. Lake Shore Dr., 312-742-7529

The largest urban park in the world, Lincoln Park is really many parks in one along nearly seven miles of lakefront. The main body of the park boasts two lakes with rental pedal boats on either side of the zoo (see below). Pathways go through gardens both formal and surprisingly wild. The conservatory north of the zoo is a showplace for plants and ornamental gardening. Going north along the lake, there's a driving range at Diversey Parkway, a yacht harbor at Belmont Avenue, and a lovely crescent of beach at Montrose Avenue. The main path is popular with bikers, joggers, rollerbladers, and walkers. A regal statue of park namesake Abraham Lincoln stands near North Avenue behind the Chicago Historical Society.

Lincoln Park Conservatory

2391 N. Stockton Dr., Lincoln Park, 312-742-7736

Three acres are under glass at this gem of a greenhouse, modeled after London's Crystal Palace. Popular stalwarts include palms, orchids, and thousands of other plants that thrive in the carefully controlled conditions. Special shows are held throughout the year, with one of the most popular being the lilies and flowering bulbs in spring. *Open daily 9 a.m.–5 p.m.*

Lincoln Park Zoo

2200 N. Cannon Dr., Lincoln Park, 312-742-2000

One of Lincoln Park's main attractions is this gem of a zoo that dates back more than 100 years but that, thanks to generous funding, boasts modern and lavish exhibits showing animals in their natural habitat. The new Regenstein Center for African Apes will house the zoo's families of gorillas and chimpanzees. The Regenstein African Journey brings together giraffes, elephants, anteaters, and more in a realistic setting. Numerous other areas span the animal kingdom, and in winter, people gather to marvel at the pink flamingos who enjoy cavorting in the snow. Best of all, the zoo is free so you can pop in and out and not feel like you need to justify your investment. *Open daily 9 a.m.–5 p.m. (until 6 p.m. summer).*

Museum of Science and Industry
5700 S. Lake Shore Dr., Hyde Park, 773-684-1414

What makes this vast museum of technology so cool? Not just a place to visit in the fourth grade, the MSI is a richly funded interactive treasure trove in Hyde Park displaying icons of the 20th century, including the German U-boat U-505, the Art Deco icon Pioneer Zephyr train (once the world's fastest), the Apollo 8 command module (the first manned spacecraft to visit the Moon and return), a huge United Airlines 727 hanging from the ceiling, and much, much more. The building that houses this great museum is a landmark itself, having been the Palace of Fine Arts during the Columbian Exposition in 1893. A recent campaign has poured more than $100 million into the museum, and its displays are engaging and well thought-out. But beware of the MSI's size. You'll never see everything, so grab a free map and plot your strategies. *Open Mon.–Sat. 9:30 a.m.–4 p.m., Sun. 11 a.m.–4 p.m.; summer until 5:30 p.m.* $

Newberry Library
60 W. Walton St., Gold Coast, 312-255-3595

This Chicago gem is a privately endowed research library with over 1.2 million documents and books covering the humanities of Europe and the Americas from the Middle Ages. The reading room in this 1890 building boasts soaring ceilings and rich tiling. Regular special exhibits are renowned for the depth of their scholarship. Recent examples include one documenting the facts and fiction of Sherlock Holmes and a look at the history of patriotism and dissent in the United States. The building has a good view of Washington Square, which, although serene today, was once known as "Bughouse Square" and was notorious 100 years ago for its gatherings of anarchists and other agitators. *Open Mon., Fri.–Sat. 8:15 a.m.–5:30 p.m., Tues.–Thurs. 8:15 a.m.–7:30 p.m.* $

Old Town School of Folk Music
4544 N. Lincoln Ave., Lincoln Square, 773-728-6000

A Chicago institution, the school has largely left Old Town for great new quarters in thriving Lincoln Square. Regular performances throughout the week showcase folk music from around the world. And while you probably don't have time for an intensive course in, say, Gaelic lyrics, you can sign up for one of the daily single-session two-hour classes that introduce you to the harmonica, bongo drums, or other instruments. *Open Mon.–Thurs. 10 a.m.–10 p.m., Fri. 10 a.m.–6 p.m., Sat.–Sun. 10 a.m.–5 p.m.* $$

NEIGHBORHOOD CHICAGO

Oriental Institute
University of Chicago, 1155 E. 58th St., Hyde Park, 773-702-9514

One of Chicago's underappreciated treasures, the Oriental Institute is the showplace for the huge collection of materials held by the University of Chicago. In three major galleries—Mesopotamian, Egyptian, and Persian—ancient treasures are displayed. Among the most impressive are the room-size artifacts from the ancient royal city of Perseopolis. Ongoing renovations have added excellent explanatory material, and new treasures are put on display regularly. Be prepared to be awed by the reliefs that once decorated the palace of King Sargon II (721–705 BC). *Open Tues., Thurs.–Sat. 10 a.m.–4 p.m., Wed. 10 a.m.–8:30 p.m., Sun. noon–4 p.m.* $

Osaka Gardens

Located in Jackson Park, a Frederick Law Olmsted creation that runs along the lake from 56th to 67th Streets, the Osaka Gardens replicate the grand gardens Japan built on the site for the landmark 1893 Columbian Exposition. These in turn were modeled on traditional gardens at a holy site near Kyoto. The simple and serene structures, which were restored in 1981, were a major influence on a young Frank Lloyd Wright, who wrote about his affinity for their simple, clean lines and harmony with nature.

Robie House
5757 S. Woodlawn Ave., Hyde Park, 773-834-1847

Located next to the University of Chicago campus, the Robie house was built in 1910–11 and for many is the epitome of Frank Lloyd Wright's Prairie style. Its long and low parts effectively harmonize as a whole and typify the low-slung style of his homes. The bricks are not the standard ones used by the billion throughout the city, but rather special long narrow bricks modeled on those used in ancient Rome. Stained glass and leaded windows are the major ornaments seen from the outside. Inside, the rooms are carefully calculated to lead you from one to the next through strong geometric features interlaced with glimpses of the space beyond. Recent renovations have mostly returned the home to its state at completion. *Tours Mon.–Fri. 11 a.m., 1 p.m., 3 p.m., Sat.–Sun. every 30 minutes 11 a.m.–3:30 p.m.* $

Sydney R. Marovitz Golf Course
3600 N. Recreation Dr., Lakeview, 312-742-7930

This popular par 3 nine-hole course is right up the lakefront at the northern end of Lincoln Park. It's very popular with golfers who take a "long lunch with clients" or have several "important sales calls to make" on weekdays. The Chicago Park District keeps the course in top shape, and the views of the lake are great. Opening hours vary. *Opening dates vary by the weather.* $$$$

University of Chicago
Hyde Park, 773-702-1234

This famous school tips the usual balance of students on its head: there are 4,000 undergraduates and 8,000 graduates. Nobel prize announcements are almost an annual event, and the school is known for its research and scholarship. The classic campus dates to 1890 and was built around some of the infrastructure of the Columbian Exposition of 1893. A notable artifact is the Midway Plaisance on the south side of the campus, a vast grassy area that was a grand entrance to the fair. The campus is well worth a ramble, and there are useful maps in kiosks at most corners. The older buildings are classic neo-Gothic; don't miss the 1925 Rockefeller Memorial Chapel and the cloistered 1926 Joseph Bond Chapel. On Ellis Avenue north of 57th Street, look for the bronze *Nuclear Energy*, which is close to the site where the atom was first split in 1942. The U of C is also home to the Court Theatre, a consistently strong and engaging professional nonprofit theatre company (5535 S. Ellis Ave., 773-753-4472).

Urban Oasis
12 W. Maple St., Gold Coast, 312-587-3500

"Salt glow" doesn't do justice to the effects you'll feel while sitting under warm infrared lights as you have various oils and salts gently massaged into your skin. Needless to say, you'll be going back for more. A full range of massage styles is on offer including hot stone, Thai, and Swedish. The staff will take the time to help you decide what is best for you. If you can't make it to the sleek little shop, you can arrange an outcall to your hotel. *Open Mon.–Fri. 10 a.m.–8 p.m., Sat. 9 a.m.–7 p.m., Sun. 9 a.m.–5 p.m.* $$$$+

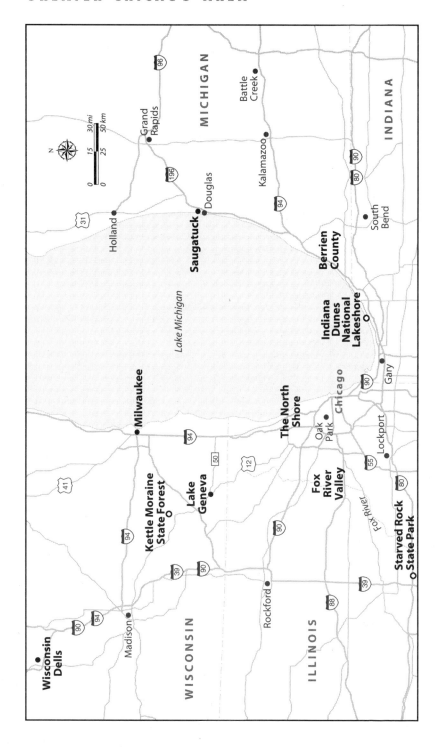

Leaving Chicago

It's easy to think that Chicago is the only thing going in the Midwest, and, well, it is, in terms of what's "happening." But look beyond the corn and soybeans and you'll find there's beautiful countryside out there. When you've had your fill of urban fun, follow the lakeshore north through the leafy and gracious North Shore. Inland, discover the many state parks and the natural beauty of Lake Geneva—or the classic kitsch of the Wisconsin Dells. Dip around the bottom of Lake Michigan to visit the Indiana and Michigan coasts, the favored summer retreats of Chicago's elite. If you only stick to the Windy City, you'll miss out on the real majesty of the Midwest.

Berrien County, MI

The Lowdown: Berrien County, in the southwest corner of Michigan, is Chicago's place to play. In the beachside town of New Buffalo you see more Illinois plates than Michigan ones all summer long. There are little beach towns like Union Pier and Stevensville right up the coast, to the twin port towns of St. Joseph and Benton Harbor. Inland there are rolling hills, which help trap the sun and extend the growing season so that the region is renowned for its cherries, strawberries, and other produce. But what really draws people are the many wineries, which use grapes grown locally on the sunny hills.

Doing It: Spending a good part of the summer at the beach in Berrien County has been a Chicago tradition for decades. People of all walks come to unwind (even Mayor Richard Daley can be regularly seen riding his bike). The lake waters are fresh and clean, slowly warming as the summer progresses. The white sand beaches are uncrowded away from the towns, and because this is the east side of the lake, when the sun finally sets at the end of the long days (it's an hour earlier in Michigan), it does so in a beautiful fashion over the lake. There are hundreds of rental cabins and scores of B&Bs. Late at night, the glow from Chicago across the waters gives people a smug reminder of what they're not missing. New Buffalo is the center of commerce and has a few good restaurants and cafes, grocery stores, and an open-air farmers market. The inland wineries are conveniently laid out along a "wine trail," which makes for easy tasting amid the grapes.

Getting There: Take I-90 East, which becomes the Indiana Toll Road at the border with Chicago. At Exit 21, change over to I-94 East, which follows the lake into Michigan. You can turn off at Exit 22 and take the very scenic U.S. Hwy. 12 the rest of the way, or stay on and exit for New Buffalo at Exit 4 across the border in Michigan.

Berrien County Contacts

Southwest Michigan
Wine Trail
185 S. Mt. Tabor Rd.
Buchanan, MI
269-422-1161

Southwestern Michigan
Tourist Council
2300 Pipestone Rd.
Benton Harbor, MI
269-925-6301

40 miles

Fox River Valley, IL

The Lowdown: The Fox River Valley is a beautiful part of Northern Illinois less than an hour from the Loop. You can't legitimately call it hilly, but it's not as flat as everything else in sight. The river itself is fairly large and provided the power for the two old industrial towns of Elgin and Aurora, which bracket the north and south ends of the valley, respectively. In between, it's all bucolic, with large estates and horse farms belonging to Chicago's old money. The little towns of St. Charles and Geneva are in the heart of the valley, and each has a restored, charming downtown. There are lots of antique stores, boutiques, cafes, and the requisite array of fudge and ice cream shops, as well as bicycling along the river or rowing in it. In summer, the vegetation is lush, and this part of the Fox River was home for centuries to the Pottawatomie Indians, who enjoyed the valley's rich fishing and game.

Doing It: Hwy. 31 follows the west bank of the river and Hwy. 25 runs along the east bank. As you explore the valley, you'll cross back and forth between the two often. Of the two towns, St. Charles has the most to offer visitors. More than 100 antique dealers can be found in old buildings in the 150-year-old downtown. Park your car and prowl around for a while before getting a treat and taking a break along the river. During the summer there are fun paddlewheel boat excursions along the tree-lined banks of the river. On the first Sunday each month, the legendary Kane County Flea Market is one of the largest gathering of antique dealers in the U.S. There are dozens of B&Bs in the valley should you decide to spent the night.

Getting There: Take I-90, the Illinois Tollway, west from Chicago to Elgin and turn south on Hwy. 31. Or take I-290 west to I-88, the East-West Tollway. At Aurora turn north on Hwy. 31. Alternately, you can ride the Metra Union Pacific West Line to Geneva.

Fox River Valley Contacts

Geneva Chamber
of Commerce
8 S. Third St.
Geneva, IL
630-232-6060 /
866-443-6382

Kane County Flea Market
Randall Road and Rte. 64
St. Charles, IL
630-377-2252

Metra Rail
312-322-6777

St. Charles Convention &
Visitors Bureau
311 N. Second St., # 100
St. Charles, IL
630-377-6161 /
800-777-4373

Indiana Dunes National Lakeshore, IN

The Lowdown: Sand dunes line more than 25 miles of shoreline at the southern end of Lake Michigan in Indiana. Besides making for beautiful beaches, the dunes are backed by forests, bogs, meadows, and other natural areas. The Indiana Dunes National Lakeshore covers much of this area, and the Indiana Dunes State Park covers the rest (except for a couple of shore segments given over to a power plant and steel mill). The entire region is laced with hiking trails, campgrounds, and nature preserves. Vacation homes for Chicagoans (including Oprah) are discreetly hidden among the trees in the little villages of Ogden Dunes and Beverly Shores.

Doing It: Mount Baldy near Michigan City, at the east end of the park, is a 123-foot-high dune overlooking a popular beach. As with beaches throughout the parks, merely walking a few hundred yards beyond the sections close to the parking lots yields pristine stretches of sand, free of crowds. The Baily-Chellberg Visitor Center and Trail is the center for Dunes information. It's a good place to get maps of the trails and shoreline. A signposted nature trail explores the diverse ecosystems of the dunes. Combine sandy fun with education at West Beach, where a long trail around a bog shows how nature works to convert the dunes into land supporting trees and other plants.

Getting There: Take I-90 East, which becomes the Indiana Toll Road at the border with Illinois. At Exit 21, change to I-94 East and then take Exit 19 north to Hwy. 12, which runs the length of the dunes. Alternately, the Metra South Shore Line has frequent trains with stops at Beverly Shores, Dune Park, and Ogden Dunes, which are convenient to various park features and beaches.

Indiana Dunes National Lakeshore Contacts

Indiana Dunes National Lakeshore 1100 N. Mineral Springs Rd. Porter, IN 219-926-7561 x 225	Indiana Dunes State Park 1600 North 25 E. Chesterton, IN 219-926-1952	Metra Rail (312) 322-6777

105 miles

Kettle Moraine State Forest, WI

The Lowdown: More than 21,000 acres of forest in southern Wisconsin includes a beautiful range of features, including glacial hills and cliffs, kettles, pine woods, hardwood forests, large and small lakes, and restored prairies. Glaciers of the last Ice Age 20,000 years ago left weird and dramatic rock formations that are linked by a network of trails for all levels of difficulty. Hikers are rewarded with iconic vistas of pristine lakes, rolling hills, lush forests, and dramatic cliffs of carved limestone. Few Midwestern summertime activities can compare with a long day of hiking and exploring followed by a refreshing plunge in a lake.

Doing It: A well-signposted road allows to you to see the major sights of the park over the course of a few hours. The neighboring towns of Eagle, Whitewater, and Campbellsport have classic Wisconsin supper clubs featuring multicourse meals of hearty fare that usually includes prime rib and lake fish. The towns also have small motels and sporting goods and equipment rental stores. There are large campgrounds in the park, but reserve in advance for summer weekends. The Henry Reuss Ice Age Visitor Center does a good job of explaining the geological forces that shaped the park. The park has 160 miles of trails, the star being a 32-mile stretch of the Ice Age National Scenic Trail, which follows the course of the glaciers and is an excellent choice for overnight trips. Popular activities year-round include fishing on the lakes and rivers as well as canoeing and kayaking. Park vendors lead horseback rides. In winter there is snowmobiling.

Getting There: Take I-94 West north to Kenosha and turn west on Hwy. 50. At Lake Geneva turn north on U.S. Hwy. 12 north to La Grange. Take County Road H into the park.

Kettle Moraine State Forest Contacts

Kettle Moraine
State Forest
S91 W39091
Highway 59
Eagle, WI
262-594-6200

Whitewater Area
Chamber of Commerce
402 West Main St.
Whitewater, WI
262-473-4005

Lake Geneva, WI

The Lowdown: For more than 140 years, Lake Geneva has been a cultured summertime retreat for Chicagoans. Initially it was home to large mansions built by the city's wealthiest citizens, and Lake Geneva soon acquired the nickname "Newport of the West." The legacy of this past can be found today in the gracious architecture, lakeside parks, and attractions like little wooden bandshells, which give the lake its rarified atmosphere. Of course not everything at Lake Geneva involves listening to sunset classical music concerts—there's a vast range of recreational opportunities, ranging from the usual water sports to more esoteric fun like hot-air–balloon flights and the classic summer vacation pursuit—golf.

Doing It: There are a huge number of rental homes, motels, and B&Bs. In addition, there are restaurants spanning the spectrum from drive-ins to fine dining (in the latter category, many chefs from Chicago have local operations here to cater to the refined tastes of vacationers). One of the most popular activities for young and old is taking a cruise aboard one of the lake-touring boats. This is a good way to see mansions around the lake, which include 1856 Golden Oaks Mansion, 1888 Black Point Mansion, 1900 Stone Mansion, and 1870 Maple Lawn. Back on land, many of these beautiful homes and their ornate grounds can be toured. The popular lakeside trail is 21 miles around and winds in and among the lavish estates. For a lake tour at your own pace, rent a power boat. Nearby pleasures include greyhound racing and horseback riding. And just so you know that not all the fun takes place in and around the water, the game Dungeons and Dragons was invented here by two disaffected teens one summer who were too cool to go outside.

Getting There: Take I-94 West north to Kenosha and turn west on Hwy. 50.

Lake Geneva Contacts

Lake Geneva Area
Convention &
Visitors Bureau
201 Wrigley Dr.
Lake Geneva, WI
262-248-4416

Lake Geneva Cruise Line
Riviera Docks
812 Wrigley Dr.
Lake Geneva, WI
262-248-6206

90 miles

Milwaukee, WI

The Lowdown: In many ways a smaller Chicago, Milwaukee has enough of its own unique charms to make the city a top weekend escape. Certainly there are parallels with the city to the south: vibrant downtown districts, interesting revitalized historic neighborhoods, and summer fun on the lakefront. But unlike Chicago, Milwaukee is closely linked to one ethnic group: Germans. And immigrants from Central Europe are responsible for the city's beer-brewing reputation and its industrial base as a tool manufacturer. German tradition also continues in numerous restaurants downtown.

Doing It: The cultural star is the Milwaukee Art Museum, which has a diverse collection housed in a lakefront building with a new—and much hailed—wing by Spanish architect Santiago Calatrava. Just south is the site of Milwaukee's center for summer fun, Summerfest. This early July event features dozens of top-name bands performing over several days. It has spawned numerous city-sponsored clones, so there is pretty much a huge lakefront party every summer weekend. If you're looking for Milwaukee's brewing tradition, however, you may be disappointed. Schlitz is gone, and recently Texas investors bought Pabst Blue Ribbon, closed the brewery, and fired hundreds of employees, and now has it manufactured by contractors. Miller does have a huge brewery, and you can enjoy free tours and free tastings of its products, but best for beer buffs are the free tours of the local microbrewer Sprecher. The place to stay downtown is the Pfister Hotel, a luxurious classic. Sample tasty German fare at Mader's.

Getting There: Take I-94 West north. Better yet, avoid the dull drive and take one of Amtrak's several daily fast trains (a 90-minute ride). Milwaukee is easily walked, or you can take cabs.

Milwaukee Contacts

Miller Brewing Company
4251 W. State St.
Milwaukee, WI
414-931-2337

Mader's German
Restaurant
1037 3rd St.
Milwaukee, WI
414-271-3377

Milwaukee Art Museum
700 N. Art Museum Dr.
Milwaukee, WI
414-224-322

Milwaukee Visitor Center
101 W. Wisconsin Ave.,# 425
Milwaukee, WI
414-273-7222

Pfister Hotel
424 E. Wisconsin Ave.
Milwaukee, WI
414-273-8222

Summerfest
Henry Maier
Festival Park
414-273-3378

The North Shore, IL

The Lowdown: A string of venerable suburbs lines the lakeshore north of Chicago. These charming towns range from affluent to very affluent. There are lots of stately mansions to peek at, and they're interspersed with parks and beaches. It's easily the most scenic drive in the Chicago area. The first town past Chicago is Evanston, which is really a small city and is home to the Gothic towers of Northwestern University. Wilmette continues the march of leafy lakefront enclaves, which in succession (and in value, like the upscale march on the Monopoly board from Pacific Avenue to Boardwalk) are Kenilworth, Winnetka, Glencoe, Highland Park, and Lake Forest.

Doing It: Sheridan Road hugs the lake and links the towns of the North Shore. At any time, however, you can head west and have a quick trip back to the city on U.S. 41 and I-94 East. Downtown Evanston is a good place for strolling, with little shops and cafes. Just north, Northwestern University is also a good place to wander; it's one of the nation's best schools. In Wilmette, the Baha'i Temple is a concrete confection surrounded by lush gardens that conjures the Taj Mahal. Glencoe is home to the vast Chicago Botanic Garden, featuring 33 gardens in 285 acres. There are many fine restaurants that make good stops for lunch throughout the North Shore. Two to seek out: Prairie Moon in Evanston, with light and innovative American fare, and Frank and Betsie's in Winnetka, with French-inspired luncheons. Both have outdoor seating. And Highland Park is home to the Ravinia Festival, North America's oldest outdoor music festival (see page 144).

Getting There: Take Lake Shore Drive north to Sheridan Road and the stay on this road through the North Shore. The CTA El Purple line serves Evanston, Northwestern University, and Wilmette.

North Shore Contacts

Baha'i Temple
100 Linden Ave.
Wilmette, IL
847-853-2300

Chicago Botanic Garden
1000 Lake Cook Rd.
Glencoe, IL
847-835-5440

Chicago's North Shore
Convention
& Visitors Bureau
847-763-0011

Frank and Betsie's
51 Green Bay Rd.
Winnetka, IL
847-446-0404

Northwestern University
633 Clark St.
Evanston, IL
847-491-3741

Prairie Moon
1502 Sherman Ave.
Evanston, IL
847-864-8328

Saugatuck, MI

The Lowdown: Saugatuck is a town of 1,000 right on the shores of Lake Michigan but increases its head count by a factor of ten on warm summer weekends. The downtown has more than 100 antique and other stores, as well as dozens of cafes and restaurants. There is a large local arts community, and this is more than evident in the many local galleries. The crowds spill over to Douglas, just to the south, and there are scores of inns and B&Bs in the communities. Ten miles to the north is the larger town of Holland, which misses no opportunity to milk its Dutch heritage, boasting a wooden shoe factory and an annual tulip festival.

Doing It: Spring, fall, and weekdays in the summer in Saugatuck are quite bearable. But be warned that on a summer weekend, unless you've booked a quiet place ahead of time, you may end up driving into the lake to save your sanity. At least it's a pretty lake, and the town's harbor on the Kalamazoo River does it proud. Take a little ferry across the mouth of the harbor to Mount Baldhead on the other side. There are views from the top of this 200-foot sand dune, and lovely beaches stretch for miles along this part of Michigan's shore. Three miles farther north is Dunes State Park, which manages to avoid some of the crowds of Saugatuck. In Holland, Windmill Island has an actual 18th-century windmill from the Netherlands.

Getting There: Take I-90 East, which becomes the Indiana Toll Road at the border with Chicago. At Exit 21 change to I-94 East, which follows the lake into Michigan. Just past Benton Harbor, take I-196 East north to Exit 36 for Douglas and Saugatuck.

Saugatuck Contacts

Saugatuck/Douglas
Convention
& Visitors Bureau
269-857-1701

Saugatuck Dunes
State Park
269-637-2788

Holland Convention
& Visitors Bureau
76 E. 8th St.
Holland, MI
616-394-0000

Holland Museum
31 W. 10th St.
Holland, MI
616-392-9084

Windmill Island
7th St. at Lincoln Ave.
Holland, MI
616-355-1030

Starved Rock State Park, IL

The Lowdown: Starved Rock State Park is another legacy of the Ice Age 20,000 years ago. It has 18 canyons that were carved into the limestone by the glaciers and their runoff. The walls are steep and sharp, and after rainfalls, each is backed by a waterfall fed by runoff. The park on the Illinois River is a beautiful retreat year-round. In summer it's predictably busy, but like so many spots, it has numerous quiet retreats away from the hordes. The park takes its name from a 130-foot-tall sandstone butte, which has a tragic past: in 1769 a band of Indians took refuge on the top after a conflict and starved to death. Adjoining the park is Matthiessen State Park, which extends the boundaries of the protected area to include additional cliffs and waterfalls. The nearby town of Utica has stores and places to stay for those not camping in the parks or day-tripping from Chicago. The town is also the end point of the old Illinois & Michigan Canal.

Doing It: There are more than 15 miles of hiking trails in Starved Rock. A popular trail leads to St. Louis Canyon, where the waterfalls are spring-fed and thus active most of the year. Matthiessen has another five miles of trails, and both parks' networks are linked. In addition, the latter park has a reconstructed French Colonial–era fort. In Starved Rock, continue on trails past Wildcat Canyon, which—at about one mile from the main parking lot— is as far as 90% of the park's visitors are willing to go. La Salle Canyon is a good destination on a sunny winter day, as there's usually a tall pillar of ice.

Getting There: Take I-55 South to I-80 West. Exit south for Utica and the parks at Exit 81.

Starved Rock State Park Contacts

Heritage Corridor
Convention &
Visitors Bureau
81 N. Chicago St.
Joliet, IL
800-926-2262

Matthiessen State Park
Hwy. 78
Utica, IL
815-667-4868

Starved Rock State Park
Hwy. 71
Utica, IL
815-667-4906

210 miles

Wisconsin Dells, WI

The Lowdown: The original draw of the Dells, as everybody calls it, are deep limestone canyons in the Wisconsin River, which were carved by Ice Age glaciers. In fact, the canyons are stunning, especially when viewed from one of the flotilla of tour boats. However, the Dells are not about nature anymore. The real draw here is the kitsch factor of the densest collection of amusement parks and themed attractions in the Midwest. In alphabetical order, some of the major sights include: Family Land, a huge aquatic park; Lost Canyon, which has wagon rides to a limestone canyon that is "found" by thousands daily; Noah's Ark, a 36-slide water park with a Christian motif; Ripley's Believe It or Not, a celebration of the improbable; Riverview Park and Waterworld, thrill rides and more water slides; Storybook Gardens, gardens populated by nursery-rhyme characters; Tommy Bartlett Thrill Show, a stunt-filled show by water-skiers; and Wax World of the Stars, which should need no explanation.

Doing It: Choosing among the many opportunities to get wet, it's probably best to go with the one offering the best deals. Of the many attractions, the best is easily the Tommy Bartlett Thrill Show, since the water-skiers show genuine skill and talent in performing a cunning array of stunts. Food options range from mere super-size to all-you-can-eat portions of classic American fare. There are dozens of motels, some with theme rooms featuring waterbeds and other diversions. On your way up, watch for the Mars Cheese Castle, just over the border in Kenosha. No kitschy trip is complete without a stop at this landmark.

Getting There: Take I-90 West, the Northwest Tollway, to Rockford and then I-39 North to Wisconsin Dells. Amtrak has daily trains between Chicago and the Dells.

Wisconsin Dells Contacts

Amtrak
800-USA-RAIL

Wisconsin Dells Visitor
& Convention Bureau
608-254-8088 /
800-223-3557

Mars Cheese Castle
(800) 655-6147

The Chicago Calendar

January	February	March
	Chicago Auto Show	St. Patrick's Day

April	May	June
Earth Day Festival	Art Chicago* Cinco de Mayo Festival	Chicago Blues Festival* Chicago Gospel Music Festival Neighborhood Festivals Pride Chicago Summerfest* Taste of Chicago*

July	August	September
Chicago's Independence Eve Venetian Night	Bud Billiken Parade Chicago Air & Water Show Viva! Chicago Latin Music Festival*	Around the Coyote Chicago Jazz Festival

October	November	December
Chicago International Film Festival Chicago Marathon	Magnificent Mile Lights Festival	Navy Pier New Year's Eve

* *The Fun Seeker's Top Five Events*

The Chicago Calendar

Weather guides Chicago's calendar: the warmer the weather, the busier the calendar. During the summer, there are dozens of neighborhood festivals, with beer and food vendors, live music, and lots of locals hanging out. But there are even bigger fish to fry here. The events listed in this section are major events that are not only worth knowing about when you're here, they're worth planning a trip around. Here's when to be here and why.

February

Chicago Auto Show

America's largest auto show is held each February at McCormick Place, one of the largest trade show venues in the U.S. with 2.2 million square feet of exhibit space (and still growing). Besides hosting multiple American and world premieres of new cars, the show also offers a look at the complete range of passenger cars, trucks, SUVs, and experimental and concept cars (more than 1,000 different vehicles in total), plus auto-related exhibits, media personality appearances, and displays of antique and collector cars.

Contact: *630-495-2282, www.chicagoautoshow.com*

March

St. Patrick's Day

One of the most important holidays of the year for official Chicago happens every March 17. The parade south down Dearborn Street starts with Illinois politicians leading the way (in election years watch the tussle as candidates vie for the front row). The rest of the parade is a collection of union floats, high school bands, girls of varying talents dancing the Irish jig, and more. But the big event is hanging out in bars throughout the city, where green beer flows like—well, like the Chicago River, which is also dyed for the day, an alarming radiator-fluid green.

Contact: *312-942-9188, www.chicagostpatsparade.com*

April

Earth Day Festival

The third Saturday of the month Lincoln Park fills with booths from green organizations set against a backdrop of speeches by lefty politicos and music by earnest folk groups. Chicago doesn't have a recognized liberal tradition in the way places like San Francisco do, so this is a chance for the city's progressives and liberals to strut their stuff.

Contact: *773-665-4682, www.chicagoearthmonth.com*

May

Art Chicago*

Usually early in May, this important art-world show at Navy Pier features works of art by more than 3,000 artists, and most of what's on show is for sale. There are also educational programs and lectures by noted experts and academics. Special exhibits often include museum-caliber shows bringing together the works of one artist or other thematic group. Overall, this is an excellent opportunity to see a lot of art shown by people who truly care about the work.

Contact: *312-587-3300, www.artchicago.com*

Cinco de Mayo Festival

Events all over town coincide with the anniversary of Mexico's May 5, 1861 victory over the French. Many festivals are scheduled for the nearest weekend and the biggest parade is in Pilsen. Chicago's Hispanic community is fast-growing and is rapidly changing the city's traditional image as a place populated solely by blacks and whites. The parades have an addictive vibrancy, and you can't help but get caught up in the spirit with the many displays of pride in cultural heritage.

Contact: *312-744-3315, www.ci.chi.il.us/specialevents*

June

Chicago Blues Festival*

The world's largest blues festival is Chicago's largest music event. Close to 100 performers take to the open-air stages over four days, with major headline events at night. Best of all, it's free. For sustenance, vendors sell a range of foods. The dates vary each year; although usually in early June, it has been held in late May.

Contact: *312-744-3315, www.ci.chi.il.us/specialevents*

Chicago Gospel Music Festival

Gospel music is a Chicago institution (hallelujah!). This festival is held on a weekend either before or after the blues festival in Grant Park. One of the real qualities about this festival that makes it one of the best is the way it makes Chicago's gospel music so accessible. There's no getting up early and trying to find a particular church on the South Side—rather, you get to see choirs at the top of their game in the lovely surrounds of the park. And it's free.

Contact: *312-744-3315, www.ci.chi.il.us/specialevents*

Neighborhood Festivals

From June through September there are literally dozens of neighborhood festivals held every weekend throughout the city. These events are often quite large, not just a block party but usually a long stretch of a major street, closed to traffic and full of food, clothing, gift, and art vendors and with live entertainment. They offer a great way to join locals indulging in the opportunity to drink beer outside with their friends while eating a wide range of foods (usually a mix of local restaurants' stands plus a number of places that set up at all the fests) and listening to a band or two on entertainment stages scattered along the street(s) involved (larger fairs often have multiple stages). A few of the biggest and most popular: the hipster Taste of Lincoln Avenue (usually in July); Northalsted Market Days, the see-and-be-seen street fair of the gay community (usually at the end of August); Hyde Park's 57th Street Art Fair (usually the first weekend in June); and the Old Town Art Fair (usually mid-June).

Contact: *312-744-3315, www.ci.chi.il.us/specialevents*

Pride Chicago

June is Gay Pride month in cities throughout America, since the community officially counts the events at the Stonewall Bar in June 1969 as its inception as a civil rights movement (gay patrons at that bar first fought back against then-common police raids). Chicago does Pride proud, usually hosting between 70 and 80 events during the month, ranging from fundraisers, award ceremonies, workshops, choral concerts, and art shows to political and sports events. The monthlong celebration culminates in the annual Pride Parade (usually the last Sunday), which begins on north Halsted St. and ends in Lincoln Park, with somewhere around 5,000 participants and estimates of as many as 400,000 spectators. It's exuberant, hot (literally and metaphorically— historically it's always been hot and sunny, and there's lots of flesh on display), and hard-partying (well, after the more serious events of the rally in the park conclude).

Contact: *773-348-8243, www.chicagopridecalendar.org*

Summerfest* (Milwaukee, WI)

It's not in Chicago, but it might as well be for the number of Chicagoans it draws, and besides, it's a short hop, and well worth the trip. This 11-day music extravaganza takes place in late June and early July each year along 75 acres of Lake Michigan lakefront in neighboring Milwaukee (see Leaving Chicago, p. 201). With 13 different stages offering live music all day and night (noon–midnight), plus a range of food and shopping venues, Summerfest is one of the official Fun Seeker's 96 Most Fun Places to Be in the World at the Right Time. Nearly a million people attend each year, and artists span the entire spectrum of the music world, so there's literally something for everyone. Whether you're looking for Tim McGraw, Buckwheat Zydeco, Angelique Kidjo, Styx, Buddy Guy, Rufus Wainwright, The Roots, Paul Oakenfold, or even Britney Spears, they'll be here (these were all on the 2004 roster, among many others).

Contact: *800-273-3378, www.summerfest.com*

Taste of Chicago*

Another official Fun Seeker's 96 Most Fun Places to Be in the World at the Right Time—the largest food festival in North America features ten days of eating and drinking the foods and beverages of more than 100 Chicago restaurants. Don't expect culinary wonders—the selections are geared to what can be prepared in tents and served to the 2.5 million attendees who overrun Grant Park. But that doesn't mean that the food isn't good—it's often quite good, but more than anything the event is geared to fun, and the weather usually provides a perfect setting for a day out walking in the park with friends while trying treats that are a little out of the ordinary. From ribs and pizza to Thai noodles and chichi concept concoctions, it's all here.

Contact: *312-744-3315, www.ci.chi.il.us/specialevents*

July

Chicago's Independence Eve

The July 4 fireworks in Chicago are always actually held on July 3 as part of Taste of Chicago, and it's usually quite a spectacle. But the events on this night are many. The fireworks are shot off over the lake directly in front of Buckingham Fountain at dark, usually around 9:30 p.m. Hundreds of boats vie for position to watch (if you know somebody with a boat, now is the time to get chummy). On land, families enjoy picnics and free music, some of it timed to complement the fireworks. The key to enjoying this mobbed event is to not be in a hurry. Make a picnic or enjoy Taste of Chicago and arrive early to get a good spot. Despite the size of the crowds, everyone's always in good cheer and things stay orderly and peaceful.

Contact: *312-744-3315, www.ci.chi.il.us/specialevents*

Venetian Night

The Chicago Yacht Club sponsors this nighttime event in late July or early August, which features a parade of gaily decorated and illuminated yachts. But what really draws people to the lakefront and Grant Park is the fireworks; some years the show surpasses the July 3 show.

Contact: *312-744-3315, www.ci.chi.il.us/specialevents*

August

Bud Billiken Parade

Named for a fictional icon in Chicago's African American community, this large community parade runs south along Martin Luther King Drive from 39th Street to Washington Park. Big with families, there are huge picnics galore in the park after the parade. Some of the best fun is just watching the variety of floats and marchers since pretty much anybody is allowed in, and many groups make up for organizational challenges through infectious enthusiasm.

Contact: *312-225-2400*

Chicago Air & Water Show

There's relatively little happening on the lake, so the name is misleading. The real action is overhead, as acrobatic planes, military precision fliers like the Blue Angels, and an array of airpower in the form of bombers and fighters fly over the lake along Lincoln Park. This is a great opportunity for wearing as little as possible (except sunblock) and enjoying the beauty of the lake and the park while the excitement thunders overhead. Held in mid-August, the event attracts more than two million people.

Contact: *312-744-3315, www.ci.chi.il.us/specialevents*

Viva! Chicago Latin Music Festival*

Viva! showcases a variety of styles of Latin music including salsa, pop, rumba, meringue, cha-cha, mariachi, and Spanish rock. Held in Millennium Park over two days in late August, the festival attracts the best of Chicago's vibrant Latin music players as well as some national acts. This, along with Cinco de Mayo, is a fine chance to see Chicago's Hispanic community strut its stuff. Be prepared for dancing in the park as the music hits its stride in the evening.

Contact: *312-744-3315, www.ci.chi.il.us/specialevents*

September

Around the Coyote

This cutting-edge arts festival in Wicker Park and Bucktown features dozens of open studios and galleries. The city's arts community is thriving, and young artists abound, helping the event keep a discernable edge year in and year out. Live music and theatre performances add to the fun; local bars and restaurants set up stands and peddle treats. Usually takes place in mid-September.

Contact: *773-342-6777, www.aroundthecoyote.org*

Chicago Jazz Festival

Chicago's second largest music event draws an international lineup of big-name performers to Grant and Millennium Parks over Labor Day weekend. Everything is free. From top-name heavyweights and jazz-crooner crowd pleasers to more modern and fusion artists, they're all here on several stages, with concerts throughout the day and evening plus ancillary events held outside the park.

Contact: *312-744-3315, www.ci.chi.il.us/specialevents*

October

Chicago International Film Festival

For more than 40 years the Chicago International Film Festival has been attracting films from around the world and the U.S. to this juried competition. Look for more than 100 films to premiere at theatres around town, usually the second week of Oct. There's scores of press about the festival in the local papers, and during the festival it's worth reading about it to ferret out the real gems among the program.

Contact: *312-425-9400, www.chicagofilmfestival.org*

Chicago Marathon

Held the second Sunday of the month, the marathon winds through a good part of the city and attracts leading international runners as well as thousands of local hopefuls. Although at first the appeal of watching thousands of sweaty people run past you may seem elusive, this event draws incredible energy for spectators and has had an amazing run (!) of luck in being held on classically beautiful Midwestern fall weekends.

Contact: *312-904-9800, www.chicagomarathon.com*

November

Magnificent Mile Lights Festival

On the Saturday before Thanksgiving, lights in trees along North Michigan Avenue north of the river are first lit in a show that goes on daily until January. The effect is magical, especially during and after snowfalls. There is usually a parade and other festivities to mark the official lighting ceremony, but don't feel you've missed out if you miss this. The real deal is the lights themselves, and you can enjoy their magical charm every day.

Contact: *312-409-5560, www.themagnificentmile.com*

December

Navy Pier New Year's Eve

New Year's Eve on Navy Pier changes from year to year, but expect various events and concerts in the ballroom and Festival Hall and in other onsite venues, plus family programming all day and a huge fireworks show at midnight.

Contact: *800-595-7437, www.navypier.com*

The Chicago Black Book

Where was that great Latin fusion sushi place I read about? And I need the phone number of that cool theatre to make a reservation. Help! No one should ever have to get along without a little Black Book to keep all the important names and numbers at one's fingertips. Ours is also cross-referenced to help you find in a flash which Chicago Experience it's in and whether it's one of our "Bests."

The Fun Seeker's Chicago Black Book

Hotels

NAME	ADDRESS WEB SITE	AREA*	PHONE 800#	EXPERIENCE PERFECT	PAGE PAGE
The Belden-Stratford	2300 N. Lincoln Park West www.beldenstratford.com	LP	773-281-2900 800-800-8301	Neighborhood	176
The Drake	140 E. Walton Pl. www.thedrakehotel.com	GC	312-787-2200 800-774-1500	Classic	76
Fairmont Chicago	200 N. Columbus Dr. www.fairmont.com	LO	312-565-8000 800-257-7544	Luxe	124
Four Seasons	120 E. Delaware Pl. www.fourseasons.com	GC	312-280-8800 800-819-5053	Luxe Plush Hotel Rooms	124 58
Hard Rock Hotel	230 N. Michigan Ave. www.hardrock.com	LO	312-345-1000 877-762-5468	Hot & Cool	100
Hilton Chicago	720 S. Michigan Ave. www.chicagohilton.com	SL	312-922-4400 800-774-1500	Classic	76
Hotel Allegro	171 W. Randolph St. www.allegrochicago.com	LO	312-236-0123 800-643-1500	Hipster	152
Hotel Burnham	1 W. Washington St. www.burnhamhotel.com	LO	312-782-1111 877-294-9712	Hipster	152
Hotel Monaco	225 N. Wabash Ave. www.hotelmonaco.com	LO	312-960-8500 800-546-7866	Hipster	153
House of Blues Hotel	333 N. Dearborn St. www.loewshotels.com/hotels/chicago	RN	312-245-0333 800-235-6397	Hipster	153
Le Meridien Hotel	521 N. Michigan Ave. www.lemeridien.com	NN	312-645-1500 800-543-4300	Luxe	125
Majestic Hotel	528 W. Brompton St. www.cityinns.com	LV	773-404-3499 800-727-5108	Neighborhood	176
Millennium Knickerbocker	163 E. Walton Pl. www.millenniumhotels.com	GC	312-751-8100 866-866-8086	Classic	77
Omni Ambassador East	1301 N. State St. www.omnihotels.com	GC	312-787-7200 800-843-6664	Classic	77
Palmer House Hilton	17 E. Monroe St. www.chicagohilton.com	LO	312-726-7500 800-774-1500	Classic	77
Park Hyatt Chicago	800 N. Michigan Ave. www.lemeridien.com	NN	312-335-1234 800-543-4300	Luxe Plush Hotel Rooms	125 58
The Peninsula Chicago	108 E. Superior St. www.chicago.peninsula.com	NN	312-337-2888 866-288-8889	Luxe Plush Hotel Rooms	126 58
Ritz-Carlton Chicago	160 E. Pearson St. www.fourseasons.com/chicagorc	NN	312-266-1000 800-819-5053	Luxe	126
Sofitel Chicago Water Tower	20 E. Chestnut St. www.sofitel.com	GC	312-324-4000 877-813-7700	Hot & Cool	100
Sutton Place Hotel	21 E. Bellevue Pl. www.suttonplace.com	GC	312-266-2100 800-606-8188	Hot & Cool	100

* AV= Andersonville; BT= Bucktown; CH= Chinatown; GC= Gold Coast; HI= Highland Park; HP= Hyde Park; LA= Lansing; LE= Lemont; LI= Little Italy; LO= Loop/Downtown; LP= Lincoln Park; LS= Lincoln Square; LV= Lakeview; NN= Near North; OB= Oak Brook; OT= Old Town; PI= Pilsen; RN= River North; SL= South Loop; SS= South Side; UP= Uptown; UK= Ukrainian Village; WH= Wheaton; WL=West Loop; WP= Wicker Park; WV= Wrigleyville

Hotels (cont'd.)

NAME	ADDRESS WEB SITE	AREA	PHONE 800#	EXPERIENCE PERFECT	PAGE PAGE
W Chicago City Center	172 W. Adams St. www.whotel.com	LO	312-332-1200 800-621-2360	Hot & Cool	101
W Chicago Lakeshore	644 N. Lake Shore Dr. www.whotel.com	NN	312-943-9200 888-625-5144	Hot & Cool	101
The Whitehall Hotel	105 E. Delaware Pl. www.thewhitehallhotel.com	GC	312-944-6300 800-948-4255	Neighborhood	177
Willows Hotel	555 W. Surf St. www.cityinns.com	LV	773-528-8400 800-787-3108	Neighborhood	177

Restaurants

NAME	ADDRESS	AREA	PHONE	EXPERIENCE PERFECT	PAGE* PAGE
Albert's Café & Patisserie	52 W. Elm St.	GC	312-751-0666	Classic	72, 78
Ambria	2300 N. Lincoln Park West	LP	773-472-5959	Luxe	123, 127
Ann Sather	929 W. Belmont Ave.	LV	773-348-2378	Neighborhood	174, 178
Argo Tea Café	958 W. Armitage Ave.	LP	773-388-1880	Neighborhood	171, 178
Atlantique	5101 N. Clark St.	AV	773-275-9191	Neighborhood	173, 178
Atwood Café	1 W. Washington St.	LO	312-368-1900	Hot & Cool	95, 102
Avenues	108 E. Superior St.	NN	312-573-6754	Luxe	123, 127
Bar Louie	226 W. Chicago Ave.	RN	312-337-3313	Late-Night Eats	54
Ben Pao	52 W. Illinois St.	RN	312-222-1888	Hot & Cool	98, 102
The Berghoff	17 W. Adams St.	LO	312-427-3170	Classic Classic Restaurants	73, 78 42
Billy Goat Tavern	430 N. Michigan Ave.	NN	312-222-1525	Classic	71, 78
Bin 36	339 N. Dearborn St.	RN	312-755-9463	Hot & Cool	99, 102
Bistro 110	110 E. Pearson St.	GC	312-266-3110	Hipster	149, 154
Blackbird	619 W. Randolph St.	WL	312-715-0708	Hipster	148, 154
Boka	1729 N. Halsted St.	LP	312-337-6070	Luxe	122, 128
Bongo Room	1470 N. Milwaukee Ave.	WP	773-489-0690	Hipster	150, 154
Brasserie Jo	59 W. Hubbard St.	RN	312-595-0800	Hot & Cool	99, 103
Café des Architectes	20 E. Chestnut St.	GC	312-324-4063	Hot & Cool	98, 103
Café Matou	1846 N. Milwaukee Ave.	WP	773-384-8911	Neighborhood	175, 179
Café Spiaggia	980 N. Michigan Ave.	GC	312-280-2750	Luxe	121, 128
Caffe Deluca	1721 N. Damen Ave.	WP	773-342-6000	Hipster	150, 155
Caliterra	633 N. Saint Clair St.	NN	312-274-4444	Luxe	123, 128
Carmine's	1043 N. Rush St.	GC	312-988-7676	Hot & Cool	97, 103
Carson's	612 N. Wells St.	RN	312-280-9200	Classic	75, 78
Charlie Trotter's	816 W. Armitage Ave.	LP	773-248-6228	Luxe Fine Dining	122, 129 47
Chicago Chop House	60 W. Ontario St.	RN	312-787-7100	Classic Steak Houses	73, 79 66

*Italic = listing in Itinerary; Roman = description in theme chapters

Restaurants (cont'd.)

NAME	ADDRESS	AREA	PHONE	EXPERIENCE PERFECT	PAGE PAGE
Ed Debevic's	640 N. Wells St.	RN	312-664-1707	Classic	73, 79
Emperor's Choice	2238 S. Wentworth Ave.	CH	312-225-8800	Classic	74, 79
Erawan	729 N. Clark St.	RN	312-642-6888	Luxe	119, 129
Everest	440 S. La Salle St., 40th Fl.	LO	312-663-8920	Luxe Fine Dining	123, 130 47
Follia	953 W. Fulton Ave.	WL	312-243-2888	Hipster	149, 155
Fox & Obel	401 E. Illinois St.	RN	312-410-7301	Luxe	119, 130
Frontera Grill	445 N. Clark St.	RN	312-661-1434	Hipster Always-Hot	151, 155 36
Fuse	71 E. Wacker Dr.	LO	312-462-7071	Luxe	120, 130
Gene & Georgetti	500 N. Franklin St.	RN	312-527-3718	Classic Steak Houses	73, 80 66
Gioco	1312 S. Wabash Ave.	SL	312-939-3870	Hipster	151, 156
Giordano's	730 N. Rush St.	RN	312-951-0747	Chicago Pizza	41
Grill on the Alley	909 N. Michigan Ave.	GC	312-255-9009	Luxe	119, 131
Heat	1507 N. Sedgwick St.	OT	312-397-9818	Luxe	123, 131
Hillary's Urban Eatery	1500 W. Division St.	WP	773-235-4327	Hot & Cool	98, 103
Hop Leaf	5148 N. Clark St.	AV	773-334-9851	Neighborhood	175, 179
Iggy's	700 N. Milwaukee Ave.	WP	312-829-4449	Hipster Late-Night Eats	151, 156 54
Ina's	1235 W. Randolph St.	WL	312-226-8227	Hot & Cool Breakfast/Brunch	95, 104 39
Italian Village	71 W. Monroe St.	LO	312-332-7005	Classic Classic Restaurants	75, 80 42
Japonais	600 W. Chicago Ave.	RN	312-822-9600	Hipster Trendy Tables	149, 156 68
Kevin	9 W. Hubbard St.	RN	312-595-0055	Hot & Cool	97, 104
La Petite Folie	1504 E. 55th St.	HP	773-493-1394	Neighborhood	173, 179
La Tache	1475 W. Balmoral Ave.	AV	773-334-7168	Hipster	150, 157
La Vita	1359 W. Taylor St.	LI	312-491-1414	Neighborhood	172, 180
Le Colonial	937 N. Rush St.	GC	312-255-0088	Hot & Cool	95, 104
Leo's Lunchroom	1809 W. Division St.	UK	773-276-6509	Hipster	148, 157
Lloyd's Chicago	200 W. Madison St.	LO	312-407-6900	Luxe	120, 131
The Lobby (The Peninsula Chiacgo)	108 E. Superior St.	NN	312-573-6760	Luxe	119, 132
Lou Mitchell's	565 W. Jackson Blvd.	WL	312-939-3111	Classic Breakfast/Brunch	71, 80 39
Lutz Café & Konditorei	2458 W. Montrose Ave.	LS	773-478-7785	Neighborhood	172, 180
LT's Grill	1800 W. Grand Ave.	WL	312-997-2400	Hipster	147, 157
Marche	833 W. Randolph St.	WL	312-226-8399	Hipster	148, 158
Melrose Diner	3233 N. Broadway St.	LV	773-327-2060	Hipster	148, 158
Mirai	2020 W. Division St.	UK	773-862-8500	Hot & Cool	99, 105
MK	868 N. Franklin St.	RN	312-482-9179	Hot & Cool	98, 105
Mod	1520 N. Damen Ave.	BT	773-252-1500	Hipster	151, 158

Restaurants (cont'd.)

NAME	ADDRESS	AREA	PHONE	EXPERIENCE	PAGE
				PERFECT	PAGE
Mon Ami Gabi	2300 N. Lincoln Park West	LP	773-348-8886	Neighborhood	*172*, 180
Morton's	1050 N. State St.	RN	312-266-4820	Luxe	*122*, 132
				Steak Houses	66
Nacional 27	325 W. Huron St.	RN	312-664-2727	Hot & Cool	*96*, 105
				Trendy Tables	68
Naha	500 N. Clark St.	RN	312-321-6242	Luxe	*121*, 132
Nine	440 W. Randolph St.	WL	312-575-9900	Hot & Cool	*96*, 106
NoMi	800 N. Michigan Ave.	NN	312-239-4030	Luxe	*120*, 133
				Restaurants w/View	59
North Pond	2610 N. Cannon Dr.	LP	773-477-5845	Neighborhood	*173*, 180
				Restaurants w/View	59
Oak Tree	900 N. Michigan Ave.	GC	312-751-1988	Classic	*72*, 81
Ohba	2049 W. Division St.	UK	773-772-2727	Hipster	*150*, 159
one sixtyblue	160 N. Loomis St.	WL	312-850-0303	Hot & Cool	*98*, 106
Opera	1301 S. Wabash Ave.	SL	312-461-0161	Hipster	*149*, 159
				Romantic Rendezvous	60
Orange	3231 N. Clark St.	LV	773-549-4400	Hot & Cool	*97*, 106
				Breakfast/Brunch	39
Original Pancake House	22 E. Bellevue Pl.	GC	312-642-7917	Classic	*71*, 81
Palace Grill	1408 W. Madison Ave.	WL	312-226-9529	Classic	*74*, 81
Pegasus	130 S. Halsted St.	WL	312-226-3377	Neighborhood	*172*, 181
				Ethnic Dining	46
Penny's Noodle Shop	3400 N. Sheffield Ave.	LV	773-281-8222	Neighborhood	*174*, 181
				Ethnic Dining	46
Pierrot Gourmet	108 E. Superior St.	NN	312-573-6749	Hot & Cool	*97*, 107
Pizzeria Uno	29 E. Ohio St.	RN	312-321-1000	Classic	*71*, 81
				Chicago Pizza	41
Portillo's Hot Dogs	100 W. Ontario St.	RN	312-587-8930	Classic	*73*, 82
Puck's	220 E. Chicago Ave.	RN	312-397-4034	Hipster	*149*, 160
Pump Room	1301 N. State Pkwy.	GC	312-266-0360	Classic	*72*, 82
				Classic Restaurants	42
Ranalli's	2301 N. Clark St.	LP	773-244-2300	Chicago Pizza	41
Red Light	820 W. Randolph St.	WL	312-733-8880	Hipster	*148*, 160
				Always-Hot	36
RJ Grunts	2056 Lincoln Park W.	LP	773-929-5363	Neighborhood	*171*, 182
RL	115 E. Chicago Ave.	NN	312-475-1100	Hot & Cool	*95*, 107
Russian Tea Time	77 E. Adams St.	LO	312-360-0000	Classic	*72*, 82
				Ethnic Dining	46
Seasons	120 E. Delaware Pl.	GC	312-649-2349	Luxe	*123*, 133
The Signature Room (at the 95th)	John Hancock Center, 875 N. Michigan Ave.	NN	312-787-9596	Classic	*72*, 83
				Restaurants w/View	59
Silver Cloud	1700 N. Damen Ave.	BT	773-489-6212	Hipster	*150*, 160
Spring	2039 W. North Ave.	WP	773-395-7100	Neighborhood	*175*, 182
Sushi Wabi	842 W. Randolph St.	WL	312-563-1224	Hipster	*147*, 161
SushiSamba Rio	504 N. Wells St.	RN	312-595-2300	Hot & Cool	*99*, 107
				Trendy Tables	68

Restaurants (cont'd.)

NAME	ADDRESS	AREA	PHONE	EXPERIENCE PERFECT	PAGE PAGE
Tempo	6 E. Chestnut St.	GC	312-943-4373	Classic Late-Night Eats	74, 83 54
Topolobampo	445 N. Clark St.	RN	312-661-1434	Hipster	151, 161
Tournesol	4343 N. Lincoln Ave.	LS	773-477-8820	Neighborhood	173, 182
Trotter's To Go	1337 W. Fullerton Ave.	LP	773-868-6510	Hot & Cool	97, 108
Tru	676 N. Saint Clair St.	NN	312-202-0001	Luxe Fine Dining	120, 134 47
Twin Anchors	1655 N. Sedgwick St.	OT	312-266-1616	Classic	75, 83
Twisted Spoke	501 N. Ogden Ave.	WL	312-666-1500	Hipster	147, 161
Valois	1518 E. 53rd St.	HP	773-667-0647	Neighborhood	173, 182
Vermilion	10 W. Hubbard St.	RN	312-527-4060	Hipster	149, 162
Vong's Thai Kitchen	6 W. Hubbard St.	RN	312-644-8664	Hot & Cool	99, 108
Wave	644 N. Lake Shore Dr.	NN	312-255-4460	Hot & Cool	96, 108
Wishbone	1001 W. Washington Blvd.	WL	312-850-2663	Hipster Always-Hot	147, 162 36
Zealous	419 W. Superior St.	RN	312-475-9112	Luxe	120, 134

Nightlife

NAME	ADDRESS	AREA	PHONE	EXPERIENCE PERFECT	PAGE PAGE
Aragon Ballroom	1106 W. Lawrence Ave.	UP	773-561-9500	Neighborhood	175, 183
Back Room	1007 N. Rush St.	GC	312-751-2433	Hot & Cool	96, 109
The Bar (The Peninsula Chicago)	108 E. Superior St.	NN	312-573-6766	Luxe Swanky Hotel Bars	120, 135 67
Base Bar (Hard Rock Hotel)	230 N. Michigan Ave.	LO	312-345-1000	Luxe Scene Bars	122, 135 61
The Baton	436 N. Clark St.	RN	312-644-5269	Hipster	151, 163
Berlin	954 W. Belmont Ave.	LV	773-348-4975	Hot & Cool Dance Clubs	99, 109 44
Bernie's	3664 N. Clark St.	WV	773-525-1898	Sports Bars	65
Betty's Blue Star Lounge	1600 W. Grand Ave.	WL	312-243-1699	Hipster	149, 163
Beviamo	1358 W. Taylor St.	LI	312-455-8255	Neighborhood	172, 183
Big Chicks	5024 N. Sheridan Rd.	AV	773-728-5511	Neighborhood Gay Bars	175, 183 49
Big Wig	1551 W. Division St.	UK	773-235-9100	Neighborhood	172, 184
Black Beetle Bar and Grill	2532 W. Chicago Ave.	UK	773-384-0701	Neighborhood	173, 184
Buddy Guy's Legends	754 S. Wabash Ave.	SL	312-427-0333	Classic Blues Bars	75, 84 38
BUtterfield 8	713 N. Wells St.	RN	312-327-0940	Hot & Cool	96, 109
Chicago Symphony Orchestra	220 S. Michigan Ave.	LO	312-294-3000	Classic	75, 84
ComedySportz	2851 N. Halsted St.	LV	773-549-8080	Hot & Cool	99, 110
Coq d'Or (The Drake)	140 E. Walton St.	GC	312-932-4622	Classic Swanky Hotel Bars	72, 84 67

Nightlife (cont'd.)

NAME	ADDRESS	AREA	PHONE	EXPERIENCE PERFECT	PAGE PAGE
Crobar	1543 N. Kingsbury St.	OT	312-266-1900	Hot & Cool Dance Clubs	99, 110 44
Domaine	1045 N. Rush St.	GC	312-397-1045	Luxe Over-the-Top	122, 135 57
Double Door	1572 N. Milwaukee Ave.	WP	773-489-3160	Hipster Clubs for Live Music	148, 163 43
Empty Bottle	1035 N. Western Ave.	UK	773-276-3600	Hipster Clubs for Live Music	151, 164 43
Excalibur	632 N. Dearborn St.	RN	312-266-1944	Classic	74, 85
Exit	1315 W. North Ave.	WP	773-395-2700	Hipster Late-Night Hangouts	150, 164 55
Funky Buddha Lounge	728 W. Grand Ave.	RN	312-666-1695	Hipster	148, 164
Gamekeeper's	1971 N. Lincoln Ave.	LP	773-549-0400	Sports Bars	65
Ghost	440 W. Randolph St.	WL	312-575-9900	Hot & Cool Scene Bars	98, 110 61
Green Dolphin Street	2200 N. Ashland Ave.	LP	773-395-0066	Luxe Jazz Clubs	123, 136 53
Green Mill	4802 N. Broadway St.	UP	773-878-5552	Classic Jazz Clubs	72, 85 53
Harry's Velvet Room	56 W. Illinois St.	RN	312-527-5600	Luxe Sexy Lounges	122, 136 62
Hi-Tops	3551 N. Sheffield Ave.	WV	773-348-0009	Sports Bars	65
Hideout	1354 W. Wabansia Ave.	WP	773-227-4433	Hipster	150, 164
HotHouse	31 E. Balbo Dr.	LO	312-362-9707	Hipster	151, 165
Improv Olympic	3541 N. Clark St.	WV	773-880-0199	Hot & Cool	99, 111
Jazz Showcase	59 W. Grand Ave.	RN	312-670-2473	Classic Jazz Clubs	75, 85 53
Jilly's	1007 N. Rush St.	GC	312-664-1001	Classic	74, 85
Joffrey Ballet Chicago	50 E. Congress Pkwy.	LO	312-902-1500	Luxe	120, 136
Katacomb	1909 N. Lincoln Ave.	LP	773-230-3333	Neighborhood Late-Night Hangouts	174, 184 55
Kingston Mines	2548 N. Halsted St.	LP	773-477-4646	Classic Blues Bars	75, 86 38
Kit Kat Lounge and Supper Club	3700 N. Halsted St.	WV	773-525-1111	Neighborhood Over-the-Top	172, 184 57
Lava Lounge	859 N. Damen Ave.	UK	773-772-3355	Neighborhood	175, 185
Le Bar (Sofitel Chicago Water Tower)	20 E. Chestnut St.	GC	312-324-4000	Hot & Cool Swanky Hotel Bars	98, 111 67
Le Passage	937 N. Rush St.	GC	312-255-0022	Luxe Hipster Hangouts	120, 136 52
Liar's Club	1655 W. Fullerton Ave.	LP	773-665-1110	Neighborhood	174, 185
Lookingglass Theatre	821 N. Michigan Ave.	NN	312-337-0665	Hot & Cool Celebrity Launching	96, 111 40
Loop Theatre District	Various locations	LO	n/a	Classic	72, 86
Map Room	1949 N. Hoyne Ave.	BT	773-252-7636	Neighborhood	173, 185

Nightlife (cont'd.)

NAME	ADDRESS	AREA	PHONE	EXPERIENCE PERFECT	PAGE PAGE
Marie's Rip Tide Lounge	1745 W. Armitage Ave.	BT	773-278-7317	Hipster	*150*, 165
Matchbox	770 N. Milwaukee Ave.	WP	312-666-9292	Neighborhood	*172*, 185
Metro	3730 N. Clark St.	WV	773-549-0203	Hipster Clubs for Live Music	*148*, 165 43
Moda	25 W. Hubbard St.	RN	312-670-2200	Luxe Sexy Lounges	*122*, 137 62
Music Box Theatre	3733 N. Southport Ave.	WV	773-871-6607	Classic	*73*, 86
Narcisse	710 N. Clark St.	RN	312-787-2675	Luxe Sexy Lounges	*123*, 137 62
Ontourage	157 W. Ontario St.	RN	312-573-1470	Hot & Cool	*98*, 112
Pops for Champagne	2934 N. Sheffield Ave.	LV	773-472-1000	Classic Romantic Rendezvous	*72*, 87 60
Rainbo	1150 N. Damen Ave.	WP	773-489-5999	Hipster	*148*, 165
Redhead Piano Bar	16 W. Ontario St.	RN	312-640-1000	Classic	*75*, 87
Rednofive	440 N. Halsted St.	WL	312-733-6699	Hot & Cool	*98*, 112
Riviera Theatre	4746 N. Racine Ave.	UP	773-275-6800	Neighborhood	*175*, 186
Rosa's Lounge	3420 W. Armitage Ave.	BT	773-342-0452	Neighborhood Blues Bars	*172*, 186 38
The Second City	1616 N. Wells St.	OT	312-337-3992	Classic Celebrity Launching	*72*, 87 40
Side Track	3349 N. Halsted St.	LV	773-477-9189	Neighborhood Gay Bars	*174*, 186 49
Simon's	5210 N. Clark St.	AV	773-878-0894	Neighborhood	*175*, 187
Smart Bar	3730 N. Clark St.	WV	773-549-4140	Hipster Dance Clubs	*148*, 166 44
Sonotheque	1444 W. Chicago Ave.	WP	312-226-7600	Hipster Hipster Hangouts	*151*, 166 52
Spin	800 W. Belmont Ave.	LV	773-327-7711	Neighborhood Gay Bars	*174*, 187 49
Steppenwolf Theatre Company	1650 N. Halsted St.	OT	312-335-1650	Hot & Cool Celebrity Launching	*96*, 112 40
Sugar	108 W. Kinzie St.	RN	312-822-9999	Luxe Over-the-Top	*123*, 137 57
Syn	1009 N. Rush St.	GC	312-664-0009	Luxe	*120*, 138
Tini Martini	2169 N. Milwaukee Ave.	BT	773-269-2900	Hot & Cool	*96*, 112
Too Much Light Makes the Baby Go Blind	5153 N. Ashland Ave.	AV	773-275-5255	Neighborhood	*174*, 187
Victory Gardens Theater	2257 N. Lincoln Ave.	LP	773-871-3000	Neighborhood	*172*, 187
Whiskey Bar	1015 N. Rush St.	GC	312-475-0300	Luxe	*120*, 138
Whiskey Sky	644 N. Lakeshore Dr.	NN	312-943-9200	Hot & Cool	*97*, 113
Y/Sound-Bar	224–226 W. Ontario St.	RN	312-274-1880	Hot & Cool Scene Bars	*96*, 113 61
Zentra	923 W. Weed St.	OT	312-787-0400	Hot & Cool Late-Night Hangouts	*99*, 113 55

Attractions

NAME	ADDRESS	AREA	PHONE	EXPERIENCE PERFECT	PAGE PAGE
Adler Planetarium	1300 S. Lake Shore Dr.	SL	312-922-7827	Classic	75, 88
Armitage Avenue	West from Lincoln Ave. to Sheffield Ave.	LP	n/a	Shopping Streets	63
Art Institute of Chicago	111 S. Michigan Ave.	LO	312-443-3600	Classic	73, 88
				Luxe	119, 139
				Don't-Miss Attractions	45
Buckingham Fountain	Grant Park	LO	n/a	Romantic Rendezvous	60
Carson Pirie Scott & Co.	1 S. State St.	LO	312-641-7000	Architecture Sightings	37
Chicago Board of Trade	141 W. Jackson Blvd., 5th Fl.	LO	312-435-3590	Hot & Cool	95, 114
Chicago Cubs	1060 W. Addison St.	WV	773-404-2827	Neighborhood	174, 188
Chicago Cultural Center	78 E. Washington St.	LO	312-744-6630	Classic	71, 89
				Hip Museums	51
Chicago Historical Society	1601 N. Clark St.	LP	312-642-4600	Neighborhood	171, 188
Chicago Mercantile Exchange	20 S. Wacker Dr.	LO	312-930-2390	Hot & Cool	95, 114
Chicago White Sox	333 W. 35th St.	SS	312-674-1000	Neighborhood	174, 189
Damen Avenue	North of Milwaukee Ave. to Webster Ave.	BT	n/a	Shopping Streets	63
Donald Young Gallery	933 W. Washington Blvd.	WL	312-455-0100	Gallery Spaces	48
Du Sable Museum of Afro-American History	740 E. 56th Pl.	HP	773-947-0600	Neighborhood	173, 189
Field Museum	1400 S. Lake Shore Dr.	SL	312-922-9410	Classic	75, 90
Flat Iron Building	1579 N. Milwaukee Ave.	WP	n/a	Gallery Spaces	48
Gallery 37	66 E. Randolph St.	LO	312-744-7274	Hipster	147, 168
Glessner House	1800 S. Prairie Ave.	SL	312-326-1480	Classic	74, 90
				Architecture Sightings	37
Grant Park/Millennium Park Concerts	n/a	LO	312-742-7529	Classic	75, 91
				Outdoor Activities	56
John G. Shedd Aquarium	1200 S. Lake Shore Dr.	SL	312-939-2438	Classic	75, 91
John Hancock Center	875 N. Michigan Ave.	NN	888-875-8439	Classic	72, 91
Lakefront/Lincoln Park	600–5800 N. Lake Shore Dr.	n/a	n/a	Neighborhood	171, 190
				Don't-Miss Attractions	45
Lincoln Park Conservatory	2391 N. Stockton Dr.	LP	312-742-7736	Neighborhood	171, 190
Lincoln Park Zoo	2200 N. Cannon Dr.	LP	312-742-2000	Neighborhood	171, 190
Merchandise Mart	222 Merchandise Mart Plaza	RN	312-527-7990	Luxe	121, 143
Mexican Fine Arts Center Museum	1852 W. 19th St.	PI	312-738-1503	Hot & Cool	97, 116
				Hip Museums	51
Millennium Park	n/a	LO	n/a	Hot & Cool	99, 116
Museum of Contemporary Art	220 E. Chicago Ave.	NN	312-280-2660	Hipster	149, 168
				Hip Museums	51
Museum of Contemporary Photography	600 S. Michigan Ave	SL	312-663-5554	Hipster	147, 168
Museum of Science and Industry	5700 S. Lake Shore Dr.	HP	773-684-1414	Neighborhood	173, 191
National Vietnam Veterans Art Museum	1801 S. Indiana Ave.	SL	312-326-0270	Classic	74, 92

Attractions (cont'd.)

NAME	ADDRESS	AREA	PHONE	EXPERIENCE PERFECT	PAGE PAGE
Navy Pier	600 E. Grand Ave.	NN	312-595-7437	Classic	*73*, 92
Newberry Library	60 W. Walton St.	GC	312-255-3595	Neighborhood	*175*, 191
North Michigan Avenue	Chicago River to the lake	NN	n/a	Don't-Miss Attractions	45
Oak Street	Michigan Ave. & Rush St.	GC	n/a	Shopping Streets	63
Oak Street Beach	n/a	GC	n/a	Hot & Cool	*97*, 117
Old Town School of Folk Music	4544 N. Lincoln Ave.	LS	773-728-6000	Neighborhood	*171*, 191
Oriental Institute	1155 E. 58th St.	HP	773-702-9514	Neighborhood	*173*, 192
Osaka Garden	Jackson Park	HP	n/a	Neighborhood	*173*, 192
Ravinia Festival	200–231 Ravinia Park Rd.	HI	847-266-5100	Luxe Outdoor Activities	*122*, 144 56
Richard Gray Gallery	875 N. Michigan Ave., Ste. 2503	NN	312-642-8877	Gallery Spaces	48
Robie House	5757 S. Woodlawn Ave.	HP	773-834-1847	Neighborhood Architecture Sightings	*173*, 192 37
Sears Tower	233 S. Wacker Dr.	LO	312-875-9696	Hot & Cool	*95*, 117
University of Chicago	Hyde Park	HP	773-702-1234	Neighborhood	*173*, 193
Wicker Park	North, Milwaukee, & Damen	WP	n/a	Hipster Hangouts	52
Willie Dixon's Blues Heaven Foundation	2120 S. Michigan Ave.	SL	312-808-1286	Classic	*74*, 93

Golf

NAME	ADDRESS	AREA	PHONE	EXPERIENCE	PAGE
Butler National Golf Club	2616 York Rd.	OB	630-990-3333	Luxe	*121*, 139
Chicago Golf Club	25 W. Warrenville Rd.	WH	630-665-2988	Luxe	*121*, 139
Cog Hill Golf and Country Club	12294 Archer Ave.	LE	630-264-4455	Classic	*73*, 89
Harborside International Golf Center	11001 S. Doty Ave. E.	SS	312-782-7837	Hot & Cool	*98*, 115
Sydney R. Marovitz Golf Course	3600 N. Recreation Dr.	LV	312-742-7930	Neighborhood	*174*, 193

Spas/Fitness/Beauty

NAME	ADDRESS	AREA	PHONE	EXPERIENCE PERFECT	PAGE PAGE
Cheetah Gym	5248 N. Clark St.	AV	773-728-7777	Neighborhood	*172*, 188
East Bank Club	500 N. Kingsbury St.	RN	312-527-5800	Luxe	*123*, 140
Face & Facial Co.	104 E. Oak St.	GC	312-951-5151	Luxe	*121*, 141
Four Seasons Spa	120 E. Delaware Pl.	GC	312-280-8800	Luxe	*120*, 141
Holmes Place	355 E. Grand Ave.	NN	312-467-1111	Hot & Cool	*96*, 115

Spas/Fitness/Beauty (cont'd.)

NAME	ADDRESS	AREA	PHONE	EXPERIENCE PERFECT	PAGE PAGE
Honey Child Salon and Spa	735 N. LaSalle St.	RN	312-573-1300	Hot & Cool Spas	*99*, 115 64
Marilyn Miglin Salon	112 E. Oak St.	GC	312-943-1120	Luxe	*123*, 143
Nordstrom Spa	55 E. Grand Ave.	NN	312-464-1515	Classic Spas	*73*, 93 64
The Peninsula Spa	108 E. Superior St.	NN	312-337-2888	Luxe Spas	*120*, 144 64
Urban Oasis	12 W. Maple St.	GC	312-587-3500	Neighborhood	*175*, 193

Services

NAME	ADDRESS	AREA	PHONE	EXPERIENCE PERFECT	PAGE PAGE
Art on the Move	Various locations	n/a	847-432-6265	Hot & Cool Guided Tours	*97*, 114 50
Bike and Roll	North Avenue Beach Navy Pier, 600 E. Grand Ave.	LP NN	773-327-2706 312-595-9600	Hot & Cool	*97*, 114
Chi Healing Center	1733 N. Milwaukee Ave.	WP	773-278-8494	Hipster	*150*, 167
Chicago Architecture Foundation	224 S. Michigan Ave.	LO	312-922-3432	Classic Guided Tours	*71*, 89 50
Chicago Neighborhood Tours	78 E. Washington St.	LO	312-742-1190	Neighborhood Guided Tours	*174*, 189 50
Chicago River Canoe & Kayak	3400 N. Rockwell St.	n/a	773-252-3307	Hipster Outdoor Activities	*147*, 167 56
Chicago Sailing Club	Belmont Harbor, Dock B	LV	773-871-7245	Luxe	*123*, 140
Chicago Tour Guides Institute	27 N. Wacker Dr., Ste. 400	LO	773-276-6683	Luxe	*119*, 140
Chopping Block	1324 W. Webster Ave.	LP	773-472-6700	Hipster	*151*, 167
Ethnic Grocery Tour	2010 W. Chase Ave.	n/a	773-465-8064	Hipster	*150*, 168
Flight School Midway	4943 63rd St.	SS	773-767-8100	Luxe	*121*, 141
French Pastry School	226 W. Jackson Blvd.	LO	312-726-2419	Luxe	*123*, 142
The Golden Triangle	72 W. Hubbard St.	RN	312-755-1266	Luxe	*121*, 142
Jane Hamill	1117 W. Armitage Ave.	LP	773-665-1102	Hot & Cool	*98*, 115
Leslie Hindman Auctions	122 N. Aberdeen St.	WL	312-491-9522	Luxe	*121*, 142
Lori's	824 W. Armitage Ave.	LP	773-281-5655	Hot & Cool	*98*, 116
Marshall Field's	111 N. State St.	LO	312-781-1000	Classic	*73*, 92
Morlen Sinoway Atelier	1052 W. Fulton Market	WL	312-432-0100	Luxe	*121*, 143
p.45	1643 N. Damen Ave.	WP	773-862-4523	Hipster	*150*, 169
Randolph Wine Cellar	1415 W. Randolph St.	WL	312-942-1212	Luxe	*123*, 144
Reckless Records	3161 N. Broadway St.	LV	773-404-5080	Hipster	*149*, 169
Rolph Achilles	n/a	n/a	773-477-8138	Luxe	*119*, 145
Sun Aero Helicopters	Lansing Municipal Airport	LA	708-895-8958	Luxe	*119*, 145
Tattoo Factory	4408 N. Broadway	UP	773-989-4077	Hipster	*148*, 169
Uncle Fun	1338 W. Belmont Ave.	LV	773-477-8223	Hipster	*149*, 169

Greenline Publications
Extraordinary Guides for Extraordinary Travelers

The Fun Also Rises Travel Series

The world's most fun places to be at the right time ...

The Fun Seeker's destination guides to each of the world's hottest cities ...

Look for other titles in the series:

The Fun Seeker's Athens

The Fun Seeker's Las Vegas

The Fun Seeker's London (2005)

The Fun Seeker's Miami

The Fun Seeker's New Orleans

The Fun Seeker's New York (2005)

The Fun Seeker's San Francisco

Greenline's Historic Travel Series

Available wherever extraordinary travel books are sold
Be sure to visit us at **www.greenlinepub.com**